WEBSTER'S NEW WORLD™

P O C K E T
INTERNET
DIRECTORY
— and —
DICTIONARY

By Bryan Pfaffenberger, Ph.D.
Faithe Wempen, Editor

LYCOS

que

Dear Prodigy Internet Member,

Empowering members to use the Internet as a productivity tool has enabled Prodigy Internet to become one of the fastest growing Internet service providers in the United States. In fact, we have a saying about our service. It's a tool for living.™ This pocket guide, like our service, is designed to help you find what you need on the Internet quickly and easily. Enjoy it with our compliments and thanks!

The first part of this book is a mini-directory of interesting and useful Web sites. One of my favorite Web sites is CNNfn (p. 25). If you don't have time to read the newspaper, this site will quickly update you on business news. And since I use Prodigy Internet not only for work, but also for fun (remember the living part!), I find that SkiNet (p. 257) is a great way to get updated information on worldwide ski conditions and news. In the personal address section at the end of the book, you can list your own favorite Web sites.

The second part of this book is a glossary of over 500 Internet terms, with everything from ActiveX to ZModem. Use it to look up Internet lingo you don't understand. You'll feel like an Internet pro in no time!

For other ways to maximize your time online, be sure to read the "Tool List" on the following page.

I hope you enjoy and use this gift. Thanks for joining our growing family of Prodigy Internet members!

Prodigy Internet. It's a tool for living.™

Very truly yours,

Samer Salameh
President & CEO

Prodigy Internet
http://www.prodigy.com.

Tool List

Prodigy Internet. It's a tool for living.™
http://www.prodigy.com

Your Home Page allows you to tailor Prodigy Internet to your needs. Here's a sample of easy tools you can find right on your Prodigy Internet Home Page:

A Tool for Simplicity
Our enhanced search technology lets you find things using plain English. Planning a trip to Bermuda? Just type, "I want to go to Bermuda" in the **Search** area and get all of your travel information.

A Tool for Learning
As a Prodigy Internet member, you can take a course at the **Prodigy Learning Center**. It offers interactive multimedia training and performance support on the latest software applications. Or you can visit the **Teach Me** section of our online **Member Center** for tutorials, tips, and tricks.

A Tool for Value
The **Personal Value Center** is your key to unlocking the value of the Internet. We have a constantly changing menu of special offers and exclusive savings for Prodigy Internet members only.

A Tool for Investing
Trade stocks for less, manage your portfolio, and get quotes in **My Stocks**.

A Tool for Communicating
PAL/Instant Messaging tells you when your buddies are online and lets you chat with them in real time. You can also check out up-coming Chat events, post and read messages on our **Message Boards,** or create your own Personal Web Pages, in **My Community.**

A Tool for Saving
Our **Travel Channel** can help you find the best prices on flights and hotel rooms. And get a great deal on a new or used car with the information in our **Autos Channel**.

A Tool for Growth
Find a new job, build your résumé, or manage your career through our **Careers Channel**.

Introduction

We live in a computerized society—and, increasingly, computer proficiency paves the way to personal and professional advancement. And the fastest-growing segment of the computer industry in the last few years has, of course, been the Internet. Currently, 40 to 45 million people in the U.S. alone use the Internet, and these numbers are projected to grow to 100 million by 1998. Has the Internet changed your life yet? If not, it will very soon.

This book is really two books in one. First, it's a mini-directory of Web sites, the top sites in every Lycos category by content. That means the sites you'll read about here are the cream skimmed from the top of the entire Internet. You can use them for education, entertainment, or to get ideas for building your own Web site. Their presentation is phenomenal across the board, and their content will make you laugh, cry, and most of all think.

The second part of the book is a dictionary of over 500 Internet-related terms, taken from the *Webster's New World Computer Dictionary*. Being up on your Internet terms can really make a difference. According to a *Money Magazine* survey, the biggest pay increases in 1996 went to computer workers at all levels. You'll be wise to know the difference between Java and Javascript, how push technology is changing Internet marketing, and whether ActiveX or JavaBeans represents the best choice for adding active content to a Web page.

Best of all, this book is so small that you can take it with you wherever you go! It neatly fits in a pocket or briefcase, and the waterproof cover protects it from most minor disasters. Good luck with it, and happy Web travels!

About Lycos, Inc.

In the brief time since the world has had point-and-click access to the multigraphic, multimedia World Wide Web, the number of people going online has exploded to 30 million at last count, all roaming about the tens of millions of places to visit in Cyberspace.

As the Web makes its way into our everyday lives, the kinds of people logging on are changing. Today, there are as many web-masters as novices, or newbies, and all are struggling to get the most from the vast wells of information scattered about the Web. Even well-prepared surfers stumble aimlessly through cyberspace using hit-or-miss methods in search of useful infor-mation, with few results, little substance, and a lot of frustration.

In 1994, the Lycos technology was created by a scientist at Carnegie Mellon University to help those on the Web regain control of the Web. The company's powerful technology is the bedrock underlying a family of guides that untangle the Web, offering a simple and intuitive interface for all types of Web surfers, from GenXers to seniors, from net vets to newbies.

Lycos (http://www.lycos.com) is a premium navigation tool for cyberspace, providing not just searches but unique editorial content and Web reviews that all draw on the company's extensive catalog of over 60 million Web sites (and growing).

Destination, Lycos

Lycos designed its home base on the premise that people want to experience the Web in three fundamentally different ways: they want to search for specific subjects or destinations, they want to browse interesting categories, or they want recommen-dations on sites that have been reviewed for quality of their content and graphics. Traditionally, Internet companies have provided part of this solution, but none has offered a finding tool that accommodates all degrees and types of curiosity. Lycos has.

Lycos utilizes its CentiSpeed spider technology as the foundation for finding and cataloging the vast variety of content on the World Wide Web. CentiSpeed processes a search faster than earlier technologies, featuring Virtual Memory Control, User-Level Handling and Algorithmic Word Compaction. This advanced technology allows the engine to execute more than 4,000 queries per second. CentiSpeed provides faster search results and unparalleled power to search the most comprehensive catalog of the World Wide Web. Lycos uses statistical word calculations and avoids full-word indexing, which helps provide the most relevant search results available on the Web.

In mid 1995, Lycos acquired Point Communications, widely recognized by Web veterans for its collection of critical reviews of the Web. Now an integrated part on the Lycos service, Point continues to provide thousands of in-depth site reviews and a thorough rating of the top Web sites throughout the world. The reviews are conducted by professional reviewers and editors who rate sites according to content, presentation and overall experience on a scale of 1 to 50. Reviews are presented as comprehensive abstracts that truly provide the user with subjective critiques widely heralded for their accuracy and perceptiveness. In addition, Point's top five percent ratings for Web sites receive a special "Top 5% Badge" icon, the Web's equivalent to the famed consumer "Good Housekeeping Seal."

And for Web browsers who don't need a touring list of well-reviewed sites but who may not be destination-specific, Lycos offers its Sites by Subject. Organizing thousands of Web sites into subject categories, Lycos Sites by Subject gives the cyber-surfer at-a-glance Web browsing, including sports, entertainment, social issues, and children's sites. A compilation of the most popular sites on the Internet by the Lycos standard—those with the greatest number of links from other sites—the directory provides Web travelers with a more organized approach to finding worthwhile places to visit on the Web.

Spiders on Steroids

Lycos was originally developed at Carnegie Mellon University by Dr. Michael "Fuzzy" Mauldin, who holds a Ph.D. in conceptual information retrieval. Now chief scientist at the company, Dr. Mauldin continues to expand the unique exploration and indexing technology. Utilizing this technology, Lycos strives to deliver a family of guides to the Internet that are unparalleled for their accuracy, relevance, and comprehensiveness. Lycos is one of the most frequently visited sites on the Web and is one of the leading sites for advertisers.

The Lycos database is constantly being refined by dozens of software robots, or agents, called "spiders." These spiders roam the Web endlessly, finding and downloading Web pages. Once a page is found, the spiders create abstracts which consist of the title, headings and subheading, 100 most weighty words, first 20 lines, size in bytes, and number of words. Heuristic (self-teaching) software looks at where the words appear in the document, their proximity to other words, frequency, and site popularity to determine relevance.

Lycos eliminates extraneous words like "the," "a," "and," "or," and "it" that add no value and slow down finding capabilities. The resulting abstracts are merged, older versions discarded, and a new, up-to-date database is distributed to all Lycos servers and licensees. This process is repeated continuously, resulting in a depth and comprehensiveness that make Lycos a top information guide company.

Online providers or software makers can license Lycos—the spider, search engine, catalog, directory, and Point reviews—to make them available to users.

Lycos, Inc., an Internet exploration company, was founded specifically to find, index, and filter information on the Internet and World Wide Web. CMG Information Services, Inc.

(NASDAQ: CMGI) is a majority shareholder in Lycos, Inc. through its strategic investment and development business unit, CMG@Ventures. CMGI is a leading provider of direct marketing services investing in and integrating advanced Internet, interactive media, and database management technologies.

Acknowledgements

The book you hold in your hands was a real team effort. The idea for the book came from Marie Butler-Knight at Macmillan Publishing. Bryan Pfaffenberger wrote the Internet definitions, and Bryan Hicquet compiled the Web site addresses (from the Lycos search engine at http://www.lycos.com). Faithe Wempen turned the raw material into a manuscript, and the Macmillan Publishing proofreading and layout groups made sure that the design and layout looked good.

Table of Contents

INTERNET DIRECTORY

Over 600 Top-rated Web
Sites From Lycos

Arts and Humanities

Architecture

The City Beautiful: The 1901 Plan for Washington, D.C.
http://xroads.virginia.edu/~CAP/
CITYBEAUTIFUL/dchome.html

Julie K. Rose, author of the excellent hypertext history of The World's Columbian Exposition, takes us on another trip back to the turn of the century in a story of the planning of Washington, D.C. in 1901. Based on an idea of "The City Beautiful," the planners set out to make a bunch of powerful, "vaguely classical" buildings that would be such an inspiration that the world (and the downtrodden residents) would be overwhelmed with a sense of nobility and destiny. Rose first explains the ideology behind the plan, then the plan itself—and the pages look gorgeous (in a powerful, vaguely classical way).

HotWired: Pop
http://www.hotwired.com/pop/

Formerly known as Renaissance, Pop is the portion of HotWired magazine that offers its take on everything from the art of Damien Hirst to the latest from Demi Moore. In between, you'll find an examination of other Web pages, a look at the flea circus currently in residence at San Francisco's Exploratorium, and a review of "The Prince, the Showgirl, and Me," Colin Clark's book about the filming of The Prince and the Showgirl, which starred Marilyn Monroe and Lawrence Olivier. Also available on our last visit was a gossipy look at the latest from Keanu Reeves, Julian Schnabel, and Tuscadero.

Humanities HUB
http://www.gu.edu.au/cgi-bin/
g-code?/gwis/hub/qa/hub.home.html

Students and researchers in the humanities and social sciences
will fall in love with this multi-faceted index of e-journals,
databases, and other pertinent Web resources. Topics range from
anthropology to computing, theology, film & media, women,
"Kibble & Ill-defined" ... well, you get the picture regarding
the HUB's extent. Yet, its vast quantity of attractions appears
to be directly proportional to their quality. For instance, a
"Hellenistic and Roman" pointer is there under Architecture,
but nothing like, say, "Top Ten U.S. Strip Malls."

Islamic Architecture in Isfahan
http://www.anglia.ac.uk/~trochford/isfahan.html

Thomas Rochford, a computer services head at the University
of Cambridge (and dilettante, in the best sense of the word),
created this elegant hypertext tour of Isfahan, Iran's "most interesting and unusual" architecture sites and styles. Photos are
provided in the GIF format, while exposition on, for instance,
the Gonbad Dome includes explanation of domes' religious
implications (they're "amongst the innumerable ways of con-
cretizing the Universe"), plus further references for those who
would dig deeper. Anyone interested in architecture or Islam
will appreciate this well integrated and still developing study.

Art Associations

Arts-Online
http://www.arts-online.com/

Arts-Online is an ambitious attempt to bring together artists
of all genres—visual arts, music, dance, theater, fashion, film—
and create a venue for publicizing and promoting their work.
Massachusetts-based and with a definite New England bias,
Millennium Productions' Arts-Online boasts a long list of artists
and art-related companies looking for exposure on the Net.
The site gives small bands a place to create a home page, galleries a place to show their works, and everyone a place to
make themselves known.

ArtsUSA
http://www.artsusa.org/

Here's the latest buzz on the Beltway arts wire, courtesy of the American Council for the Arts (which, despite the current political brouhaha, comes down firmly in favor of expanded public support for the arts.) The ACA offers insights on art advocacy, including tips on organizing grass roots initiatives, plus full texts of pending cultural legislation. Jump into the fray of the ArtsUSA Cafe for virtual dialectics. A vital resource for artists and activists interested in public policy.

Fine Art Forum Directory of Online Art Resources
http://www.msstate.edu/Fineart_Online/
art-resources/

Serving as a "resource and jumping-off place for people interested in art, and in the possible relationships between art and technology," this massive directory is maintained by Jeliza Patterson, a Masters candidate in art history at Tufts University. Patterson points browsers to advocate organizations like the American Council for the Arts (where activists can learn about current legislation for arts funding), and DIA Center for the Arts, a multi-disciplinary organization based in New York City. The pile of links to museums, galleries, artists, and journals should keep historians and enthusiasts enthralled for hours.

San Francisco Open Studios
http://www.retronet.com/openstud/docs/
default.htm

Based on a real-life art show of 600 amateur artists in San Francisco (it's over, unfortunately), this site is an impressive online excerpt. Nearly 100 artists are represented here, each displaying several works online. Predictably, the site's design is attractive and inline images are pleasantly small, with the larger versions just a click away. The works themselves, understandably, are too varied to describe collectively. Don't expect to slip in for a few minutes and get the whole picture, though. This is a site to be savored.

Other Art Displays

Inward Vessels
`http://www.mcad.edu/home/faculty/szyhalski/`
`spl/Inward.html`

This site, which could loosely be described as an art magazine, almost seems to explore your mind while you're reading it. Inward Vessels is full of low-key, high-impact art and prose, and rather than being hampered by the Web interface, it thrives in it. Some vessels, like Fire Serpents and The Unchangeable, require you to scroll sideways to read the text as the pictures go by; others, like Moving Force, use Netscape's auto-refresh feature in interesting ways. Be sure to check the viewing suggestions so you can get the full impact—there's lots of "impact" to get, here.

Paintings of Vermeer
`http://www.ccsf.caltech.edu/~roy/vermeer/`

In an unlikely marriage of fascinations, CalTech computer engineer Roy Williams has taken time off from parallel computing to create this homage to Dutch master painter Jan Vermeer. The artist's uncanny understanding and manipulation of light raised his renderings of ordinary people to near-holy heights, none of which is lost on the viewer in this electronic gallery. A perfect example: Vermeer's well-known Woman With a Water Jug, an innocuous scene that is made memorable by the master's magic stroke. A splendid clickable map locates other Vermeer classics from Amsterdam to Washington. Excellent selections and reproduction.

The Photojournalist's Coffee House
`http://www.intac.com/~jdeck/index2.html`

Not just for photojournalists, this beautifully-designed site is of interest to anyone who appreciates a story told in pictures. Powerful black and white photo essays by site creator John Decker and Tahra Makinson-Sanders tell better than words about those who struggle to live. Follow the lives of migrant carnival workers, or "carnies," as they pass through small-town Ohio. Or see profiles of teen mothers in Ohio and homeless people in Kentucky. This is a site that stays with you.

The Swiftsure Project
http://www.swifty.com/

The Swiftsure Project aims to make talent from the British Columbia, Canada area available on the Internet. And those Canadians must have a lot of creative people—there's a wide range of talent here. The Artists' section alone has a wide range of ability, from the serious BC Chapter of the Graphic Designers of Canada to the kids' DodoLand in Cyberspace. That section alone could keep you occupied for a while, but there are bookstores, magazines, art galleries... an impressive array of sites in one place.

Art Education

Art Crimes: The Writing on the Wall
http://www.gatech.edu/desoto/graf/

Graffiti: is it the people's art, or the people's misdemeanor? Whether it's on a bathroom wall or the side of a subway train, it's become a kind of universal expression that needs no translation. What does often require translation is the nature of the act, when "gang style" territorial markings make the viewer wonder whether s/he's seeing "art" or merely vandalism. These are some of the issues explored on this site, a collaborative effort by graffiti artists and curators from around the world. Great pointers to real-time exhibits, too.

Artz
http://www.magic.ca/magicmedia/artz.html

This hip, splashy page sponsored by Magicmedia (an online 'zine from Toronto) is a collection of galleries, reviews, and news about the arts in Canada. Swing through an electronic photo gallery for a few tubby views from the Florida beaches (by Canadian photographer Stephen Stober), or grab the latest dish on the independent Canadian film world from The Nightingale Report. Lee's Cyber Palace has info on alternative music dates at Toronto's Dance Cave, not to mention an impressive (and thoroughly eclectic) array of record company links.

File Room Censorship Archive
http://fileroom.aaup.uic.edu/FileRoom/
documents/homepage.html

Here a group of Chicago artists collect and chronicle humankind's history of censorship, from Aristophanes to Annie Sprinkle. No matter how you feel about Ms. Sprinkle's act, it's hard to believe that the classical Greek comedy "Lysistrata" was considered "unmailable" in the United States until 1955. Read the sorry facts here, along with a depressingly large volume of censorship cases categorized by date, location, medium and "reasons for censorship." The latter heading spans topics from religion to politics to sexuality. The File Room is interactive; readers are encouraged to submit new cases.

Guerrilla Girls
http://www.voyagerco.com/gg/gg.html

Those masked anti-discrimination crusaders of the art world take their message online at this site, which is sponsored by the Voyager software company. When they're not busy with lectures and performances (given through gorilla masks), this group of women artists and art professionals produces posters about sexism and other forms of discrimination in the art scene as well as "the culture at large." At times the propaganda may be abrasive, but it can also be mighty clever—and it's available for sale if you want to support the Guerrilla Girls.

Art History

The Alexander Palace Time Machine
http://www.travelogix.com/emp/batchison/

Our hats are off to Bob Atchison, who has created here one of the best—if not the best history Web site we've seen. Maybe we shouldn't gush (you know, to maintain our dignity), but this tour of the Romanov Dynasty palace is absolutely beautiful, not to mention chockablock with historical information on the family of Tsar Nicholas II. It's easy to get lost here, wandering through the palace rooms as they appeared in 1916 (or as close to that as you can get, given the trashing it got during WWII). Dozens of family snapshots and portraits match brief biographical information, and even extended family members and hangers-on (Rasputin, naturally) are included. We won't waste more of your time going on and on, except to urge you to go.

Horus' History Links

http://www.ucr.edu/h-gig/horuslinks.html

At first glance Horus' collection looks like every other giant list of history links. Before skimming the contents, we recommend reading up on what the objective here is, and why they choose the sites they do. While other history departments are out chasing primary sources to study great and famous people, Horus' seems more interested in giving us the tools to learn what life was like for everybody else, that "history from the bottom up" theory. This is no new idea, of course, but the Web has certainly opened up this field, both in terms of information and methodology. This doesn't mean they neglect military and diplomatic history, or any other traditional sites. It just means they include popular culture periphery, like motion picture history, political cartoons and Unabomber manifestoes. It's a great undertaking, to be sure, and requires an investment of shopping time, but this is a tremendous educational resource.

The Nizkor Project

http://www2.ca.nizkor.org/index.html

Here's an incredible, all-encompassing research library devoted to combating one of the darker elements of the Net: the prevalence of Holocaust "revisionism." Canada-based archivist Ken McVay doesn't want to censor anti-Semites and neo-Nazis who flood the Usenet with Holocaust-never-happened spams. Instead, he wants to refute their every claim. The heart and soul of his site is the Shofar FTP Archive—something like 4,000 text documents rebutting, exposing and ridiculing every possible permutation of the revisionist theory. Nizkor is also home to the nascent HWEB Project, a volunteer effort to put the entire collection into HTML.

The World's Colombian Exposition: Idea, Experience, Aftermath
http://xroads.virginia.edu/~MA96/WCE/title.html

Julie K. Rose has done an outstanding job with this hypertext historical "essay" on the Chicago World's Fair of 1893. Although it was called The Colombian Exposition, Rose tells us that the event was only nominally a celebration of Christopher Columbus' first journey to the new world. More significantly, she casts it as a coming out party for the newly technological United States. It was big (633 acres, 65,000 exhibits, 6,000 lectures—some of which are no doubt still being used by slovenly college professors), it was popular (27 million visitors, 6 million of whom got in for FREE—sheesh!) and it was influential. After taking the excellent tour here, which is handsomely illustrated and loaded with history, be sure to read a sample of reactions from those who visited the fair. Amid all this information, Rose draws plenty of parallels between America at the end of the last century and America now, and isn't that the point of reading history? To recognize that we're doomed to repeat it no matter what?

Art Museums

The Krannert Art Museum
http://www.art.uiuc.edu/kam/

The real-time collection at the Krannert—part of the University of Illinois at Urbana-Champaign—spans over four million years, and curators have supplied a generous selection for this virtual presentation. From antiquities like Yupa, an Egyptian stone carving circa 1304 B.C., to Yves Tanguy's 1948 surrealist painting Suffering Softens Stones, the Krannert is as good a place as any to start a comprehensive art history lesson. The Krannert also posts notices of upcoming real-time exhibitions here, as well as ongoing events and series, like the Visual Learning Initiative. A stellar art site.

Royal Ontario Museum
http://www.rom.on.ca/

This museum site is a pleasant departure from the "let's put our free visitors' pamphlet online" motif used by many similar sites. Instead, this art and science museum uses the Web as a separate but complementary part of the museum itself, which is exactly as it should be. Witness the Fun Stuff section, where kids can find online activities and adults can take an archaeology-related quiz. There's also a great Online Artifact Identification project where people send in images of objects they've found and an expert in the field identifies their origins.

Whitney Museum of American Art
http://www.echonyc.com/~whitney/WMAA/

One of the most famous (and controversial) venues for modern and contemporary American art, the Whitney shows its usual imagination and aplomb with this Web site. Even the opening page is characteristically "Whitney": the background intermittently changes to reveal works by Hopper, Gottleib, Twombly, and even you—if you send your original (digital) work for display. The Whitney is not for all tastes, but the quality of the work comes through clearly here.

World Wide Arts Resources
http://wwar.com/

Links to more than 250 museums worldwide (catalogued by country), 560 galleries and exhibitions, 50 publications and 40 arts-related institutions are, believe it or not, only the tip of the iceberg here. There are also antiques, an "Arts Site of the Day," and much more. Visitors can locate a dealer who can say whether that armchair in grandma's attic is really a Chippendale or they can mine the index of major artists for links to Ernst, Esher, Picasso, Pollack, Arbus, Bosch . . . and thousands more.

Commercial Art Galleries

ArtCity
http://www.artcity.com/

This New York-based virtual exhibition hall goes a step beyond the usual gallery fare. In addition to its online studios, the page features its own contemporary art news and commentary, as well as top stories from Art & Auction magazine. At the ArtCity newsstand, Charlie Finch asks the question—which may be on the minds of many—"The Whitney Biennial: Is That All There Is?" and writer Anthony Haden-Guest tries his hand at cartooning. Exhibits rotate regularly. On our last visit, a remarkable showing of 20th century tattoo art from New York City's Drawing Center was accompanied by a rare collection of Vietnamese political paintings. Photography, works on paper and computer digitization are just a few of the media represented in this exceptional art space. And don't worry: your opportunity to buy has not been overlooked by the Webmasters.

Art Indices International
http://www.artindices.com/

This virtual exhibit offers the collector an opportunity to buy original works of art in a variety of genres at a broad range of price levels. We were impressed by the breadth and mastery of the artists represented, like printmaker Gertrude Bleiberg, whose work also appears in the San Francisco Museum of Modern Art. The exhibits rotate regularly, so there's little chance of anything growing stale, and the San Francisco-based curators are happy to take your queries about works you've browsed that have been replaced by new entries. New collectors will find the straightforward presentation a comfortable intro to the art of buying art.

dotCom Gallery
http://www.dotComGallery.com/

A textbook example of Web interface and graphic design done well, this online companion to a real-world gallery of digital art and artists is impressive in just about every way. The goal is to create a forum on and off the Web for artists working in digital composition, video, or anything else that involves technology and the dreaded "interactivity." A handful of artists are featured, along with samples of their work and extended interviews. Read about Marjan Moghaddam, who works with fractal images and tells the story of her early fascination with computers. "I remember buying a computer and never seeing daylight for the first year in the mid-to-late eighties," she says. Now is that such a bad thing? Who needs daylight when we have the Net?

The Electric Gallery
http://www.egallery.com/

Don't be fooled by whimsical titles like "Artichoke Unbound." The Electric Gallery is jam-packed with wonderful original paintings and reproduction prints for sale or just browsing. Each wing of the site focuses on a different subject matter, including unexpected genres like "Jazz & Blues" or "Haitian Art." All of the works are worth a look, though, if only for their eclectic subjects.

Computer Art

American Indian Computer Art Project
http://shell5.ba.best.com/~jantypas/

Turtle Heart, an Objibway artist in the Mojave Desert (and host of this site), tells us he has become a "scout" for the Internet. Traditionally, a tribe's scout was sent out to watch for important natural "signs"—some good, some not so good—and report back to the Chief. The scout is an important member of the tribe, for he or she must be unusually perceptive, and able to decipher and interpret the unknown. He must also be a messenger, and here Turtle Heart shares Native poetry, prose and song, while scouting for signs of Native life in the cyber world. Further explorations in the digital gallery reveal a stunning partnership between historical imagery and new art forms, bridging the gap between past and present. "We are the people of the ancient ones," writes the artist, "of the stars and the seasons of time, root and feather, and beyond." A most gratifying and enlightening stop.

MkzdK
http://www.mkzdk.org/

Mkzdk (yup, that's the name) is chock-full of art and philosophy, but the most intriguing aspect is its organization. The site's framework is based on the concept of adjoining "hubs" and "nodes." It's too complex to describe here, but it essentially comes down to this: through the use of the "mutate" button, you're able to cycle through different aspects of the same site. They all access the same information, but each view contains its own artwork, which is symmetrical, and often disturbingly organic. Even without the "galleries" and the insightful essays on the human condition, this site would be worth visiting, if just to stare at it in awe.

Ozone
http://www.winternet.com/~drozone/index.html

You have to push a lot of buttons to access this library of computer art and fun. "I just like buttons," says "Doc" Ozone, whose stirring art often has the depth of a hologram. Images range from mossy bark and textural landscapes to global thermonuclear war. Don't let the war thing scare you off, though—Ozone has a good sense of humor. (Try activating his "low-bandwidth option," for example.) When you're finished with the images (and this may take a while), follow links to The Annoying Post Brothers (a couple of greedy "twisted bad boys"), or to a place called Demonweb, which may provide your most horrific experience yet on the Net. This guy's good.

Pixel Pushers
http://www.pixelpushers.wis.net/

What's a pixel pusher? It's a digital artist who pushes around little refracted bits of light and eventually makes a picture. If that doesn't quite explain things, this totally interactive icon-driven site from a digital artists' collective will do the job. It will also take care of any sensory deprivation you've been experiencing lately. Click on a 3-D globe to access the main menu, then wander through a gallery of first-rate images that run the gambit of taste and genre, from straightforward portraits to questionable manipulations.

Literature

American Literature Survey Site

```
http://www.en.utexas.edu/~daniel/amlit/
amlit.html
```

You'll feel like you're back at school again (and that's a good thing!) browsing through the texts, discussions, and commentary of the American Literature Survey Site. Developed as part of an American Literature Class at the University of Texas at Austin, students and teachers—and surfers who've just dropped in—have contributed to discussions on American culture and history through the pages dedicated to A Raisin in the Sun, Yellow Wallpaper, and Rip Van Winkle, to name a few. A truly excellent site.

The Electronic Beowulf

```
http://www.uky.edu/ArtsSciences/English/
Beowulf/
```

This digital preservation of these readings won the 1994/5 Library Association Mecklermedia Award for Innovation Through Information Technology. Woo! (Beowulf, for those who haven't had college prep literature, is an Old English epic poem about a bunch of battling Norsemen and a very nasty creature named Grendel.) The Beowulf GIFs are beautiful, vibrant, and detailed, especially since they've been enhanced: through fiber optic backlighting and ultraviolet readings, British and Kentucky-based researchers were able to bring out words otherwise not visible to the naked eye. It's certainly a far cry from the paperback version.

Mark Twain Resources

```
http://marktwain.miningco.com/
```

With this resource for Twain sites, Jim Zwick is emerging as the Web's "Mark Twain Guy." Zwick has collected online exhibits (his own "Mark Twain on the Philippines" is one), texts, scattered writings and cartoons, and even spots where you wouldn't expect to find the cigar-chomping, quote-mongering literary giant (for instance, "Star Trek: The Next Generation" and "Babylon 5" episodes). Twain said, "My books are water; those of the great geniuses is wine. Everybody drinks water." Now millions more have access to the well. Although there's little flash to this site, it is generously sprinkled with Twain quotes, from the celebrated ones to this less-famous comment on Hawaiian volcanoes: "The smell of sulfur is strong, but not unpleasant to a sinner."

Walt Whitman Home Page
http://lcweb2.loc.gov/wwhome.html

Lost from the Library of Congress for nearly 50 years, the Walt Whitman notebooks are brought back here on the Internet. Because they are so fragile (Whitman carried them around in his shirt pockets during the Civil War), handling by the public is out of the question. The solution, part of the National Digital Library effort by the National Library of Congress, is to provide access to these pages in GIF form. You can see Whitman's loop-like script, read his thoughts on the war, and seek insight into the mind of a poet. All pages of the four notebooks have been scanned—even those left blank and the pages that have been partially ripped out.

Museums

National Museum of Natural History
http://nmnhwww.si.edu/nmnhweb.html

Most worthy of its progenitor, the Smithsonian Institution, this virtual museum should please everyone from the interdisciplinary scholar interested in Evolution of Terrestrial Ecosystems to the little kid who loves dinosaurs. Casual visitors may proceed straight to Exhibits & Programs to go, say, "In Search of Giant Squid," while the Research & Collections section offers specifics on the Museum's millions of artifacts, which are categorized under anthropology, botany, mineral sciences and other disciplines. Multimedia and descriptive texts are available, along with contact information for the Museum's departmental personnel. Lose those dunce caps, because this is a serious resource on natural history and sciences.

National Zoological Park Home Page

http://www.si.edu/organiza/museums/zoo/
homepage/nzphome.htm

The National Zoo in Washington, DC, is not your ordinary zoo. Designed around the BioPark concept, they aim "to break down the barriers between zoos, natural history museums, centers for scientific research and museums of art." This outstanding Web site provides a wide-ranging animal-encounter experience. Our favorite: the immense double-wattled cassowary ("They kill more people each year than polar bears do.") Visit the Think Tank, where they're teaching a simple symbolic language to Orangutans, and take a few lessons yourself. Or read about other worldwide research projects with man and beast. Or try the educational games sprinkled throughout this fascinating and beautifully-presented site.

On-Line Visual Literacy Project

http://www.pomona.edu/
visual-lit/intro/intro.html

Under obviously adept direction from Professor Brian Stonehill, media studies students at Pomona College created this enthralling exhibit, examining visual (as opposed to verbal) literacy. (Who says you can't judge a book by its cover?) Visitors are introduced to basic elements of visual communication (e.g. dot, line, texture, motion), and may examine those elements at play via hypertext commentary, photos, and video animations. Light is shed on Direction, for instance, by way of Edward Munch's painting, "The Scream," as well as a clip from the 1940 Disney film Fantasia. Needless to say, a fast modem is a definite plus here. Yet, even without such enthralling multimedia gadgetry, the On-Line Visual Literacy Project will likely teach you a thing or two. Wunderbar!

Smithsonian Institutions Libraries (SIL)

http://www.si.edu/newstart.htm

For those who thought the Smithsonian was just an attic filled with Archie Bunker's chair and the Hope Diamond, the SIL home page is an eye-opening discovery. Far more than just a collection of museums, the Smithsonian is an extended research complex, and you need only visit this site to discover its depth. SIL branch libraries cover everything from archeology to zoology, and they're coming online fast, offering access to the institution's collective resources. Check into the American History branch, for instance, and, under African American Resources you can link to the Amistad Research Center (a leading black cultural study center) at Tulane University. The Political History Resources page will direct you to George Washington's boyhood home in Falmouth, Virginia, as well as to other presidential libraries and archives. The History of Computers Resources section includes a link to the Chronology of Events in the History of Microcomputers.

Philosophy

Hyper Philosophy by WWW
```
http://www.physics.wisc.edu/~shalizi/
hyper-weird/philosophy.html
```

This branch of Cosma Rohilla Shalizi's Hyper-Weirdness by WWW appears to be a gateway to virtually all the Net's philosophy resources and e-texts. And don't miss the numerous annotations such as: "Confucius did not write fortune cookies. Few competent scholars today think he wrote anything at all . . ." or "Daniel Dennett is the late 20th century's answer to William James . . . that's an exaggeration, but they both focus on the mind, both are devout Darwinians . . . ." Shalizi's hypertext stands in well for a hacker's philosophical history. A boon for both serious students and those who'd surf on to the likes of "really strange beliefs" at the Kooks Museum.

Journal of Buddhist Ethics
```
http://www.psu.edu/jbe/jbe.html/
```

This "first (online) academic journal devoted entirely to Buddhist ethics" is a fine, scholarly resource. Complete hypertext articles such as "Are There 'Human Rights' in Buddhism?" are offered with notes and abstracts. Can be tricky reading: in "A Buddhist Ethic Without Karmic Rebirth?" Winston L. King discusses "Theravaada emphasis on the personal nature of karma... followed by a consideration of the evolution of a social dimension to the doctrine in the Mahaayaana... attributed to the twin influences of the Bodhisattva ideal and the metaphysics of Naagaarjuna and Hua Yen." "Ten Easy Steps to Nirvana" it ain't.

Left-Wing Lingo, Ideologies, and History
http://www.dsausa.org/Docs/Lingo.html

J. Hughes has here amassed an excellent leftist panorama. Master it, and you'll be prepared to lead a revolution, or at least teach a university political science course. Between a telling photo of Lenin's ruined (statue) head loaded in a rickshaw, and a cool ideological family tree, this hypertext document traces a rich history of the left, from its roots in Utopian, Communitarian Socialism through, for instance, Trotskyism, all the way to Eco-Feminism. Each section begins with a theory link, and includes praxis page pointers, such as to writings of Bakunin and Kropotkin under Anarchism, George Bernard Shaw under Fabianism, and Michael Harrington under Democratic Marxism. Curious intellects could spend a long and rewarding time exploring what's here.

The Tech Classics Archive
http://classics.mit.edu/

For Netheads who ain't got no cultcha, this undergrad-run MIT Web site provides an unbelievable education. A friendly search form guides you through a storehouse of 376 ancient drama, literature, and philosophy classics. Perfect if you're looking for that one, special passage in Aeschylus' Eumenides. All the big names are here: Sophocles, Plato, Hippocrates. Hard to imagine better content developers than those guys. All texts are English translations. The archive is part of The Tech; the Web site created by MIT's student newspaper of the same name. The student journalists claim their site was one of the first 100 on the Web.

Religion

Christian Resources
`http://www.webcom.com/~nlnnet/xianres.html`

This surprisingly eclectic page offers superb links to Christian Web sites around the world. Dig into your favorite cantus firmus at the Gregorian Chant Home Page (sorry, no droning monks yet), or stop by the Amy Grant fan club for something completely different. "Devotional Help" links the pious to e-mail lists for daily guidance and to great practical pages like "Keys for Kids," a changing collection of stories on "life lessons" illustrated by Bible verses. For a bizarre finale, don't miss Snake Oil: Your Guide to Kooky Kontemporary Kristian Kulture, an e-zine devoted to exposing the vagaries of certain less-than-savory televangelists. Sponsored by Agape Europe Online, an interdenominational Christian mission organization.

Christus Rex: Sistine Chapel
`http://www.christusrex.org/`

It's the next best thing to being Pope! 325 color images of the Sistine Chapel, more than 800 from around the Vatican, and 400+ from cathedrals around the world highlight this collection from Christus Rex, a non-profit group dedicated to spreading the good word through cathedral art. The pics are gorgeous (even if resolution is sometimes fuzzy), and fans of the Italian Renaissance will find many familiar names here: Giotto, Perugino, da Vinci, Raphael, and of course, Michelangelo. Catholics and disciples of papal politics will enjoy recent Papal Encyclicals accompanying the exhibition, not to mention a generous helping of Pontiff-ications, including the full text of John Paul II's pivotal June 1995 "Letter to Women." Due to the sheer volume of images, download times can be lengthy at times, but expect divine inspiration while you wait.

Jewish Web World Homepage
`http://www.nauticom.net/users/rafie/`
`judaica-world.html`

This site offers to bring even the most traditional Jews into the 1990s. Visitors can get a daily dose of religion with Torah Fax

("Torah on the spot for people on the go!") and download a Mac program that will remind them to say sefirah whenever they start their computer. The Asian Kashrus Page serves up some unusually delightful kosher recipes, like Coconut Loozena and Burmese Gin Xao Xaot (chicken with lemon grass). Amazingly diverse Jewish and Israeli resources connect to bar mitzvah lessons, Chabad servers and a host of Judaica galleries. For the kids, JWW offers space to create and display original interactive artwork, and get feedback from other kids around the globe. This is a very lively religious festival. And for even more Judaic resources, link to Jewishnet.

MonasteryNET

http://www.geocities.com/SouthBeach/Lights/
5427/mnet.html

It's a little tough to figure whether MonasteryNET is intended for amusement or edification, but it delivers both. An introduction to The Monastery, located on California's central coast, claims its "lowly and humble monks live a modest and mendicant lifestyle in the pursuit of spirituality and greater knowledge of humanity." Then we're entreated to Chez Loser, to consider, among other features, "The Life and Times of a 41-Year-Old Virgin." That's in keeping with the ascetic theme, to be sure, but... well... who are these guys? They never really say. But Friar Wally offers an extensive "Monk's Guide to Dating," good for clinical analysis of relations between the sexes (e.g. "Perper asserted that 'over half the time, the woman—not the man—initiated the courtship process.'"), and insights on flirting—"Once it has been established that there is interest (i.e., confirmed occurrences of proceptivity), the male must respond in kind (if he has not chosen to flee)." You can consult with the resident shrink, Dr. Psycho M.F.C.C.—"at the vanguard of pseudopsychotraumaneurology research"— or take in serious discourse on questions like: "Can You Be a Modern-Day Job?" Go figure. It's well worth the time.

Theater & Dance

The John F. Kennedy Center for the Performing Arts
http://www.kennedy-center.org/

The Kennedy Center's home page is as visually vivacious as a Broadway-bound show, offering a taste of the Washington, D.C. arts center to Internet patrons. Visit What's On Stage for info on current shows and ticket availability, or click on Exploring the Center for some background and history about the complex, which opened in 1971 as a living memorial to President Kennedy. The Learning Through the Arts area outlines the center's arts education classes and events. You'll also find a Fun Facts page with such trivial tidbits as the information that the Kennedy Center "was constructed using 3,700 tons of Carrara marble, a gift from Italy. Each block of marble was cut, numbered, and labeled in Italy to fit an exact spot on the Center's walls."

Laurie Anderson's Green Room
http://www.voyagerco.com:80/LA/VgerLa.html

This is the next best thing to being on the tour bus with America's premiere performance artist. The "virtual green room" whisks you across North America and Europe and behind the scenes of Laurie Anderson's 1995 multimedia extravaganza, "The Nerve Bible." Techies will drool over the details of Laurie's "drum suit" and "laser tunnel," and hungry vagabonds will want to hunt down her recipe for Hotel Hot Dogs. Most insightful are her road-diary entries, which expose the human side of this techno-artist as she ponders Dollywood, encounters good barbecue, and has an awkward conversation with a childhood friend. Voyager Co., the producer of Anderson's recent performance piece on CD-ROM, Puppet Motel, developed the visually dazzling (and gargantuan) site.

Playbill Online
http://piano.symgrp.com/playbill/home.cgi

This thorough info-site from the ubiquitous Broadway program/reader provides the latest in theater news and listings along with some exciting trivial features for theater buffs. The variety is excellent: those who would rather take in Meet Mr. Hand than Show Boat will appreciate the inclusion of Off-Broadway reports. And the site's proud search device will make your next quest for Brooke Shields references a cinch. Serious theater people will appreciate extras such as "the first theatrical video clip produced exclusively for online" (Ellen Burstyn talking about Sacrilege), and a mind-blowing 37-question "'Hello, Dolly!' Quiz."

Tap Dance
http://www.tapdance.org/tap/

With this informative site, Webmaster Paul Corr accomplishes his stated goal of providing "one-stop shopping" on tap dance and related resources—and he does it with toe-tapping cadence. Visitors can learn the difference between a "scuff" and a "shuffle" in the Tap Glossary, and learn to do the "Shim-Sham" at the Tap Steps page. A reference section gives a brief history of tap dance, and profiles "tap patriarchs" King Rastus Brown ("Mr. Tap") and "Juba," who was apparently the first to combine African steps like the shuffle and slide with jig steps. Dancers can listen to an audio clip of Gregory Hines clacking away. This is also the place to go for consumer tips on snappy items like Jiffy Tabs, those removable taps for street shoes.

Business and Investing

Advertising

50 Best TV Commercials
http://adage.com/news_and_features/
special_reports/

From Advertising Age magazine, this nostalgic and enlightening look at the ultimate commercial medium's most memorable pieces of commercialism is hugely entertaining. Using still images rather than video, making the site accessible without lengthy downloads or irksome plug-ins, A couch potato delight.

Advertising Age
http://www.adage.com/

For the daily scoop on advertising and marketing news, here's a fine source. Ad Age's Web site offers a daily briefing on the big moves in advertising. Is Energizer going to do away with the bunny? Who's doing the ads for the Well? Other cool features include several special sections, like Ad Age's "50 Best Commercials" and the "History of TV Advertising." This site stresses the latest developments in interactive media and includes some reviews of Internet sites. (American Airlines suffers from "brochure-itis," they say.) A cool site for those in the biz.

American Demographics Inc.
http://www.marketingtools.com/

The publisher of American Demographics and Marketing Tools magazines has created a Web site loaded with stuff for people who need to know how much money the average person in Sulfolk, N.Y., spends on books and magazines ($249.72 a year), or what part of the U.S. is tops in hardware store sales (Washington State). Most of the information is selected from this Dow Jones company's publications, but the online version

includes a search engine to help you find the demographic fac-
toid you need. Data files in dBase and Lotus 1-2-3 formats
accompany some of the feature articles, so keeners can download the raw data and crunch the numbers themselves.

Karakas VanSickle Ouellette Advertising and Public Relations
http://www.kvo.com/

It's generally hard to enjoy a purely commercial site, but this
Portland, Oregon, advertising agency makes it easy. Visitors can
casually join a fictional, nosy outsider on a meandering tour of
the firm and its portfolio, employees and clients. Watch out,
though: you could get caught up in the enthusiasm and end up
deciding you need your own personal PR firm. (Check out the
"Yo, Taxi" ad, in which a Powerbook powers the big Times
Square video screen.) The highlight here is really the comical
Who's Pierre? game, where you can attempt to uncover the
Pierre Ouellette (KVO's "creative big cheese") imposter.

Business News & Services

BigBook
http://www.bigbook.com/

If you run a business anywhere in the U.S., it probably already
has a "home page" in the BigBook. The BigBook team has
combined yellow-pages-like business info with detailed maps
from GeoSystems Global Corp. to build an astounding commercial directory. Search for just about any business and you'll
discover its address and phone number and see a street map you
can zoom in and out for land-based bearings. If you can't
remember the name of a business but know where it's located,
you can start your search with the maps. Absolutely a must-see.

CNNfn (The Financial Network)
http://www.cnnfn.com/

CNNfn—the Cable News Network's all-business channel—debuted on television and the Web almost simultaneously in December of 1995. If you missed those first broadcasts you can download video of opening-day preparations here. You'll find loads of fast-breaking business scoops in the site's News in a Hurry section, along with continuously updated indicators from the stocks and commodities markets (and, yes, that includes pork belly futures).

Money and Investing Update
http://update.wsj.com/

It may lack the grit of the *Wall Street Journal*, but this site created by the legendary financial newspaper has a leg up on its tree-based parent. Money and Investing Update bills itself as the Net's premier source of financial news and analysis, and it doesn't disappoint. At any time during the business day, you can log into this service and get articles analyzing the latest swings of today's trading, beating tomorrow's *Wall Street Journal* by a mile. You also get material from *The Asian Wall Street Journal*, *The Wall Street Journal Europe*, and *Dow Jones* newswires sprinkled in for valuable international connections.

The Wall Street Journal
http://wsj.com/

The newspaper for investments just made a big one itself. Taking the copy-for-money plunge is one of the nation's biggest and most-respected newspapers, *The Wall Street Journal*. While access to this site remains free until August 31 for anyone who registered before July 31 (guess they like the end of the month), it will cost money after. Is it worth it? If you like the Journal it is. You'll find just about every story in the printed edition plus updates throughout the day—those classic center-column front-page tales and the aggressive editorials. And it even looks like the Journal. Articles from the Asian and European versions are included—along with the best business reporting you're likely to find. A fabulous read—even on a monitor.

Career and Jobs

America's Job Bank
http://www.ajb.dni.us/

Linking 1,800 state employment-service offices in the United States, America's Job Bank lists upwards of 100,000 jobs at any given time—probably the largest source for job postings on the Net. And we're not talking just technical jobs. On our last visit, we found choker setter positions in logging camps throughout Oregon and Washington, and even discovered a bank president's desk ready for the filling in Savannah, Ga. Best part? All this info is free.

Employment Opportunities and Job Resources
http://www.jobtrak.com/jobguide/

Whew! If you STILL can't find a job after using this home page, something may be wrong. (Have you checked your breath?) Help-wanted servers, recruiter links, professional societies, government job listings... they're all here. Margaret Riley (this is also called "The Riley Guide") maintains this employment resource out of the Worcester Polytechnic Institute. A fine introduction explains how to use the Net to find an employee or a job; this is also a mini-course on Internet usage in general. From government and business through the arts and humanities, this guide tries to cover all the bases, with special emphasis on high-tech and computer employment. It used to take days in the library to dig this kind of stuff up.

Hard@Work
http://www.hardatwork.com/

You've got to be a real grouch not to love the name and the atmosphere of this Web site aimed at those interested in the social mechanics of the workplace. Dennis Murphy and Mark Gozonsky have both worked in the personnel management business, and now they've brought their gregarious-Texans approach to the Web. Hard@Work's mission, they say, "is to reduce the oversupply of fear and alienation in the workplace by meeting the pent-up demand for constructive communication about what's happening on the job." Here, you're invited to play "Stump the Mentor," and if the computer can't solve your difficulties motivating employees or managing the boss, it's time to create an original solution and add it to the database. Newsreader technology enables interactive discussion forums, such as the Water Cooler, where you can "tap into refreshing streams of work-related thought."

Online Career Center
   http://www.occ.com/

It's not who you know, it's what database you know. This may become the new job-hunting motto. The Online Career Center is a breeze: enter a job description and it spits out a list of up-to-the-minute postings from across the country. You can also find limited career advice—though without that tender, sensitive touch for which human career counselors are so famous. Or, you can become part of the database yourself by posting your resume. Cost to you: zero. Most helpful to computer specialists: our search found 2019 listings under the keyword unix against 159 for the keyword nurse.

Corporate Homepages

Heineken
   http://www.Heineken.nl/

With a virtual tour of international cafes and bars and a role-playing game that sends visitors on a global goose chase, giant Dutch brewer Heineken serves up a worldly Web site. It's always Happy Hour somewhere in the world, and Heineken's Time Zone page lets you spin the globe until you find it. When you're ready for serious fun, the Heineken Quest casts you as a private investigator assigned to escort a millionaire's unruly son from Amsterdam to Sydney, Australia. If you're lucky, you might win one of Heineken's monthly draws for those on the list of top players.

Hewlett-Packard
http://hpcc920.external.hp.com/

One would expect an excellent Web site from electronics whiz-kids HP, and yet they've still outdone themselves. Their state-of-the-art, icon-rich interface is a delight to navigate. Consumers will appreciate the index of product documents and catalogs (including a Windows 95 support page). Business-folk will enjoy the company briefs, news releases, and HP's Worldwide Contacts. Job-seekers can search the database of HP employment opportunities by entering the state, department, and kind of job they prefer. And everyone can check out the Palo Alto garage where Bill Hewlett and Dave Packard got started.

Microsoft
http://www.microsoft.com/default.asp

Some genuflect and some gag at the mention of Microsoft, but nearly everyone can use this site. Microsoft asks "Where do you want to go today?" then lets you get software updates, patches, and help files for its many products. A lightning-fast database lets you search by key words. (Searching for the word "bug" quickly gets you a document explaining how to become a beta tester, a sort of crash-test dummy for new software.) And a Top Ten list features the most common questions site visitors have and the pages that answer them. The massive library is likely to answer 95% of your questions. This is a marvelous substitute for long hours spent on hold for Microsoft's telephone technical support! Highly recommended.

ZD Net
http://www5.zdnet.com/

Now the publishing giant has led its flock of over a dozen magazines to the Net, where it offers an array of helpful information for computer users of all types. Hesitant to freely give away the helpful tips of "PC Magazine" and "MacUser" (just two of their high-profile publications), Ziff-Davis delivers smaller, fresher Web editions which sell you on the magazines without stealing away all-important subscriptions. ZD Net has so much to offer—from hot news and tips to just plain fun FREE stuff, it's hard to keep up in just one visit.

Investing

Chicago Board of Trade
http://www.cbot.com/

The "world's leading futures exchange" has a fattened pork belly of a site here, packed with information. Speculators will find closing prices for commodities exchanges worldwide, and agricultural market commentaries at both mid-day and closing. The Visitors Center contains histories of the market and the CBOT (dating back to the mid-19th century, when "disappointed farmers who could not find buyers dumped their grain into Lake Michigan"); a guide to "futures market jargon"; a QuickTime movie of the trading floor; even a paean to the Art Deco architecture of the Board's building. Lots of info and nice graphics to boot, though the latter can be a bit slow to load.

Finance Watch
http://finance.wat.ch/

If you can't put your money in a Swiss bank, you can at least put some time into this treasure trove of world financial information from Switzerland. (Do not adjust your set: they do spell it "wat.ch." "Ch" is the Net's country code for Switzerland.) Visitors can find exchange rates, stock market data, and even an online training course in futures and options. (The Web was pioneered in Switzerland, after all.) The regularly updated hotlist brings you the newest financial sites, from the Philadelphia Stock Exchange to global market predictions from Perception Knowledge Systems, Inc. A superbly designed site that brings into reach everything from derivatives to a financial glossary.

StockMaster at MIT
http://www.stockmaster.com/

The experimental StockMaster at Massachusetts Institute of Technology spits out historical price/volume charts for stocks trading on U.S. markets. You'll find the most recent closing prices and graphs with up to a year of historical data for some 500 companies, plus information on an assortment of mutual funds—all part of a project masterminded by MIT Artificial

Intelligence Lab regular Mark Torrance. Also available online is the raw data behind each chart. That means visitors can download the numbers and do their own analyses on companies ranging from ADC Telecommunications to Zycad Corp.

Stock Research Group
http://www.stockgroup.com/index.html

The goal of the Canada-based Stock Research Group "is to provide an environment where investors can receive up-to-date stock and investment information... about high-growth stocks on the NASDAQ, VSE, and Alberta exchanges." Visitors can read thorough profiles of companies like International Tasty Fries, Inc.—a group that SRG feels is poised "to capitalize on an entrenched product in a market that is $12 billion in North America alone." (In America? Heck, it's a $12 billion market in our office.) By focusing on "small fry" like these, SRG offers an extremely valuable service to smaller investors.

Real Estate

ComSpace Commercial
Real Estate Resource
http://www.comspace.com/

ComSpace boasts the largest listing on the Internet of commercial real estate for sale or lease. The company's searchable database contains entries from a growing listing of U.S. cities along with the latest news from the real estate game in each region. For real estate shoppers more interested in tractor-trailer access than in suite baths, ComSpace is a real find.

Cyberhomes
http://www.cyberhomes.com/

Cyberhomes has unveiled a nifty approach to house-shopping in communities across the U.S., backed by data supplied by regional multiple-listing services. We went shopping for a home near Sandwich, Illinois by clicking on a map of the state, then using the push-button interface to zoom in on the community until we could see its suburban streets. Then we selected a price range and features such as the number of baths and bedrooms to come up with our $124,900 dream home. Another great idea here is the use of links to other Web sites to provide information on weather, population stats, services, and attractions in each region. This site will improve with more listings from other areas of the country.

International Real Estate Directory and News
http://www.ired.com/

The International Real Estate Directory and News (IRED) is not just a terrific jumpstation to some 5,000 real estate sites on the Web: it's also an online magazine jam-packed with articles that both buyers and sellers will find useful. Billed as "the independent source for real estate information on the Web," IRED keeps tabs on the industry's use of the Internet in articles such as "Apartment renters and building owners finding Web useful" and "AOL offers Bank of America home loan resources."

Realty LawNet
http://www.realty-lawnet.com/

Brought to you by the New York law firm of Novick, Edelstein, Lubell, Reisman, Wasserman & Leventhal, P.C. (whew!), Realty LawNet gives you information on the wide-ranging legal ramifications of real estate. Legal forms are provided here, plus links to banking, legal, and government sites, as well as information on topics like tenant investigations, foreclosures, and the basic buying and selling of real estate. It's all geared toward the professional; the lingo may be daunting to the general consumer.

Web Consulting/ Marketing

Atomic Vision: dex
http://www.atomicvision.com/dex_now/index.html

Prepare to enter a different dimension at this stimulating minimalist site from a Web design firm. Called "dex," this e-zine

may lose you for a while, but stick with it. Once you under-
stand its purpose as a gentle promotion for the font design and
Web consulting services of Atomic Vision (cool name!), you'll
appreciate the fresh approach. Expect some debunking of the
Web's design myths, and perhaps even some ideas on what
NOT to do with your Web site.

Freerange Media
http://www.freerange.com/

Free Range Media, Web consultant/creator to the stars (Time-
Warner's Pathfinder, for one), shares some of its secrets here.
Don't miss the Showcase section where Free Range provides a
good general explanation of new technologies (great if you
don't know the difference between Shockwave and VRML),
along with examples of their work and links to download sites
for the requisite viewing software and/or plug-ins. Even though
you probably can't afford to hire them for your personal homepage, these folks are worth emulating.

infoPost
http://www.infopost.com/

This is headquarters for a California company specializing in
putting small businesses on the Web. And if volume means anything, the people at infoPost are among the more successful at
the game. Here you'll find Designs by Margarita, selling flash-
light headbands for $28.50, just a flick of the wrist away from
the Thornton Winery, where you can pick up a bottle of 1993
Pinot Noir "made the traditional way" for $16. Most of the
vendors online here make California their home, but you can
do all your shopping online.

Stoogenet
http://stoogenet.com/

Stoogenet is billed as the site for those who want to learn how
not to do business on the Internet. That's why you'll find marketing case studies here under categories such as Hall of Fame
Boners and Promotion Pitfalls. "Everybody screws up," say head
stooges Bill and Randy. "Learn from your mistakes." The people

behind Stoogenet bared all to get the site rolling, but visitors are asked to contribute their own marketing horror stories (like the guy who was so busy he posted a link to his competitor's Web pages instead of his own). It's a fun site that'll get better if others turn out to be as accident prone as Bill and Randy.

Computers and Software

Hardware, General

C | Net
http://www.cnet.com/

Formerly a promotional site for its television ventures, C | Net is now a bona fide Web heavyweight when it comes to computer industry news. No Web gadget goes unused here—RealAudio news reports, Java applets, dizzying use of frames for no apparent reason—but somehow it all works. Imagine a daily TV show covering the computer software and hardware industry, and you'll have a good idea what to expect here. The news is timely (reorganization rumors at Apple, for instance), and professionally presented. There's also a healthy dose of Net-related news, gossip, and even a little interactivity. And while the site is still an infant, it's already spawned its first progeny with the venerable shareware.com site.

Daystar Digital
http://www.daystar.com/

In the brave new world of Macintosh compatible computers, Daystar Digital is clearly looking to capture the high ground. Their flagship product, the Genesis MP, is a blisteringly fast graphics powerhouse with up to four PowerPC processors. That level of performance pushes it out of the league of Apple's Macs (in terms of both performance and price) and moves it into competition with Silicon Graphics' low-end workstations. At this site there's plenty of marketing double-talk (video cards for the MP are listed as simultaneously required and optional), but it's clear there's some truth to the hyperbole. These are some wicked fast machines.

Mac Today Online
http://www.avaloncity.com/MacToday/

Independent of Apple Computer, this e-edition of the monthly print tabloid delivers "an irreverent, off-the-wall, PC-slamming, totally-biased look at the Macintosh." It's quite generous, as readers get free access to "News From Apple," feature stories (answering questions like: "after the Win 95 hype is gone, what's really left?"), and product reviews (e.g. of the popular Suitcase font utility). That's all from Mac Today's current issue. Columns such as "Life in the Mac Lane" are also good, say, for dispelling the popular myth that Apple's advertising designer "is a serious substance abuser." (Commentator Scott Kelby thinks "it's more that he or she has completely lost touch with consumers" in an effort to win over "artsy-fartsy" ad award judges.) Efficient to browse, fun and informative to read, with lots of cool Mac links as well.

Moan and Groan Page
http://eightof.tsixroads.com/Moan/

Just about everyone's been burned by bad hardware or software at some time, but "The Moan and Groan Page" aims to change all that. By acting as an archive of war stories—"Widget for Windows erased my hard drive," or "I spent three days on hold waiting for SlimeTech's customer support"—the Net's citizens can warn each other of problem companies and products before another person gets burned. The database is large, but mostly PC-related (stop laughing, Mac users). If nothing else, it makes for an entertaining, empathetic read. And it just might save you some yanked-out hair.

Hardware, Peripherals

Adaptec, Inc.
http://www.adaptec.com/

This leading manufacturer of controller cards for PCs (and now Macs) encourages you to read about new products, get technical support, then call your broker and buy stock in the company. At our last visit, the stock was doing quite well, so something must be going right. Adaptec has expanded its business from the original SCSI hard drive controllers to a new market they call "IOware," so you'll find information about disk arrays and high-speed network cards as well. Kudos for the detailed compatibility listings, a feature that you often don't get in the computer industry until after you've already bought the product.

Black Box On-Line Catalog
http://www.blackbox.com/bb/index.html/tig7915

One of the hardest things you can do with computers is to interconnect them, and the Black Box company has been helping out for 18 years. Now they've moved their comprehensive catalog of little black boxes to the Web, and they've implemented one of the best online shopping experiences anywhere in cyberspace. We admit that they're selling pretty dull stuff like modem cables, but they do so in a manner that's both outgoing and businesslike. There's also an excellent bit-head glossary (no, the ISDN D-channel has nothing to do with Disney), with friendly technical articles, all eminently searchable.

Phoenix Technologies
http://www.ptltd.com/

Many PC users may see this company's name every time their computer starts—since Phoenix makes a popular BIOS (Basic Input/Output System) chip needed to start your computer. This site shows off new Phoenix BIOS chips that support buzzword standards like Plug-and-Play, and offers a welcome technical support library for older chips (great for solving computer mysteries). Lots of techie information; we suggest getting details on your BIOS before your computer crashes, though.

Xyplex, Inc.
http://www.xyplex.com/

Xyplex, Inc. is a company that makes network switching equipment and remote access servers. Granted, the subject matter isn't terribly exciting, and no one ever wept tears of joy over a new stackable ATM switch. (Well, we did once, but it was a weak moment.) But you can't doubt the quality of the site: there's no tortured maze of links to traverse to get the info you need, like some other corporate giants we could mention. And, even if you can't find your info quickly, a search engine is provided. For a down-to-business approach, plenty of companies could take lessons from these people.

Hardware, Personal Computers

Advanced Micro Devices (AMD)
http://www.amd.com/

If you can identify any of the following initials, this site will be a hit with you: CISC, EPROM, SRAM, CMOS, CPLD. If you guessed that they're all types of computer chips made by AMD, you're mostly right; the correct industry term is "integrated circuit." Now that you qualify, you'll find detailed technical reports and product announcements at this site, like the 120-megahertz 486 chip coming to a PC near you. And while you won't find a "Pentium" chip (that's a trademark of Intel, AMD's arch rival) you can get little-known facts about the competing K86 family of processors. (Hint: we're told the AMD K5 is 30% faster than a similar Pentium). A fine spot for computer speed freaks and electronic engineers.

Computer Hardware and Software Phone Numbers
http://mtmis1.mis.semi.harris.com/comp_ph1.htm
1#top

Until we have total global online Yellow Pages, this site will have to do. Harris Semiconductor faithfully maintains this current list of phone numbers and other electronic addresses for vendors of computer hardware and software. Sounds dull, but could be a lifesaver if you're trying to find obscure software, or if your software vendor has deftly hidden its phone number in your manual (a common practice in the fly-by-night computer industry). As a bonus, you'll find those elusive BBS numbers, since many software and hardware vendors are noticeably absent from the Net. Actually, it's kind of funny to see the silly 800-numbers that the gear-heads come up with (e.g., 800-TINY-RAM). Of course, once you get these numbers, you'll still have to spend hours listening to Muzak after the electronic operator says "Your call is very important to us."

Corey's MacOS Page
http://www.imc.sfu.ca/mac/default.html

Corey's MacOS page is clearly the work of a Mac devotee. With a fervor bordering on fanaticism, your host serves up a well-organized collection of software and other information about operating system updates (rated according to their usefulness), Apple's plans for the hardware line, and even the upcoming Windows 95 of Appledom, System 8. Better known by its working title, Copland, this Macintosh operating system redesign is given its own page to both quell and fan the fire stirring in the hearts of Mac fans everywhere. Those too anxious to wait for the much-anticipated release will find icons borrowed from pre-release versions of Copland, so that they can get at least a taste of what's to come. There's much more to the parent site, though, and it deserves some exploring.

Quantum
http://www.quantum.com/

Hard disk users who eat 10 to 20 megabytes a day will feast on this "information buffet" from Quantum Corp. If your wimpy hard drive is under 500 megabytes, you'll quickly feel like you're in the Dark Ages while browsing through detailed brochures on drives now measured in gigabytes (of which you use about 25 megabytes). Or if you only dream about that much real estate, you can enter a weekly drawing for a free hard drive. Techies will be all over the guides to jumper settings and drive specs, saving those annoying tech support phone calls. Don't miss the info on new solid state drives that could someday make hard drives measured in megabytes as outdated as trilobites.

Hardware, Servers and Mainframes

Digital Equipment Corporation
http://www.digital.com:80/info/home.html

Make no mistake: the folks at Digital want you to know their lightning-fast computers can wow even NASA rocket scientists. This catch-all site touts the new 200-plus megahertz Alpha systems (souped-up rivals to the Pentium), yet still provides support for older ("honored citizen") mainframe systems. The pages load briskly, and they'd better: after all, NASA uses Digital computers to launch the Space Shuttle.

Sun Microsystems
http://www.sun.com/

Sun workstation computers and software used to be the best-kept secret of brainy engineers. But in the world of the Web, Sun is as prominent as its namesake. This site's snazzy interface leads you through its treatises on tools that can connect you to the rest of the blue planet. Customers, job-seekers, and investors can all benefit from this site, but don't expect modesty. This cocky 12-year old company proclaims itself (with Macaulay Culkin-like charm) to have had the most successful start in the history of American business. But among corporate Web sites, they've earned a right to brag.

Tandem Computers, Inc.
http://dmzweb.tandem.com/

"Tandem Means Infobahn," we're told at this home page. Tandem is now pushing Internet servers, so technology shoppers will find a load of information categorized neatly into industry categories. No earth-shaking demos, but they at least seem to prove that their servers hold a lot of information and work reliably. Like the autobahn itself, this page is for seasoned drivers.

Unisys
http://www.unisys.com/

Unisys is one of the grand-daddies of the computer industry, and
serves up a bit of something for everyone here. Mention of the
company's workstations, servers, and software (big in the retail
and banking industries) takes back seat to the company's more
colorful projects, like a "real-time scoring" system provided for
the U.S. Open golf tournament (we learned that Fuzzy Zoeller
bogeyed the 7th in Round 4). We also read news of a new $520
million Unisys contract to provide computers and software for
the IRS "modernization" program (quick—alert your accoun-
tant). Kudos for making things interesting with ongoing golf
promotions; the rest is mostly corporate news.

Platforms, Macintosh

Apple Computer
http://www.apple.com/

Apple, Inc: mild-mannered computer maker or dangerous cult?
You decide at this mega-site, where the company with the
intensely loyal following has set an admirable standard for Web
quality. Discover the quirks of Apple's confusing array of models
named with P (Performa, PowerBook, PowerMac, Pippin—is
this some cult code?) and take a journey into the amazingly
detailed product support area. Or, check the What's New list
to get the latest hyperlinks to Apple's myriad software libraries
and QuickTime files. Also new on our last visit: a big feature
on "Why Macintosh computers are better than PCs running
Windows 95." (And if the details on processing speed and multimedia don't convince you, maybe the "Doonesbury" cartoons
will.) A must for Apple-philes; a temptation for frustrated PC
users.

The Info-Mac HyperArchive
http://hyperarchive.lcs.mit.edu/
HyperArchive.html

This is a Web interface to the Mac software archives at Stanford
University, probably the biggest single collection of Macintosh
freeware and shareware in the world. (The archive is mirrored

in many machines across the Internet.) It takes some study to use it well, and beginning users may have trouble with it, but the alternative is to get involved in FTP transfer arcana. Trust us, this is easier. A great concept that can only get better.

Metrowerks WorldWide
http://www.metrowerks.com/

Any Macintosh code hacker knows the name of Metrowerks, the company that created CodeWarrior, the popular Macintosh programming environment. On this site, you can get everything CodeWarrior you'd ever need—except CodeWarrior itself, of course. Read about the new release of CodeWarrior 8 and all its new additions; if you already have it, you can download updates to the software and get errata for the manuals (hey, it happens). You can get info on all their other products, too, which includes other programming books and tools, and even some GeekWare ("Dress for success in the latest Metrowerks fashions").

WIN Macintosh Shopping Directory
http://www.wincorp.com/windata/msd/msd.html

Don't be confused: this list of Macintosh mail-order phone numbers has nary a Window in sight. (WIN stands for the World Internet Corporation.) Part of the One World Plaza shopping mall, the page has a few links to online catalogs and even fewer graphics; instead, it's just a utilitarian list of phone numbers, perfect for anyone looking for CD-ROM drives, memory, scanners or used Macs on the cheap. Not a design award-winner, but it gives Mac maniacs good contacts.

Platforms, OS/2

Berkeley OS/2 Users Group
http://godzilla.EECS.Berkeley.EDU/os2/

OS/2 cultists, under increasing pressure from Windows 95, will find a friendly oracle at this moderately fun page from Cal-Berkeley. (Shouldn't these kids be out protesting?). The Webmasters are vigilant about posting demos and betas of new commercial releases for OS/2 (like the new OS/2 Web browser), plus the hottest shareware. The support pages range from official IBM (all done up in respectful blue), to a hip section about sound cards. Non-OS/2 computer users can find lots of great stuff, here, too, like bitmap libraries (including Homer Simpson after a doughnut), and the Fun Stuff section, which brings on the latest in Microsoft bashing and other computer-related humor, including "What if people bought cars like computers?" You must know the secret OS/2 handshake to enter.

OS/2 e-Zine!
http://www.os2ezine.com/

On the first line of the first page, you're hit with the sentence: "If you're not using OS/2, you have our sympathy." This opinion is evident in much of the writing in this informative magazine, because, after all, OS/2 is simply the best operating system, isn't it? (So they believe here, at least.) The 'zine includes reviews, locations of files you can download, and interviews with high-power execs in the OS/2 world (a recent one was Dan Porter, prez of the company that created Post Road Mailer). Definitely not to be missed by the OS/2 user.

OS/2 Warp Vs. Windows 95
http://www.austin.ibm.com/pspinfo/
os2vschg.html

Howard Cosell would have loved this matchup: "The scintillating performer takes on the muscular heir apparent!" This site offers IBM's subtle trash talk before its bout. You get a series of documents explaining with certainty that Windows 95 lacks the strength and endurance of OS/2. (Translated: "We're gonna kick hiney.") Some good technical explanations in understandable terms; will please those betting against the 900-pound Microsoft gorilla.

Rexx Language
http://rexx.hursley.ibm.com/rexx/

Finally, a programming language with a dog's name. Rexx is IBM's highly-regarded "scripting" language built into the OS/2 operating system, allowing you to customize your programs with powerful "macros." IBM's labs in the UK offer this complete guide to Rexx resources on the Web (both free and commercial), and describe how Rexx can be used on other operating systems. We're told it's simple compared to some programming languages, so beginning programmers may want to start here. No cartoon logos to play up the browser name connection—just lots of details on "logic operations" and "string handling."

Platforms, Unix

The Linux Home Page
http://www.linux.org/

Linux is a freely-distributable version of Unix, and arguably the most popular. This site contains Everything You Ever Needed To Know About Linux (But Couldn't Figure Out Who To Ask). From FAQs to searchable software indexes to other Linux resources, it's all here. If you want the power of Unix but can't afford it, and you're worried about the lack of support for a free product, take the time to read this information. The scope of this site could convince you that Linux has enough support to be reliable.

NetGenesis
http://www.netgen.com/

This staggering site from a Web software and consulting company does more than simply promote products. It offers valuable resources including the Comprehensive List of Sites and Wandex, two unique and efficient search engines. (And for good cocktail party discussion, don't miss the charts of the Web's growth). This is a satisfying trip to the Web's cutting edge.

Unix Guru Universe
http://www.polaris.net/ugu/

Unix operating systems and the people who control them are due some serious respect, and this site shows why. It's hard to say why anyone would want to make a career of Unix administration, a field notorious for turning previously respected professionals into office slaves with less seniority than temps. But for those who love to hack a shell script, who think in terms of command line arguments, it's a religion. Priests of this misunderstood faith will find their shrine at this site, an altar of Unix resources with that holiest of Web relics, a nifty text search engine. Information on anything from network security to open sysadmin positions can be found in the neatly organized categories therein. And the congregation says: amen.

The X Advisor
http://landru.unx.com/DD/advisor/index.shtml

No, this doesn't have dirty pictures—it's an online magazine for users of X Windows, a graphical interface for Unix. Articles like "Extending Widget Attributes" help programmers put a prettier face on Unix, and columns about "Using Your Client Data Luggage" offer ever-popular tips and tricks. Most articles have a technical and academic bent aimed at professionals who spend their entire day cranking away on Unix workstations. But if you qualify, this prolific commercial e-zine is a definitive resource. And keep extending those widgets, will you?

Platforms, Windows

NetEx Unofficial Windows 95 Software Archive
http://www.NetEx.NET/w95/index.html

Internet consultant company NetEx here provides a free online forum for downloading the latest Windows 95 shareware and discussing Windows 95 problems. Sure, there are ads, but strong content including Usenet-like discussion groups and frequently updated software archives makes the site worth repeated visits. In the discussion forums, Windows users help each other solve problems like configuring TCP/IP to connect to their Internet providers. It can be annoying to wait for graphics to download on pages that could have easily been designed as text, but that's a small quibble. The wealth of good downloads makes it worth the trouble.

The Ultimate Collection of Winsock Software
http://www.tucows.com/

While it may not be the "ultimate" collection, this site does have a load of software available for Windows. The acronym for the site's name is "TUCOWS," so you'll be seeing a pair of bovines pretty frequently. The software is organized by subject, and each item is provided with a short decryption, version number, byte size and the like, and is available for download. The products are also rated on a scale of (what else?) one to five cows. You're given a choice of "graphics rich" or "not so graphics rich" options; if you plan to download a lot, pick one of the 28 mirror sites around the world closest to you.

Win95 Magazine
http://www.win95mag.com/

Riding on the success of its Windows95.com sister site, Win95 Magazine is a gold mine for users Microsoft's much-ballyhooed (and almost as much maligned) Windows 95. Reviews of the first issue turned up quality articles on 95's buggy security, new shareware applications, and a tutorial on how to set up file sharing with another Windows 95 machine across the Internet (Mac users are undoubtedly now mumbling about being able to do that since the 80s). The interface is smooth, making liberal use of frames and some Netscape-specific tricks. It's not loaded down with huge graphics, though, so you won't spend all day waiting for images just to read an article.

WinSite
http://www.winsite.com/

In the world of Windows software, the reigning champ of FTP sites has always been CICA, a huge shareware archive based at Indiana University. WinSite is the commercial descendant of CICA, repackaging the archive for the Web and putting a smooth interface on what has long been accessible by FTP. WinSite carries on CICA's tradition of archiving and organizing just about every freely-distributable Windows 3.1, 95, and NT software package there is. There's not much to the interface, but tools you'd expect like a search function are there when you need them. The graphics are a little cheesy, but it doesn't matter much when all you really want is to drop in, snag some files, and scurry out.

Platforms, Windows NT

Cold Fusion
```
http://www.allaire.com/go/
go.dbm?webresourceurl=/products/
coldfusion/20/intro.cfm
```

Unlike the original cold fusion, this is no harebrained nuclear theory. This is Windows NT (and 95) software that puts databases on the Web by automatically fusing them into HTML code. If done correctly, it could save hundreds of hours of conversion and programming for companies wishing to market their valuable databases to Web users. The documentation here explains how it's done and what software configuration it requires; you can even download a free 30-day evaluation version of the software to see if it works for you. If it works as promised, it could enrich more Web sites with online conferences and searchable databases; a must-visit for Web developers.

Digital's Windows NT Home Page
```
http://www.windowsnt.digital.com/
```

This is quite a collection of resources for Windows NT, both on and off the Digital server. After you get past Digital's advertising (hey, they pay for the thing, after all), you'll find locations for hardware and software resources, developer and VAR resources, and a slew of shareware and freeware programs. There's a light note here and there: in the Tech Tips section, you can learn the cryptic sequence of commands that will turn your cursor into a spinning barber pole. (Who said all computer stuff was boring?)

The Windows NT Information Server
```
http://www.bhs.com/
```

In all the hubbub about Windows 95, has everyone forgotten about Windows NT? These folks at Beverly Hills Software certainly haven't. Not only do they offer many NT-based programs for download in an ingenious on-screen folder-based format, but they also provide a large list of NT-savvy network consultants. Lots of well-organized information, but one major complaint: the tables are often wider than most monitors can handle.

Windows NT on the Internet
http://www.microsoft.com/pages/bussys/ internet/in10000.htm

Find out how to use Windows NT as a Net server and publishing system "straight from the horse's mouth," here. But this is no gift horse—some of the key details are offered only in the Windows NT Resource Kit, which will cost you. For a free ride, use the exhaustive list of Net resources on NT.

Software, Archives

The Consummate Winsock Apps List
http://cwsapps.texas.net/

On this site, Forrest Stroud lists and reviews many popular programs available for all flavors of Windows. Its power cannot be denied: the programs are separated by topic, and each application is given a rating, short and long reviews, who makes it, where to get it—simply a wealth of information. Although its title limits its scope to winsock applications ("winsock" loosely translates into "what allows Windows to connect to the Net"), there's still some stuff on other types of programs, too.

Virtual Software Library
http://www.shareware.com/

This is the mother of all software archives on the Net. And we're talking the kind of mother that holds your hand, shows you the way, and bakes you cookies when you get home. Merely click on an icon for your computer type, enter a few search words, and a list of relevant shareware from servers around the world pops up nearly instantly. Or, if you want to know what's hot, you can get a list of the top 30 requested files. For users who've dawdled away hours trying to find software on a BBS or online service, this is staggeringly simple.

Walnut Creek CD-ROM
http://www.cdrom.com/

Walnut Creek is best known on the Net for its huge FTP site and off the net for its low-end CD-ROM titles. Their Web presence brings these two together nicely. Appealing more to the techie crowd, Walnut Creek's CD-ROM line focuses on programming tools, operating environments, and shovelware (all the freely-distributable software they can fit on a CD). The site also provides a smooth interface to the FTP site archives and an unexpected technical support area focusing on software like Linux (which they sell on CD-ROM). Walnut Creek probably won't create the next "Myst," but they've clearly found their niche.

Windows95.com
http://www.windows95.com/

If you're a Windows 95 user, getting used to the Web interface to Windows95.com should take all of a few seconds. This huge, well-organized archive of Windows 95 tips, trivia, and software looks just like the Windows 95 desktop. Funny thing is, the site isn't from Microsoft; Brigham Young University grad student Steve Jenkins has put together this beautifully-designed site with everything from reviews of Microsoft's Internet Explorer to a custom live chat system for users to share Windows war stories. And if we know Microsoft, heads rolled when word got out that someone outside the company's Redmond campus registered the windows95.com domain first.

Software, Companies

Amdahl Corporation
http://www.amdahl.com/

This site holds plenty of interest even if you're not a user of this well-known computer company's high-end systems. Visitors can start with the company's top-notch guide to Web resources, linking to selected beginner's guides, search engines, and a Hot Topics section which, on our last visit, focused on the 25th anniversary of the Internet and the 50th anniversary of the United Nations. As a good corporate citizen of California,

Amdahl also hosts the home pages of the Santa Clara County Sheriff's Office and provides forms to query real-time road conditions on California highways. California drivers will be happy to receive advance warning of construction closures and restrictions, others will simply be glad they live in, say, Wyoming.

Autodesk
http://www.autodesk.com/

Software giant Autodesk has put together a strong showing on the Web with plenty to keep customers and prospective customers busy. Alongside predictable information about their flagship product, AutoCAD, you'll find nice touches like a clickable map to find a user group in your area. Online events like an animation showcase keep the content timely and topical. If you're exceedingly bored, you can even read a speech by company chairman (yes, chairman) Carol Betz.

Open Text Corporation
http://www.opentext.com/index_4.html

Open Text makes the software behind some heavyweight Web sites like Yahoo, but the best reason to visit this corporate home page is the Open Text Index, a large, flexible Web index of keywords similar to the index frontrunner (and Point parent company), Lycos. Gleaned by automatically traversing the Web and indexing what it finds, these types of indexes (known as spiders, web crawlers, or just robots) are good at finding obscure information hidden in the nooks and crannies of the Net. This particular spider isn't as extensive as Lycos, but it's not far off. The rest of the site is primarily the domain of Open Text's marketing department, but their index is certainly a good enough reason to drop by.

RockSlide
http://www.rockslide.com/

Simultaneously a software company, music promoter, and art gallery, RockSlide does a fair job at all three. Primarily a maker of screen-saver software (featuring multimedia clips of bands), the company also hosts a site for the band King Crimson.

Finally, an impressive gallery of amateur art rounds out the site's eclectic mix. Only have time for a quick tour? Sample some of Joel Levicke's strange dark paintings.

Software, Languages and Compilers

Carl & Gary's Visual Basic Home Page

http://www.apexsc.com/vb/

Carl Franklin and Gary Wisniewski want to stick to the traditional Internet concept of free information on their site—free to users, free to companies, and free of advertising. It's not because they're hurting for content, though. New and veteran Visual Basic programmers will find a huge database of files, tutorials, newsgroup discussion, and even a bit of humor on this VB megasite. Before leaving the site, though, don't miss the history of the site, which traces its origin back to a drunken bender on New Orleans' Bourbon Street after a Microsoft technical conference. With that in mind, the rest of the site seems positively brilliant.

JavaWorld

http://www.javaworld.com/

Rather than just pointing to reference material as some other Java sites have done, JavaWorld is a full-fledged online magazine for the growing ranks of Java programmers. Produced by technical publisher IDG, the site's professionally-written articles and reviews easily set it apart from the "here's a link to a Java manual" sites that are springing up. Contributors include people like Arthur van Hoff—formerly one of Java's lead developers at Sun—so you can be sure the advice is good. Not long ago this would have been a regular paper-based publication, but thanks to the Web you can get this great information for free.

Sockets
http://www.sockets.com/

Truly a programmers-only site, Sockets is a thorough reference for the Windows sockets interface. Programmers will know that winsock allows programs to speak to other Internet hosts. Others won't care a bit. Those who do care will find a well-researched reference that's based on site creator Bob Quinn's book, Windows Sockets Network Programming. A large portion of the book's content is available online, along with supporting material and links to related sites on the Net. There's even a joke section of sorts, containing gut-busters like "Calling WSAAsyncSelect( ) with a zero Event mask just to make the socket non-blocking." We didn't get it, either.

Turbo Pascal Programmers Page
http://www.cs.vu.nl/~jprins/tp.html

Anyone who's serious about programming with Borland's Turbo Pascal will want to make this their online reference desk. Brimming with pointers to Pascal resources around the world and intelligently organized by topic (it's easy to see a programmer's hand in the design), it seems to have just about everything. A few of the documents are in Dutch, but while the site is based in the Netherlands, most of the files are in English. Look for pointers to FAQs (Frequently Asked Questions lists), summaries of books on Pascal, and a large section on Borland's very hot Delphi programming environment.

Software, Multimedia

Computer Animation Home from AAST
http://www.bergen.org/AAST/ComputerAnimation/

Two students from New Jersey's Academy for the Advancement of Science and Technology have created a mini-course in computer animation for the home viewer. A comprehensive and accessible story of the evolution of computer animation explains how it's done, who does it, and what it can be used for. There's a little bit of techno jargon here, but it isn't overwhelming. For visitors seeking entertainment the files on our last visit were regrettably thin, but the many links to other sites and sources more than made up for it.

MMWire Weekly
http://www.mmwire.com/

MMWire (which stands for Multimedia Wire) is a daily report on the multimedia industry, faxed daily to subscribers around the nation. Here MMWire boils its daily newsletter down to a weekly form. The emphasis is on commerce and corporations: you'll find reports on major players like Sony and IBM, along with little fish just starting to make a splash. The site also includes back issues, reports on conferences and trade associations, and much more. Essential reading for multimedia pros.

Photodisc, Inc.
http://www.photodisc.com/index.asp

Photodisc, Inc. is a supplier of stock photography on CD-ROM. This new home page allows you to purchase their stock images right over the Web. With its graphic interface, the Web is a natural for this—one look at the site and you'll be amazed no one thought of this sooner. Before you can buy anything, you'll have to register by phone, but once you do, you can browse their entire collection and buy one picture at a time, rather than whole CDs. Even those not interested in the photos should visit Design Mind, a hefty section with advice on design, Web creation, and other tidbits.

Voyager
http://www.voyagerco.com/

Voyager has quietly made a name for itself in the crowded CD-ROM field in just a few years, and this site gives you a good idea why. Design is key here, but along with the stylish graphics you'll find extensive sub-sites like the "Guerrilla Girls" art project and a mini-magazine called "Things To Think About." Paramount, though, are the areas devoted to promoting Voyager's always-stunning CD-ROM projects like Laurie Anderson's "The Green Room." And if you're looking to buy something, a different selected CD-ROM title is half-off each day. Truly a huge site that deserves the time it takes to explore it. Don't miss "The Killer App," a thoughtful critique of Wired magazine.

Software, Virtual Reality

QuickTime VR
http://qtvr.quicktime.apple.com/

QuickTime: It's not just for Macs anymore. This site is dedicated to distributing information about Apple's QuickTime VR technology, and just plain showing it off in the bargain. You're able to download a QTVR player for your Mac or Windows machine at no cost, and after some installation, come back to the site and go flying. The site also presents some interesting technical info on how QuickTime VR environments are made, with links to developers who are using the technology.

Silicon Studio
http://www.studio.sgi.com/

Here's a sample of the Hollyweb (or Siliwood) angle we've all heard so much about. Silicon Graphics' entertainment arm exists to develop tools to empower creative individuals, and here it shows off fabulous graphics and glossy multimedia galore. Sadly, it can all be slow to load, and in practical terms most surfers can't download the high-res video files that run to 15 megs or more. Gosh, if only we had a Silicon Graphics workstation, all those problems would be... wait a minute. We get it.

Virtual World Entertainment
http://www.virtualworld.com/

As flashy as this site appears, don't think you'll be able to experience "The World's First Digital Theme Park" from the Web—this is merely a promotional tool for interactive gaming centers located in several big cities around the world. At these centers, we learn, you shell out $7 to $9 a pop on games like "BattleTech" and "Red Planet," which are wars or races against other human players. You play from within your virtual reality pod (like a flight simulator), with as many as 100 different controller knobs and pedals (and you thought operating a mouse took motor skills). If you're town's not VR accessible, then it's at least a fun stop for the looking.

VRML Repository
http://www.sdsc.edu/vrml/

The term "virtual reality" is used recklessly on the Web, but at this international repository for VR software, it actually means something. No hype, no breathless speculation; just a rich collection of information on the new Virtual Reality Modeling Language (VRML) standard. Programmers and "visualization" researchers will appreciate the sample programs and lists of resources; connoisseurs of "Gun Down the Alien Spacecraft" games will be disappointed. Truth is, VR technology is still mostly for people with $20,000 computers: check here regularly to see it begin to reach the masses.

Education

College Home Pages

College and University Home Pages
    http://www.mit.edu:8001/people/cdemello/
    univ.html

At this site, MIT's Christina DeMello provides an extremely useful (and popular) service: a directory of university home pages. Visitors can download the entire list in compressed formats or search by letter. (For faster results, the data is "mirrored," or stored, at several sites around the world.) A glimpse at the "L" listings, for instance, yields La Salle University, Lycoming College, and dozens of other schools whose names you might not recognize. Terrific resource!

Pomona College
    http://www.pomona.edu/

Pomona, a Southern California liberal arts "college of the New England type," is home to some 1,380 students and a founding member of the renowned Claremont Colleges consortium. Their elegant Web parcel features a fine institute overview, delightfully peppered with clickable sidebars explaining such things as how "All Numbers are Equal to 47"—an astoundingly supported fact that also bears a "Star Trek" connection! Academic pointers include one to a Petrology and Plate Tectonics Teaching Tool, plus student works such as the excellent Thomas Pynchon home page and an enthralling On-Line Visual Literacy Project. Indeed, if these pages are indicative of the school's overall quality, Pomona College is state-of-the-art!

University of California, Berkeley
    http://www.berkeley.edu/

Offering 300 degree programs to over 31,000 students in a city some call "the Athens of the 20th Century," UC Berkeley has put up a Web site that reflects its diversity and high standing among the world's intellectual and research hubs. It's substance over style here, as (after a rudimentary graphic) this home page is simply a long list of pointers. While informing prospective students, though, those pointers lead far and wide—to the Museum of Paleontology's virtual Great White Shark exhibit; the Beatrice M. Bain Research Group on Women and Gender; the Center for Particle Astrophysics, and beyond. The computing resources look especially impressive here as well.

Yale University
http://www.yale.edu/

Appropriately enough, links to Yale's quite impressive array of online resources are graphically embedded in a row of shelved books, apparently classics in their own right. This is a multimedia feast for prospective students, as well as those interested in research carried on at the Ivy League institution in New Haven, Connecticut. An introductory video is provided, with Carillonneurs Guild audio, a Computerized 3D Segmented Human (one example of the Image Processing and Analysis Group's work), publications, and so much more. The "Bulldogs" don't bark up a self-aggrandizing storm here either, even though they obviously could. Great site!

Early Childhood Resources

Building Blocks to Reading
http://www.macconnect.com/~jrpotter/ltrain.spml

Karen Potter, a mother of two in Dallas, shares her copyrighted "Building Blocks to Reading" program in this helpful page for parents struggling to enliven early literacy lessons. Pages cover Potter's reading tips, monthly activity suggestions, and A-Z ideas like "Activity L: Children make great lazy lumps on logs. This is a wonderful outdoor activity." Potter doesn't seem to be selling anything here (you can't order her program online), just sharing her ideas—she also offers links to related early childhood learning sites.

Gryphon House Books, Inc.
http://www.ghbooks.com/

Gryphon House Books, Inc. is a seller of children's books, both for them and for the teachers and parents who care for them. The site is geared more towards the adults, though—the children's books aren't listed (but you can order a free catalog of them online). All their teaching books are sold here, with full descriptions... but what makes this site stand out from any commercial site is its free list of activities, sampled from their book collection. For other sites, visit the Wonder Room, their well-annotated hotlist with pointers to other child-related sites across the Web.

The Preschool Page
http://www.ames.net/preschool_page/index.html

"Hi! I'm Michael, and I'm a CyberKid!" And if you didn't click away after reading that line, you're probably one of the many parents or kids who will enjoy the Preschool Page, which Michael's Mommy created because she "thought that there should be a place on the World Wide Web that kids can visit with their Mommies and Daddies." CyberKids and their Mommies and Daddies will find pages on the zoo, the circus, worms and bugs, and other kid-tested topics.

Punky's Childcare Connection
http://www.cisnet.com/punky/daycare.html

Barbara Haake (a.k.a., Punky) has done parents, childcare providers and early childhood educators a great service by creating this info-rich, link-filled site. Its philosophy was best summed up by the Java message scooting across the bottom of the screen when we stopped by: "It is better to build a child than to re-build an adult." This vast and charming site includes a BBS for sharing ideas and problems, as well as pages on everything from toy safety to recipes for kids. Punky also includes a page on Books for Preschoolers, with recommended children's book titles. The site is rich with activities and educational ideas for keeping youngsters gainfully busy, making it a great rainy day bookmark.

Education Issues

Educational Policy Analysis Archives
http://olam.ed.asu.edu/epaa/

Arizona State University's College of Education publishes this peer-reviewed e-journal, dedicated to "education policy at all levels and in all nations." Visitors can browse issue-by-issue abstracts, and, should something strike their fancy, proceed to the article archives to read full text selections like: "An Example of Assessment in Elementary Education from Nineteenth Century Britain," or "The Educational System and Resistance to Reform: The Limits of Policy," and "Choosing Higher Education: Educationally Ambitious Chicanos and the Path to Social Mobility." Free subscriptions, welcome submissions, and discussion opportunities make this a fine site for educational policy buffs.

Mission Critical
http://www.sjsu.edu/depts/itl/

San Jose State University created this virtual lab, utilizing the Web's interactive capacities to help teach basic critical thinking skills, which are part of the transfer core curriculum in California's higher education system. Then again, these "essential tools of intellectual analysis" (e.g. deduction, induction) also play well in Peoria. Visitors are encouraged to work through detailed tutorials and multiple choice exercises on, for instance, "Vagueness & Ambiguity" and "Universal Syllogisms." Along the way, you'll learn about "Ad Hominem Attacks" and "Non Sequiturs." We're talking straight HTML presentation of literate logic lessons. Master Mission Critical, and you'll be a hoodwinker's nightmare.

Pathways to School Improvement
http://www.ncrel.org/sdrs/pathwayg.htm

Consider Pathways to School Improvement an online road map for enhancing America's educational system. The North Central Regional Educational Laboratory (NCREL)'s Pathways project has developed a schemata of critical educational issues, organized into areas such as Professional Development, School to

Work, Math, Science and Learning. Each area is broken down into "Critical Issues" and combined with links to other useful online resources. Though seemingly comprehensive in its coverage of scientific academics, professional training and policy issues, a pothole seems to have swallowed up the arts and humanities. Still, Pathways to School Improvement lights the crossroads at which American education now stands, and offers suggested routes for the future.

University of Arkansas at Little Rock College of Education
`http://www.ualr.edu/~coedept/index.html`

Thomas Teeter, Associate College of Education Dean, compiled this comprehensive educational resource index. While categories such as "Just for Graduate Students" and "...Undergraduates" are oriented toward prospective UALR students, tons of general pointers are included as well. Under "Just for Teachers," for instance, resources are indexed by subject matters ranging from English to Hearing Loss and Technology. "Just for Parents" includes a link to the Children's Literature Web Guide, among so many more. Beautiful organization, sharp annotations, and obvious discernment regarding the sites listed make this an excellent resource guide.

Financial Aid

CollegeNet
`http://www.collegenet.com/`

CollegeNet offers an efficient and, yes, even cool way to access and browse U.S. and Canadian higher education institutions. Their database is searchable by criteria, including geography (state or province), price, and enrollment. Click Massachusetts on the sensitive map, for example, and up comes an alphabetical list of schools such as Amherst College, with contact information, annual tuition ($19,152 if you want to be a "Lord Jeff"), and a pointer to their official home page. Financial aid and graduate program directories, links to standardized test discussion groups, as well as the Complete Works of William Shakespeare and other academic resources are featured. A great tool for getting into school!

Don't Miss Out: A Student's Guide to Financial Aid

http://www.infi.net/collegemoney/toc1.html

These pages are part of the larger Signet Bank College Money Matters site, but are worth special consideration in themselves. Each year, Signet produces this guide to help the ambitious college student find financial aid, and the entire text is placed online. There are some great general information chapters here, like "The Concept of Need," which explains that your eligibility for financial aid at an expensive private college isn't out of the question just because you're not poor. There's also a list of Special Opportunities and a rundown of who's giving money to students for what. The guide is good for the upcoming school year, because the folks at Signet keep it up to date.

fastWEB

http://web.studentservices.com/fastweb/

And you thought "f.a.s.t." stood for financial aid search through the Web, eh? Actually, it does stand for that. And after your first visit here you may find yourself registering for a mailbox and keying in your biography in order for this search engine to return all the Web's financial aid resources appropriate to your personal criteria. Our own entry turned up addresses for the Wal-Mart, Big 33 Football, and Thurgood Marshall scholarships, plus application advice to boot. The service is free, thanks to Student Services, Inc. It's not clear what SSI gets out of providing this service, but perhaps we should just clam up and appreciate the free help.

The Student Guide: Financial Aid from the U.S. Department of Education

http://www.ed.gov/prog_info/SFA/StudentGuide/

According to the U.S. Department of Education (and they should know), more than 80 percent of all student financial aid comes from government sources. Another 19 percent comes from school-sponsored sources. (One percent is stolen, apparently.) You can find out about the first 99% right here, straight from Uncle Sam's mouth. This page goes a long way in unraveling some of the mystery over landing that first student loan.

Higher Education

Ask Dr. Math

> http://forum.swarthmore.edu/dr.math/drmath.
> survey.html

The ultimate problem-solver, Ask Dr. Math helps kids of all ages with their toughest math questions. Not that we suggest kids should get this numerical guru to do all their homework, but for brain teasers turned tormenters, Dr. Math's answers add up. Dr. Math is actually a pseudonym for a batch of college students in the Math Forum, based at Swarthmore. Their answers are archived by grade level (Elementary, Middle, High School and College Level). Educators will find Dr. Math a treasure trove of fun math puzzlers—including such real-life queries as this one from a father and daughter: "Why is a manhole round? We think it has something to do with physics." Dr. Ken of the Geometry Forum responded, "I'd say it has more to do with Geometry than Physics. It's because a circle is the only shape that won't fall through its own hole."

ICLnet: Institute for Christian Leadership

> http://www.iclnet.org/

Since 1983, the Institute for Christian Leadership has provided publications, seminars, and other services to those concerned with critical issues in Christian higher education. In excellent fashion, and for anyone else with a literate interest in Christianity, their home page furthers that tradition. Articles such as "The Pedagogical Impulse in The Pilgrim's Progress" can be found in the electronic archive of ICL's tri-yearly Faculty Dialogue journal. Extensive Christian Web resources are indexed, with a software library, a prolific "Reading Room," and on. This vast database is searchable, and hosts electronic discussion groups too.

UnCover

`http://www.carl.org/uncover/unchome.html`

Approximately 6 million pieces from 17,000 magazines and journals are available through this "online table of contents index and article delivery service." UnCover remains in compliance with all copyright laws, because you pay individually for the articles ordered, but searching their data base is free! This looks to be an especially fine service for those needing information quickly, as UnCover will fax the goods to your computer "within 24 hours—often in less than 1 hour." They also offer special library and institutional rates. This user-friendly interface includes current and back issues of the UnCover Update newsletter, a glossary of terms like "Boolean Searching," and, yes, every one of those 17,000 periodicals are listed as well.

University of Waterloo Career Development Manual

`http://www.adm.uwaterloo.ca/infocecs/CRC/ manual-home.html`

Created by a Canadian university's job center, this converted print manual offers a five-step process to finding the career that's right for you. You begin by filling in forms to assess personal skills (sorry, hackey-sack excellence doesn't count). Next, you'll learn how to research career options and specific firms. And finally, you'll find tips on getting and keeping that right job. In measuring a company, the manual says, make sure it has "stable management," and once hired, "do not make criticisms about the job or other employers in public." Sound advice.

K-12

Cyberschool Magazine

`http://www.infoshare.ca/csm/index.htm`

Ring the bells and clap the erasers: Cyberschool Magazine is in session, and kids are likely to learn a lot from this fun educational 'zine. Each issue includes departments with articles covering science (Nuclear Newton), the arts (Bionic Bard), history (The Time Machine) and other curricular standards. A recent issue included features on stuff like the government's SETI (Search for ExtraTerrestrial Intelligence) programs and student life in the Middle Ages. And if you're ready to link out on your own, the Surfin' Librarian features hundreds of great sites worth exploring. Cyberschool Magazine makes the grade as a full-service e-ed zone, and one worth bookmarking for return visits.

Environmental Education Network
http://envirolink.org/enviroed/

This is an excellent electronic clearinghouse for environmental education information and materials. Students can explore the solar system, learn about deforestation in the world's rainforests, or poke around some old dinosaur bones in Honolulu. Teachers will find a wealth of K-12 resources, including air quality lesson plans designed to teach kids about acid rain, carbon monoxide and the ozone layer. EnviroLink, which sponsors the site, also offers links to a "Green" Market which promotes and sells eco-friendly products, and a huge library containing shelf after virtual shelf of "EnviroEvents," activist info, and government resources.

Kathy Schrock's Guide for Educators
http://www.capecod.net/schrockguide/

Kathy Schrock breaks out the yellow pencils at her Guide for Educators—but here, the pencils are merely icons, symbols of guidance for a vast assortment (more than 800 at last count) of links to educational sites online. Schrock's indices can be browsed alphabetically or categorically—she arranges her links in groupings such as Arts and Literature, Holidays, and World Information & Languages.

The SACC iProject at Wellesley College
http://www.wellesley.edu/Cheever/saccp.html

Wellesley College's Center for Research on Women is home to the renowned School-Age Child Care Project, and this page offers Internet users the benefits of its resources. The project examines issues such as day care licensing, child care subsidies and school preparedness, and publishes numerous reports and studies, many of which are outlined online (you can also buy them here). Child care professionals and parents alike will also find the site's Fact Sheet on School-Age Children helpful if chilling: It notes that "Children spend more of their out-of-school time watching television than in any other single activity. Children's television viewing has been associated with lower reading achievement, behavior problems, and increased aggression."

Libraries

Berkeley Earth Sciences & Map Libraries
http://library.berkeley.edu/EART/

Plot a course to one of the Web's best sources of digitized maps at U.C. Berkeley's Earth Sciences and Map Libraries site. From its colorful global graphics to its growing collection of online maps, the site is as visually appealing as it is informatively browsable. The digital maps are organized into areas such as nautical charts, topographic maps, transportation and communications maps, facsimile maps and reproductions, and aerial photography. You'll also find research round-ups of fire insurance maps—invaluable historical, building-by-building cartographic community portraits.

Consortium of University Research Libraries
http://www.leeds.ac.uk/library/curl/intro.html

This is a simple but highly useful collection of libraries from the British Isles. Rather than looking for, say, the Leeds University library and Oxford's Bodleian library in separated places, both (and more) are here. Each library has its own server and provides scores of resources—for instance, visitors can find experts in nearly any academic field from the London School of Economic and Political Science, among others. Drawing from places like Oxford, Glasgow University and London University, this simple gateway leads to much, much more.

LibraryWeb: Columbia University Libraries WWW Information System
http://www.columbia.edu/cu/libraries/

Columbia University seems to a have library for every field of study, from journalism to social work—and its LibraryWeb lets online users tap into some of these extraordinary resources. The nicely designed site lets you peruse the possibilities by subject or by library; it also features background pages on institutional history and collection highlights. The Columbia University Digital Library Collections included electronic texts of references and literature such as the complete Oxford English Dictionary and the Federalist Papers.

Smithsonian Institutions Libraries (SIL)
http://www.si.edu/newstart.htm

For those who thought the Smithsonian was just an attic filled with Archie Bunker's chair and the Hope Diamond, the SIL home page is an eye-opening discovery. Far more than just a collection of museums, the Smithsonian is an extended research complex, and you need only visit this site to discover its depth. SIL branch libraries cover everything from archeology to zoology, and they're coming online fast, offering access to the institution's collective resources. Check into the American History branch, for instance, and, under African American Resources you can link to the Amistad Research Center (a leading black cultural study center) at Tulane University.

Entertainment

Books

AwardWeb: Collections of Literary Award Information

http://ivory.lm.com/~lmann/awards/awardweb.html

Dominated by science fiction, AwardWeb offers current lists of major literary awards. (It's also where we learned that the crew of Apollo 11 was given a special 1969 Hugo Award for "The Best Moon Landing Ever.") Laurie Mann maintains this excellent source, catalogued by year and by decade with winners of laurels like the Arthur C. Clarke Award (best science fiction published in Britain), the Bram Stoker Award (from the Horror Writers' Association), or the James Tiptree, Jr. Award (for literary work that "explores or expands gender roles"). If this all seems a bit mainstream, more adventurous readers might explore the European Sci-Fi Awards or the French Sci-Fi Awards here (because, you know, the French aren't regular Europeans). A list of Newbery Medal winners for children's literature is also here, once you have waded through all that science fiction. Although a bit dry in presentation, this is one heck of a resource for recommended books and a font of trivia for tome gobblers.

Literary Kicks

http://www.charm.net/~brooklyn/LitKicks.html

"If Generation X is like Woodstock, the Beat Generation was like a small dark tavern at two in the morning, with a bunch of old jazz musicians jamming on stage and Jack Kerouac buying rounds at the bar," explains Levi Asher, who has developed this impressive tribute to some of his favorite writers. Asher wisely keeps his distance, with biographies of Beat authors Kerouac and Ginsberg that don't portray them as heroes, but as guys who wrote some good stuff in spite of their sometimes glaring lack of cool. He's not blind to their literary faults either, noting that while what they wrote is sometimes brilliant, "a lot of it sucked." Selected writings are provided for the uninitiated, and Ginsberg fans and critics should love the parody "Yowl," an updated version of his classic poem. Asher works in some fantastic links—his own—on topics like Bob Dylan, San Francisco, and Buddhism.

Stacey's Professional Bookstore Homepage

http://www.staceys.com/

The strength of this large and well-established California bookstore is its huge storehouse of technical and professional books, and we can tell from their online presence that they aren't kidding around. Search the database or simply use their nifty "autobrowse" method, and get an idea of the catalog. If something sounds good, chances are you'll be able to read a good chunk of it online. The samples here are truly impressive (long and varied), and other juicy bits include sections on publishers and specific authors (including recommendations updated frequently). Although it is clearly still growing, this site already commands a high position among ALL online bookstores.

WWWWebster

http://www-lj.eb.com/mw/

This online version of the Merriam-Webster Dictionary, part of the Merriam-Webster Online site, uses a simple form to let you look up entries from the famous reference book. But don't expect to find the latest technology terms here—we entered "Internet" and found four similar-sounding entries—for "Andermatt," "intermit," "interned" and "underneath"—but nary a mention of the very technology that serves as the conduit for this old-fashioned reference. A built in thesaurus lets you find words with similar meaning, however, saving the book-switching of the hard-cover version. If you're just looking for a little vocabular inspiration, the site offers a Word of the Day, offering not only a definition, but also a little background on the history of the word. Our word the day we visited was "Largesse," which, we learned, "derives via French from the Latin word largus, meaning 'abundant' or 'generous.'"

Comics and Cartoons

The Dilbert Zone
http://www.unitedmedia.com/comics/dilbert/

What could be better than the chance to see a major cartoonist holding a sock puppet? That's just one key opportunity available at this home for Dilbert, the popular comic strip about a computer geek and his dysfunctional office. Creator Scott Adams is a well-known figure on the Web, and he and United Media have put together a terrifically silly home page. Besides reprints of the strip (they show up here one week after they're in your daily paper), the big winners here are the Prehistory of Dilbert, the story of Adams' troubled cartooning youth, and A Day in the Life, a photo tour of how Adams creates the strip. And yes, T-shirts are available. This is a Web site worthy of the swell strip it represents.

Hitoshi Doi's Anime Pages
http://www.tcp.com/doi/doi.html

Hitoshi Doi loves his anime, and has apparently poured his heart and soul into this database of character guides, inside facts and a hefty section on seiyuu (voice actors). At first glance this doesn't look like much, but some digging yielded amazing anime facts and fun that doesn't seem to show up on any of the scores of like-minded pages. Did you know, for example, that Mitsuishi Kotono, voice of Sailor Moon, is blood-type A and wears size 23.5 cm shoes? She's also a member of the singing group Peach Hips (among others), and Doi kindly keeps track of the careers of other seiyuu, with their appearances on TV and CD. There's plenty here to take in, from "Voogie's Angels" to "Super Catgirl Nuku Nuku." Well done, Hitoshi!

Warner Bros. Home Page
http://www.warnerbros.com/

Even though they own half the world, they still take pride in their cartoons. Warner Brothers' home is a monument to cartoons, but to really appreciate it you'll need to keep up with the Joneses in a big way. From Madonna ballads to Babylon 5 and on to the Animaniacs, Warner's showing off they're VERY impressive catalog of entertainment, so there's plenty here to occupy any viewer for... forever. But to get the full punch you'll need a top-grade system and the latest Web gear. Then you'll be able to get all the really cool stuff like the Superman radio serial and all the cartoony sound files. Nevertheless, this is a chance to see some new cartoon projects like "Earthworm Jim" (featuring Professor Monkey-for-a-Head) and "Sovereign Seven" ("Fantastic Four" adjusted for inflation), and families should enjoy "Kids WB," with features on cartoons including a great storyboard of "How We Make Cartoons."

WebComics Index
http://www.webcomics.com/

Bucknell student David de Vitry created this site "so that normal netzians like you and me could easily find most all the comics on the net." He's collected and presented scores of dailies, weeklies, and editorial cartoons. They include the latest episodes of popular dailies like "Dilbert," and samples from and links to Websites "Dr. Fun," "Buzz the Fly," and "Lily Wong," among others. Both online entries and familiar newspaper strips are available, like the weird oldie "Marmaduke," the new weirdie "Rose is Rose," and "Soft Targets" (a kind of contemporary Canadian "Pogo"). This site is well-organized and well-executed, with lots of pretty colored background to spice up what is really simply a comics directory. For some reason, Web comics tend to be PG-13 material or stronger, and the selection here is no exception.

Famous and Infamous People

Elvis Costello
http://east.isx.com/~schnitzi/elvis.html

One of the United Kingdom's best punk-era angry young men was born Declan Patrick MacManus, but you know him better as Elvis Costello. To know him even better, stop by this wonderful Costello kiosk built by fan Mark Schnitzius. Offerings include an amazing, album-by-album compilation of song lyrics, some with guitar tablature; the usual "what's he up to?" news; links to home pages of "artists often mentioned in the same breath as Elvis Costello" (Bob Dylan, the Beatles); links to "other EC-related stuff," including a page done by Warner Brothers; instructions on how to get some decent fanzines; and the news that Costello recorded his first album, My Aim Is True, with Clover, an American Country & Western band whose singer was Huey Lewis!

The Andy Kaufman Home Page
http://fly.hiwaay.net/~bkm/akhome.htm

The Andy Kaufman Page is a tenderly funny tribute to the weirdly wacky comedian who died of lung cancer in 1984 at the age of 35. B.K. Momchilov, the page's creator, offers a brief bio and several pages that deepen and enhance the Kaufman story. These include a witty timeline of Kaufman's life and career, and a collection of FAQs about the star, who was best known for his portrayal of Latka on "Taxi" and for his lunatic "Saturday Night Live" appearances. The timeline describes his first SNL performance: "October 11, 1975—On the inaugural broadcast of 'Saturday Night Live' Andy lip-synchs 'The Theme from Mighty Mouse.'" The Kaufman Chronicles page offers up tidbits about "all things Andy," including David Letterman's definitive take on the often over-the-edge comic: "Sometimes when you look Andy in the eyes you get the feeling someone else is driving."

Harry Shearer
http://www.timecast.com/channels/comedy/shearer/

It doesn't get any funnier than Harry Shearer's home page—unless you're O.J. Simpson. The comedian's official Web site offers for sale Shearer's "O.J. on Trial: The Early Years" CD, featuring his juiciest O.J. material from his syndicated radio program "Le Show." Another Simpson—Homer, that is—also frequently gets skewered by the comic: Shearer does the villainously nasal voice of Homer's nasty boss, nuclear power plant owner Mr. Burns, on "The Simpsons." If you doubt it, you can download audio clips of classic Burnsian vocalizations, such as his evil "heh-heh-heh" snicker. He also does the voice of Burns' sniveling sidekick Smithers. Sound clips abound throughout Shearer's page. Though his "Le Show" is well represented with lots of funny bites, die-hard fans will click right to the Spinal Tap site, with its gallery of images from the heavy metal mockumentary *This is Spinal Tap* and a few audio clips of Shearer as headbanger Derek Smalls.

Virtual Voyager—In Search of Elvis
http://www1.chron.com/voyager/elvis/

Is Elvis a religious icon? Does his soul live on in the body of a 21-year-old Vietnamese impersonator? To find out, we took a virtual voyage with David Galloway, a writer and content developer for the Houston Chronicle Interactive. The site details his visit to the First Annual International Conference on Elvis Presley, "six days of intensive Elvisia" at the University of Mississippi (with side excursions to Memphis and Tupelo). Galloway turns the trip into a personal quest to find Elvis, and he tracks the magic of the "poor old boy from Mississippi" with unusual vigor, even by the standards of Elvis fanatics. Galloway's witty travelogue ("Day 3: Elvis goes to College") is never dull, and breathes new life into an entirely worn-out subject. Bonus: a collection of fantastically tacky portraits of the King displayed at the "Velvet Gallery."

Food & Cooking

The Brewery
http://alpha.rollanet.org/

Don't scuttle around in that dark cellar! Beer brewing is legal! (In many places, anyway.) This site holds a kettle full of tips, from mouthwatering recipes (like "Lazy Sunday Steam Beer" and "Mongrel Ale") to advice on beer tasting (we need advice for this?). Enthusiasts can get more complete "Brewhaha" from software by the same name. All of the entries here come from homebrewers. Get hoppy!

Epicurious
http://food.epicurious.com/

This elegant e-zine from CondeNet features "the combined gustatory wisdom of Bon Appetit and Gourmet." The site goes far beyond simple recipes and food preparation instructions to offer such clever fare as In Polite Company, a guide to "coping with problem foods" like artichokes and shellfish, and Victual Reality, "archetypes from the culinary collective unconscious." (On our last visit, the icon on display was an imprint of Julia Child's hand.) An online guide offers the pick of the restaurant litter in ten American cities; we find that "those liable to be irritated by a veal chop flavored with vanilla bean should stay away" from Boulevard Bistro in Houston (but we're not that easily riled). It may take a few tries to initiate a successful search of the extensive recipe database, but eventually it yields tasty results.

Peter Crombecq's Benelux Beerguide
http://www.dma.be/p/bier/beer.htm

Everything you always wanted to know about Belgian and Dutch beer (but didn't know whom to ask) is right here on this page from Antwerpian beermeister Peter Crombecq. If you're trying to figure the difference between Lambic Banana Beer and Old Brown Flemish Beer, Crombecq's got the answer (one's old & brown, the other's made with bananas, right?). At the top of his list of 100 irresistible beers is Vleteren Alt, 8% alcohol with a "sweety" taste. And there's plenty more to blow your head off: beer guides, beer pubs, beer shops, beer clubs... whew! Bring a bottle opener.

Roadside on the Web
http://www1.usa1.com/~roadside/

Hold the mayo! This e-version of the funky northeast road food quarterly Roadside is as great looking as it is stick-to-your-ribs filling, with its boomerang background and EAT HERE graphics. And once you've settled down for a byte of countertop culture, you're in for a treat: real diner stuff abounds, from the Find-a-Diner page that lets you hunt for eateries in the northeast, to Napkin Notes, featuring road trip tidbits. Reviews and reports on American diners are the focus of Diner to Diner, though you won't find any dirt dished on these greasy spoons: Roadside's "Prime editorial policy is if we can't say anything nice, we won't say anything at all." That is, unless a wayward owner plans to remodel a classic diner; in that case, the Countertop editorial may urge readers to protest at public hearings. Roadside sees itself as the standard bearing publication of classic diner heritage—and cooking. Every issue features a piping hot diner recipe, with all the trimmings. Yummm. And after you've had your fill, hit the road again with a great collection of travelin' links.

Games

Chess Space
http://www.chess-space.com/

Gather 'round, chess fans—here's a site for all facets of the chess nut in you. There are, of course, links to significant chess sites, like the Internet Chess Library and related resources. But there's a more eclectic mix of links here, some of which may have an only tangential connection to the game, like home pages of other chess enthusiasts, and audio clips (really!) of HAL saying "Would you like to play a game of chess?"

DoomGate
http://doomgate.cs.buffalo.edu/

DoomGate is on the Net, and it's just WAD the doctor ordered. (That's a Doom-junkie pun.) Here you get all the latest shareware releases of Doom, Doom II, and Heretic; spoilers, cheat codes, and screen shots; utilities, editors and add-ons; more WADs than you can count; themes that cover everything from the Simpsons to Star Trek; plus a kazillion docs and FAQs, including "The Wadster's Guide" and "DEU For Dummies." Stop us when you've had enough. There's even a section on iFrag (for playing DOOM over the Net). If none of the above makes any sense to you, you can safely skip this site, which is really aimed at dedicated Doomsters. In that sense, this page is to Doom what Stonehenge is to Druids.

The Games Domain
http://www.gamesdomain.co.uk/

Could there be a more complete source than this for the home computer gamer? The Games Domain has built its popularity on its huge array of direct links to games and tip sheets around the Internet. You'll find pointers to games, mailing lists to discuss games, and resources to help you play games; or, if you can't solve your own file transfer software, you can download files directly through your Web browser. In recent times, the Domain has added The GD Review, an online magazine "by gamers, for gamers" with the hottest reviews and sneak peeks available. (We don't know if they're really "the hottest"; that's just according to these guys). Programmers will like The Nexus, with its links to resources for creating games. Face it: you're not a true gamer if you haven't memorized the location of this site.

The Mortal Kombat WWW Pages
http://www-dept.cs.ucl.ac.uk/
students/A.Espindola/mk/

Mortal Kombat has become (to some parents' consternation) one of the most popular video games ever created, and this frequently-updated site has almost all the detail you'd ever want about the game. Along with the expected FAQs, game play tips, and statistical esoterica, there's tidbits you'd be hard-pressed to find in any one location, like rumors and news about MK4 (which will be a 3D polygon game like Virtua Fighter), and some glitches in Ultimate MK3 that let you get games for free (!!).

Gardening

Great Blue Productions
http://www.grtblue.com/index.html

Great Blue's mission is to produce Websites that celebrate nature and educate visitors on the necessity of conservation programs. They won't beat you over the head with some hardline manifesto; they WILL show you how cool nature is, and the rest is up to you. Specifically, this is a group of birding pages, including the excellent magazine, The Virtual Birder.

Other fine features include birding in New England, with some wonderful photos of the "Bird of the Month." Birders, go see the Great Grey Owl and the Barred Owl here. A bonus for more than just birders are Paul Rezendes' pages on animal tracking.

Ohioline's Yard and Garden
http://www.ag.ohiostate.edu/
~ohioline/lines/hygs.html

This is a giant library of fact sheets, a sub-site of Ohioline, which is a general guide to living thanks to the Ohio State University College of Food, Agriculture and Environmental Sciences (go, OSUCFAES!). Text rules here, with hundreds of articles on...on whatever you can name having to do with the yard and garden. Pests, of course, get top priority, and this place gets specific. Scab of peach or the hairy chinch bug been messing with your mind? Turn to this place for the straight poop. Learn the right way to mow your lawn ("Don't Bag It"), build a cold frame, or detect and treat (or avoid) human lice. Fruits and vegetables get more airtime than flowers, but why quibble? Different authors represent different viewpoints on the organic/chemical treatment debate, and there's no searching here—it's wade or die. Still, we keep coming back here to find the answers to our gardening questions.

The Orchid House
http://sciserv2.uwaterloo.ca/orchids.html

"In the world of flowers," boasts this lovely site, "orchids are the undisputed champions." (And we have to admit, they are beautiful.) Here's a mammoth guide to the much-loved blossom, complete with species-by-species breakdowns of color, size, ideal temperature, humidity... even appropriate fertilizers. Orchid myths are exploded right and left: they don't need a greenhouse to get started, not all blooms come from the jungle, and they're no longer just "a rich man's hobby." Once you feel secure in your orchid expertise, you can check the index of show regulations to prepare your handiwork for judging by the pros. Aimed at the orchid hobbyist, the Orchid House also includes a nifty H.G. Wells story, "Flowering of the Strange Orchid."

The Virtual Garden

http://www.pathfinder.com/@@dJPtCQQA98bLEVHf/
vg/Welcome/welcome.html

This first-class home gardening resource from Time-Life looks great and offers up some of the best online info around. Reference materials include a terrific book list (complete with lengthy excerpts),and a superb interactive plant encyclopedia. And if your thumb is only green indoors, consult the House Plant Pavilion for advice on choosing the best plants for your home. Fun, easy how-to projects take you step-by-step through building a rock garden or digging a lily pond. Nice botanical tours are included, too. Of course, the folks at Time-Life hope you'll buy a book or two while you're here, but it's hard to hold that against them, considering the quality of the material they offer here. This is one of the sunniest garden spots on the Web.

Hobbies

AquaLink

http://www.aqualink.com/

AquaLink is a searchable trove of info and resources pertinent to tropical fish tanks, and virtually all other aspects of hobby aquarium-dom. It was created primarily by University of Washington oceanography student David Kreg, who has since enlisted a staff of "help service" volunteers. Visitors get access to a free commercial product locator (great for those hard to find freshwater plants, and aquaria software!), nutrition FAQs, columns like Dean Grant's "This Old Reef," chat rooms... the livestock catalog would do Noah proud, featuring everything from African Pygmy Angelfish to Wisteria (Synnema triflorum). And don't forget to check the stunning results of the last live rock survey!

Collector's Coin Universe

http://www.coin-universe.com/index.html

Numismatists of every denomination will want to put a book-mark in this excellent home page for coin and currency collecting. Among the offerings at this online collector's 'zine are news of upcoming coin shows, dealer ads, a U.S. Coin Directory, and a "Coin Dealer Newsletter." At the catalog for Heritage Rare Coin Galleries, we found quite a selection, including an American coin from 1793 selling for more than $50,000! Links and searchable indexes will put you in touch with the "Israeli Government Coins and Medals Corp.," "Frank Chlebana's Coins Page," "Scott Travers' Rare Coin Consumer Protection" and lots more. There's even (inevitably) coin software. Enjoyable "Coin Market Slang" file includes the meanings of "bellybutton dollar," "onepapa," and "whizzing."

Western Square Dancing
http://suif.stanford.edu/~rfrench/wsd/
index.html

This hearty, jumbled compilation takes you through the ropes of western square dancing—right down to ordering the dance shoes. Recreational "squares" can get acquainted with others across the globe. ("Hi! My wife Blanche and I square dance at all levels....") Those in search of career opportunities can enroll at the "Famous Callers School." A "Callerlab" professes definitive stylings on "Box the Gnat" and "Slip the Clutch," and a guide to excruciatingly correct square-dance behavior reminds, "Shower, use deodorant, and brush your teeth" before hitting the floor.

Wonderful Stitches
http://www.needlework.com/

Few navigate the no-man's-land between folk art and technology better than The Needlepoint Gazette (a publisher of stitch collection books). With meaningful links at every turn, its site offers needlepoint and cross-stitch patterns, as well as a very politely presented selection of books for sale. The craft is easy to learn: "One only need know that each stitch begins in a specific hole and ends in a specific hole." Once you've mastered the basics, a "Decorative Stitch of the Month" lets you try techniques like the Scotch Check and Corn on the Cob. Well-organized and photographed (including close-ups), the patterns run the gamut of styles and patterns, but our favorite was a mix of old and new—Cybersampler 1 depicts numbers, the alphabet, and a sampling of designs based on pixel patterns in MacPaint. How techno-retro-homespun-chic!

Humor

Evil Little Brother Excuse Generator
http://www.dtd.com/excuse/

Your evil little brother always seemed to get out of trouble, didn't he? Leaving you holding the bag, right? This site lets you put his Unholy Power in your hands for a change. From "I never return your calls" to "Sorry I burnt down your house," this Evil Little Brother zips to the rescue with an apology, a rationalization, and a spiteful grin. You choose a general description of your problem, then type in the recipient's name and other excuse-specific details. Forgot your mother's birthday? Key in the appropriate information and receive a custom phrase of rapprochement: "I have made a kelp cake stuffed with gnocci, your favorite, if I remember correctly." It's strange, but it's fun.

Real Newspaper Headlines
http://pubweb.acns.nwu.edu/~bil874/comedy/
occup/news-hea.htm

We don't know if they are real, but they sure are funny. This is smart: not a giant list of funny headlines, only about 30, so there's no burn-out before the fun is done. These headlines may be urban legends—after all, there's no, you know... documentation—but even so, who wouldn't be proud to make up "BRITISH LEFT WAFFLES ON FALKLAND ISLANDS?" Brighten your day with the inadvertently comic (2 SISTERS REUNITE AFTER 18 YEARS IN CHECKOUT COUNTER) or the just-plain-boneheaded (COLD WAVE LINKED TO TEMPERATURES). Brought to you by the Mole Hole Comedy page out of Northwestern University.

Scotland
http://www.scotland.com/

Why don't they have countries like this in the real world? Scott Thompson, late of the Canadian sketch comedy outfit "Kids in the Hall," is the creative force and founding father behind this nation where everything and everyone is pretty funny. A quick application is required for citizenship before all areas of the land are accessible. And after that it's requested that new citizens affiliate themselves with one of Scotland's political parties. Responsible citizenship requires participation, after all. We chose the "Dry Martini Party." We also considered the "Martyr Party" whose leader, Fran, says "Why do I want to be Prime Minister? I don't know. I just know that I was a mother and all my kids have left the nest and I got nothing to do. My husband's sitting around at home—he's retired—he's getting in my hair and I know that I got to find something that's not volunteer work." That's as good a reason as any, these days.

Twisted Tunes
http://www.twistedtunes.com/index.html

Seattle station KISW radio morning DJ Bob Rivers regularly restocks his jukebox full of song parodies in the Weird Al Yankovic mode. Rivers and his cohorts record the "twisted tunes" in his 24-track home studio and he sells his CDs on the site. But Rivers is a generous soul. Offering a choice of TrueSpeech or RealAudio formats, he had 12 songs available for real-time listening on his site when we stuck in our quarter. Don't miss his uncanny version of the Janis Joplin classic, "Mercedes Benz," here rendered for the '90s as "Honda Accord." Willie Nelson's "On the Road Again" becomes "Pick My Nose Again." Bob's wit will never be categorized as overly highbrow. If you dig Weird Al, or for that matter, Mad magazine, you'll twist to Bob's tunes.

Movies and Videos

The Complete X-Files Page
http://www.geocities.com/Hollywood/3142/

By way of France comes this meta-site for the popular (yet still "cult") TV show. Yes, lots of photos and sounds; yes, reprints of magazine interviews and individual pages on the stars, Gillian Anderson and David Duchovny (there's even a page called "Mulder and Scully Romance Archive"). Agent Mulder might think it a little suspicious that there would be such a voluminous place all about his piddly little government job, but fans will love the easy access to Websites, IRC lines, fan-fiction and (many) FAQs.

Cyber Film School
http://www.cyberfilmschool.com/

Impact Picture's Cyber Film School is the place for Scorsese wannabes who're unwilling to shell out the thousands of dollars necessary to attend NYU or UCLA. Whether you're a novice or a professional, CFS covers moviemaking basics like writing, producing, directing, acting, shooting, lighting, sound recording, and editing. Once in the Classroom, click on screenwriting, and you'll get a primer on proposal writing and screenplay format, as well as hints for naming your characters (Abbott, Griswold, Adora, and Liana are among the cool names listed) and coming up with movie ideas. The Lecture Hall spotlights exceptional films, filmmakers, and screenplays and Artists in Residence lets you exchange e-mails with folks like award-winning Canadian producer Stavros Stavrides.

Film Scouts
http://www.filmscouts.com/

Film Scouts comes in as one of the better all-around movie houses on the Web. It's similar to others in the design ("walk" into a movie theater and pick a screen), but with deeper reserves of reviews, interviews, commentary and, of course, movie clips. Not simply trailers, but also video clips of interviews, short ones and long ones. Recent major releases are covered extensively, and they don't stop there. Film festivals from all over are highlighted, and within these sections there are reviews and comments on what's playing at the festivals! If you can't stand the time required to download any of the clips (let alone view them all), catch up on recent movie releases by reading the brief reviews or entertainment news. Even the "usher" had a movie that we saw in one of the darker corners of this cyber-cinema, a small super-8 movie of Times Square. He'll also help you sneak back in anytime for free.

The Internet Movie Database
http://www.imdb.com/

Nearly any Web site you've seen on a movie or a movie star has dipped into this pool in one way or another because it's the best there is. Filmographies and biographies from a database with over 70,000 titles is only the beginning. Thousands and thousands of visitors are familiar with searching here, but everyone should check out the neglected tour to discover the IMDB's hidden gems of awards, reviews and gaffes. For any movie fan, this is the most essential bookmark there is.

Music

AudioNet
http://www.audionet.com/

Striving to be the definitive Internet radio site, AudioNet uses the best-known real-time player, RealAudio to offer a range of programming far wider than any individual radio station. And unlike over-the-air stations, AudioNet offers its programs on demand. From a pretty good selection of full-length CDs available for instant play (Pick of the Week when we tuned in: Grease: The Soundtrack) to interviews with celebrities, authors, and athletes—AudioNet even offers a wine tasting program. The home page presents an exhaustive list of links to other RealAudio radio stations. AudioNet ranks near the top of the Web's aural wallpaper pages.

CDnow
http://cdnow.com/

CDWow is more like it. This online superstore offers a mind-blowing collection of music and related products (over 145,000 items and two-day delivery), but it also includes some invaluable information resources—like a guide for building a classical-music library, and a dictionary with definitions for musical terms from a cappella to zither. The scope of the CD database is almost unbelievable. A search under Donald Fagen (one of our own favorites) turned up his personal biography, a discography with descriptions and star ratings, and a list of import titles (even telling us that his Japanese EPs were not in stock but could be back ordered). It also revealed a Fagen video we didn't know existed. Multiply this entry by every jazz, pop, country and classical artist you can think of, and you get a sense of this site.

Rocktropolis
`http://www.rocktropolis.com/rt4/`

Unsigned musicians and pop icons lurk about in this splashy rock and roll fantasy theme park. Soma and Droog, two comic-book rock babes, escort you through a city that looks like Vegas meets Blade Runner. (Their juicy red lips say things like "Click me if you wanna go really fast... huh-hee!") Cruise the "strip" and check out its "clubs"—from chat lounge to poetry-tinged Jim Morrison Hotel. In sharp contrast to the babes, a Rock and the Environment "building" delivers p.c. messages from artists like Live and Midnight Oil.

At close look, this all seems a clever concept for enticing re-cord labels to buy virtual billboard space to promote artists. But the city's neon glare and distractions emancipate Rock-tropolis from a state of commercial hell. Commercial or not, it still rocks.

SonicNet
`http://www.sonicnet.com/`

Here you can grab "the best" of the alternative Net from a group of former New York City BBSers. They've moved their board to the Web, and brought with them a jackpot of idio-syncrasies suited to all manner of unconventional palates. The chat zone features provocative sessions with artists like Meat Puppets, Laurie Anderson, and Talking Head David Byrne, who discusses the "Muzaking" of "Burning Down the House" ("I thought it was a pretty ridiculous idea... but they did it and I've yet to hear it in an elevator"). An animated cyber-musical, Ralph Steadman's "Project No. 1: The Fouling of America" puts a gruesome (but artful) spin on the mugs of Laurel & Hardy. For an encore, see why spooning, bikini waxing, and dumping your boyfriend have never been easier in the "Indie Rock Guide to Dating."

Personal Homepages

Anti-Imperialism in the United States, 1898–1935

http://www.rochester.ican.net/~fjzwick/ai198-35.html

Syracuse University doctoral candidate Jim Zwick, better known on the Web for his excellent Mark Twain Resources page, presents an occasionally astounding archive on the issue that may have attracted him to Twain in the first place. The great American satirist and curmudgeon was staunchly opposed to U.S. military escapades overseas. And here Zwick digs up dozens of essays, speeches, and articles from other anti-imperialists from the early 20th century, focusing on the Anti-Imperialist League, a group "created to protest the annexation of Cuba, Puerto Rico, Guam, and the Philippines after the Spanish-American War." The anti-imperialist debate (couched in different terms) has resurfaced since the demise of the Soviet Union leaving the U.S. pondering whether it should act as the planet's only superpower, or just another good neighbor in the community of nations.

DeeT's 70's Page

http://www.rt66.com:80/dthomas/70s/70s.html

Can't get enough H.R. Pufnstuf? Kick it back to DeeT's 70s page, where the disco decade is still writhing strong. Dave B. Thomas (who confesses he was only 10 in 1976 but bonded to the decade anyway) has compiled a cool collection of 70siana, from commercial soundbites to cartoon theme songs. Name a show, from "Speedbuggy" to "Donny & Marie!" and he has the theme. Name a product, from Wrigley's Spearmint Gum to Playdoh Fun Factory, Jr., and he's got the ad audio. You'll even find classic sound-effects such as Samantha's nose-twitch ringy-dingy from "Bewitched" (OK, that was more of a 60's show; don't quibble with greatness). And fans of Sid and Marty Krofft, innovators of such overstuffed kid's shows as "H.R. Pufnstuf" (Barney's ancestor) will find a fact sheet about their work. You can't go home to the 70s again, but you can visit at this wonderfully tacky tribute that covers the era like wall-to-wall shag carpeting.

Fly By Night
http://www.jgeoff.com/

Freelance Web and desktop publishing designer J. Geoff Malta's home page is a gateway to the half-dozen-plus sites that the rambunctiously creative Malta authors and manages. These include his awe-inspiring Godfather Trilogy site, which has already made Malta something of a minor Web celeb. He seems to have a healthy (if it can be called that) fascination with gangster fiction, because he also runs a popular site for the Cuban-crime flick *Scarface* and is developing an "official unofficial" site for *Godfather* author Mario Puzo's novel *The Last Don*. Both are reachable through his home page. But Malta's interests are not limited—also found here are his home-brew beer page, a site devoted to Mr. Johnson, a local New Jersey band and Puberty 101. In the latter site, Malta—who it turns out, in his secret identity, is a certified psychological counselor—offers advice for teens. Malta is a Web renaissance man, indeed.

The Land of Pitman
http://www.greyware.com/authors/pitman/

The proprietor of this overstuffed site, Mark Pitcavage, is a historian fascinated by militias. His dissertation was on state militias 1783-1858, but he's equally concerned about the "neo-militia" movement and is authoring a book on it—but more to the point, he displays copious amounts of his own research on militias here on his site, which is home to The Militia Watchdog e-zine. The lighter side of Mark Pitcavage is also on display on the "Satanic Side of the Web" in which Satan himself issues a press release endorsing Pat Buchanan as the "candidate of Hell." Pitcavage also posts the lyrics to songs from Nixon: The Musical, the little-known original version of the Oliver Stone-directed biopic. Good for big guffaws.

Pets and Animals

Adopt a Greyhound
http://delta1.org/~greyhound/

Greyhound info galore! On the technical/functional side of this page you'll find greyhound backgrounds, advice on successful adoptions (get a lot of sleep before you bring them home), and tips on doggie dentistry. On the warm fuzzy side, you can peruse the top 10 reasons for owning a greyhound ("People stare at your dog instead of you") and visit the greyhound in art and literature from Shakespeare to "The Simpsons." The page also includes a heartwarming photo gallery of adopted greyhounds all over the country. Also here are greyhound clip art and a variety of greyhound supplies and treatises.

AquaLink
http://www.aqualink.com/

AquaLink is a searchable trove of info and resources pertinent to tropical fish tanks, and virtually all other aspects of hobby aquarium-dom. It was created primarily by University of Washington oceanography student David Kreg, who has since enlisted a staff of "help service" volunteers. Visitors get access to a free commercial product locator (great for those hard to find freshwater plants, and aquaria software!), nutrition FAQs, columns like Dean Grant's "This Old Reef," chat rooms... the livestock catalog would do Noah proud, featuring everything from African Pygmy Angelfish to Wisteria (Synnema triflorum). And don't forget to check the stunning results of the last live rock survey!

NetVet
http://netvet.wustl.edu/

NetVet marks out its territory here with a colorful list of veterinary home pages. Vets and zoologists will frolic amidst these fields of links to colleges, labs, and animal-rights groups. The site features a Pick of the Litter (the best animal page of the week), and it's also the Web home of the USDA's Animal Welfare Information Center, which covers topics like "ruminant anesthesia problems." Pet owners who just want to know how much to feed a two-headed calf will have more trouble. Finding anything can be hard here, since the links are piled up behind complex categories like Informatics and Virtual Library. Still, veterinarian Dr. Ken Boschert deserves a scratch behind the ears for his hard work in compiling this site. Good boy!

Sherlock Bones, "Tracer of Missing Pets"

http://www.bdt.com:80/home/sherlock/

John Keane has been finding lost pets for nearly 20 years, and this site has all the poop (so to speak) on his unusual service. Keane tells you about his service and how to get in touch with him for a telephone consultation (for a fee). The page also offers a kennel-full of info as well as a BBS of currently missing pets. If "Come back, little Sheba!" is your plaintive wail, the venerable Mr. Bones may be able to help.

Photography

All Pictures

http://www.cse.unsw.EDU.AU/NO_ACCESS.html

A beachworthy Claudia Schiffer (sans David Copperfield, guys!) greets you at this Australian site that is, as the name implies, a massive collection of pictures. The links are heavy on pretty girls, natch—expect a dozen listings for Alicia Silverstone and not a single one for, say, Margaret Thatcher. Still, All Pictures does include an impressive bunch of links to places like the "Kodak Home Page," "Aerospace Images," and "Sydney Bush Fires." And there are guys, too: the "Kevin Bacon Game," anyone? Still the real attractions here are the girls, girls, girls. From "The Spew Presents Linda Evangelista" to a goldmine of Anna Nicole Smith JPEGS, the biggies are all represented. And if All Pictures doesn't include your favorite celeb, you can make a request.

Ansel Adams: Fiat Lux

http://www.book.uci.edu/AdamsHome.html

In 1968, the University of California commissioned Ansel Adams to produce a "current portrait" of the university for that its centennial celebration. Three decades later, this fascinating site presents the Web premiere of the exhibition, Ansel Adams: Fiat Lux. You can read essays or interviews about the project here—even hear audio clips of the artist talking about how he set up some of the shots—but the real joy comes in exploring Adams' characteristically eloquent images, which capture the life and landscapes surrounding University of California campuses. Visitors will find page after page of crystalline images of subjects such as a stockpile of sugar beets and "segregating pupae" in a lab. And rarely has California looked as strangely beautiful as it does in Adams' black-and-white landscapes.

Bill Schwab Photography
http://earthscape-press.com/schwab/

The sound of an auto shutter release opens this slick, professional page from Detroit photographer Bill Schwab, who showcases both fine art and commercial projects. Schwab's commercial work is impressive, particularly an image he created for Petroleum Research, which reminds one more of the film Brazil than of gasoline products. Schwab has also done work for the IRS and a variety of big-shot CEOs, not to mention a fine portrait of Malcolm Jamal Warner.

Time Life Photo Gallery
http://www.pathfinder.com/@@A5m3@QUA6MgQMTuv/
photo/sighthome.html

Yanked from the files of Time, Life, People and Sports Illustrated, this extraordinary collection of photographs spans more than a century of global history. Early photos from the American Civil War include a shot of President Lincoln (in that crazy stovepipe hat) at Antietam. A gallery of photos from the '50s includes—what else?—hula hoops, rock and roll, and a bomb shelter. And Elizabeth Taylor has never looked as fetching as she does in this site's celebrity wing. "Your Picks" is a virtual request line, and a photo links page will take you to a Sports Illustrated baseball photo gallery or to a "Full Moon Rave" with Life. The page is sort of halfway commercial; you can order calendars, prints and posters from the collection, but there's plenty to look at even if you don't.

Pop Culture

Interesting Ideas
http://www.mcs.net/~billsw/home.html

What the heck is this site? Beats us, but it sure has Interesting
Ideas. It's an eye-popping pop culture compendium that celebrates Americana in all its often bizarre forms. Don't think too
hard about it, just dive right in to musings on Don Knotts
("Tell the world!!! The Ghost and Mr. Chicken, The Reluctant
Astronaut, and The Love God? are all finally coming to home
video!!!") Sluggo and Nancy (you know, those speechless comic
kids), and Dick Van Dyke, among many other pop topics.
There's so much to see and do here, it's kind of like an online
fun house: check here for a great image collection of Roadside
Attractions, or click there for "The Gyro Project" (spotlighting
gyro signs of Chicago)... here a click, there a click, everywhere
a click, click. And when your brain's nearly been fried by the
poetical musings in the Rants and Raves section, which address
sizzling subjects such as White Castle hamburgers ("Gutbusters,
gluies, stomach bombs, sliders: let us speak the names of the little square things with their five stigmata inexplicable"), click
once more, to the page of Lackadaisical Links that lead to more
wacked out wonderlands of the Web.

No Place for a Woman: The Family in Film Noir
http://www.obs.net/Noir/noir-toc.html

John Blaser manages the Web site for the American Dental
Association and also spends a lot of time pondering cinema and
how it reflects American societal and cultural values. The result
is this quite scholarly but highly readable hypertext essay about
the critique of the traditional family in such films as *Out of the
Past, Double Indemnity* and others in that post-World War II
genre that came to be known as film noir. That means "dark
film" for those of you who know absolutely no French at all.
These films dealt with themes that usually didn't find their way
into mainstream Hollywood fare that generally requires
"happy" endings and a celebration of courage, virtue and other

traditional values. Not so in noir, in which evil often triumphs and fear rules the day. Interestingly, these films often presented strong, progressive images of women. Read Blaser's excellent essay to learn more.

View-Master
http://redwood.northcoast.com/~shojo/View/vm.html

What kid didn't first visit the Grand Canyon, the Empire State Building, or the Golden Gate Bridge through the double-visioned vantage point of a trusty View-Master? Those stereoscopic gadgets are honored at this picture-perfectly kitschy site. It takes a wide-angle lens to the popular toy, offering a list of View-Master Reels—they depicted everything from Niagara Falls to Woody Woodpecker—as well as overviews of View-Masters through the years. You'll even find pages devoted to View-Master projectors (watch with your friends!) and accessories, such as the Personal Stereo Camera, which featured a "built-in Expo-Sure calculator which makes setting easy... and Filmiser that gives more pictures for less money." Real ad copy and goofy pictures make this site downright 3-D-lightful!

Yesterland
http://www.mcs.net/~werner/yester.html

Werner Weiss created this tilt-a-whirlwind tour through the land of lost rides and attractions that have magically disappeared from Disneyland. He's a real theme park addict—his site also has lots of links to other parks—but his heart belongs to the yesterday's Tomorrowland, from whence many of these attractions came. Yesterland lets you hitch one last ride on the Rocket to the Moon, take a final Adventure Thru Inner Space and enjoy dozens of other missing amusements. Some were downright prescient in their vision: Climb aboard General Electric's Carousel of Progress (circa 1967), where you can read the script for the futuristic animatronic family. Father: "Our television console is more than just a TV set. It has a built-in video tape recorder." Mother: "Now we can record our favorite shows for viewing at a more convenient hour. And television programming is so much improved today." This, mind you, was more than a decade before G.E. bought NBC, and more than twenty years before Disney bought ABC. Wow!

Romance

Ask Dr. Tracy

http://www.loveadvice.com/

Dr. Tracy Cabot is the author of How to Make a Man Fall in Love With You and other popular relationship books. Online she's also an advice columnist, taking questions from visitors three at a time. Her advice is usually pretty sensible, sometimes crummy (she tells a lonely woman to "join a group of people who dress like you do"). Cabot also maintains her library of love lit here, more advice on a wide range of topics, from "giving too much" to cyberlove. Even if you don't like her advice, eavesdropping on relationship tales is endlessly entertaining, and some of the best come from Dr. Tracy her own bad self, like this tale of a bum she once dated: "The worst was the night he backed over my puppy and killed it while he was on his way to see another woman." Yow!

Match.com

http://www.match.com/link.cgi/437924350170/
welcome.tpl

This fun personals site asks you to "just leave your bags behind," along with "those blind dates, bar scenes, hang-ups, put-downs..." (What a life you must lead!) First you have to register (it's not free). Then you can either browse categories ranging from "All" to "Women Seeking Women" to "Men Seeking Women," or try your search by region with their geographical browser. Detailed information on the listed singles is available, like the California woman who likes "candlelight dinners and music (everything from Snoop Doggy Dogg to Pavarotti)." Match.com Zine has features on dating, covering modern dilemmas like actually meeting your date face to face. The site's coolest feature, however, measures the distance between you and each person whose ad you peruse. That way you'll know you're just 313 miles from that mystery date in Pittsburgh.

Romance Novel Database

http://www.sils.umich.edu/~sooty/romance/
romance.html

Here's a nice tool if you want the lowdown on the latest Jude Deveraux tome. Categorized by title, author, and subgenre, the Romance Novel Database presents a thorough catalogue of more than 50 titles ("Angel Rogue" and "Maiden of Inverness" among them) with publisher info, a one-to-four heart rating system and in some cases, a review of the book. You can even submit your own rating of the book if you found it to be lustier than the given review indicates. A service of the University of Michigan's School of Information and Library Services, the site was created by Chris Powell, a graduate of the department, as part of her senior project.

The Romance Web

http://www.public.com/romance/

The Romance Web bills itself as a "sanctuary for hope & love as a human condition." Cherubs and angels adorn this site, which offers humorous reflections on romance, a personal quiz (is naked Twister really appropriate on a first date?), and a dissertation titled "Every Man Can Be A Romeo." And if you don't like the suggested titles on this list of romantic poetry ("Sonnets from the Portuguese: #43" and "She Walks In Beauty," to name a few), there's a link to the Random Love Poem Server, which will "choose a love poem from around" the Web. This site also includes links to personal ads with about 17,000 potential mates. Brought to you by the folks at L&L Information Services, who are also quite willing to deliver a pitch on their other ventures.

Science Fiction

Cracks in the Web

http://www.directnet.com/~gmorris/title.html

Cracks in the Web is a weekly espionage techno-thriller based in the spy-laden secret underbelly of today's society. (Isn't your underbelly spy-laden?) On June 26th, 1995, the Space Shuttle Atlantis blasted into space to dock with the Russian Space

Station Mir. This site gives you a fictional weekly serial of everything the government Doesn't Want You To Know, from massive cover-ups to deadly computer programs to (yes, of course) love affairs. Scanned pictures of actors give a personal feeling throughout the story, and the Daily Flap, a near-daily collection of e-mail and responses, shows a personal side of the author.

Earth2: A Gaian Hypothesis
http://www.arcade.uiowa.edu/proj/earth2/
index.html

For a show that lasted just 22 episodes and was preempted 11 times in its 33-week lifespan, NBC's "Earth2" sprouted much food for thought—at least for the University of Iowa's Karla Tonella. The utopian series—produced by Steven Spielberg's Amblin entertainment—focused on a band of humans trying to make a new home on a pristine planet after Earth's own resources have been dried up. In addition to the usual fan page flotsam (cast list, episode guide, fan fiction) Tonella offers her own well-written essays on how the show dealt with gender issues, environmentalism, and "Gemeinschaft and Gesellschaft." This short-lived series spawned an inordinate number of Web sites. Tonella's is perhaps the most worthwhile read among them.

Science Fiction Resource Guide
http://sf.www.lysator.liu.se/sf_archive/
sf-texts/SF_resource_guide/

This site offers links to virtually every galaxy in the sci-fi universe. We're talking Cheap Truth (an electronic cyber-punk fanzine), Silly Little Troll Publications, and whimsical oddities like "WWWF Grudge Match (Enterprise vs. Death Star, Khan vs. Lex Luthor)," plus scads of archives and newsgroups. This collection of sci-fi related pages is far more inclusive than most of its competitors, with rarely recognized sites that feature African-American, French, Japanese, Jewish, and Gay and Lesbian fan pages. Wonderfully presented, and because each item contains a brief description of the site, there is less "linking to the void;" you'll actually have an idea of what to expect. A small but worthwhile section is "Art and Artists," including

Frank Kelly Freas, winner of 10 Hugo Awards and granddaddy of post-WWII science fiction cover art.

The Star Wars HUB
http://empire.res.wabash.edu/david.htm

This personal home page by David Coates has an impressive collection of "The X-Files" trading cards, to be sure, but the centerpiece is his Star Wars HUB, a mammoth collection of images, sounds, and plain ol' stuff from the movies, comics, and game videos. Hundreds of stills and sound samples (the latter reveal a fondness for blaster sounds and Chewbacca growls) support an archive that includes comic book covers, scripts, and rocketship blueprints. Don't be afraid that you'll be spending too much time here—you will be. You will be.

Television & Radio

Bloomberg Online—WBBR-AM 1130
http://www.bloomberg.com/wbbr/index.html

Bloomberg Business News bills itself as the world's fastest growing news service. Actually it may be the only growing news service. Bloomberg has branched out into virtually every area of the media. Their 24-hour news radio station now comes to the Internet through the Streamworks real time audio player (non-Mac versions play rudimentary video, too). These are live broadcasts, the exact same ones you'd hear if you switched on the radio. If you're out of range of a Bloomberg affiliate and you absolutely must have your business news—here it is! Otherwise, it seems a little silly to soak up the memory resources of your computer, not to mention your phone line, for the exact same broadcast you'd get by switching on the radio. In any case, this is one of the best business news services available, with Bloomberg's general news and sports material on-line via Streamworks as well.

CourtTV
http://www.courttv.com/

From the people who brought you the O.J. Simpson trial comes—the O.J. Simpson trial! Along with dozens of other intriguing cases and several four-drawer file cabinets' worth of legal news-you-can-use. Probably not by accident, cable TV's all-law channel is the most entertaining legal site out there, as well as one of the most informative. The "case files" should satisfy any law junkie's Juice jones. CourtTV even provides downloadable sound bites (Judge Ito: "I'm not going to tolerate that kind of stuff anymore!"). But that's not all—the Menendez brothers, the OK bombing and, staggeringly, the Yugoslavian War Crimes Tribunal are all here, too. An even greater bounty of juicy court filings turns up under a "cases involving celebrities" heading: the Bob Dylan palimony suit ("disenfranchised woman left homeless by Mr. Dylan, after 20 years, when he pulled the plug on her at his whim"), the John Grisham plagiarism case, REM vs. Hershey's Chocolate, Spam vs. the Muppets. You get the picture.

Mentos—The Freshmaker!
http://www.lido.com/tv/mentos/

This brilliant page offers, believe it or not, witty and detailed analysis of all known Mentos TV commercials—you know, the ones where life's little difficulties are solved by enterprising young people with the aid of "the Freshmaker." The site offers synopses and made-up titles for each ad, and so much more! You'll find "concrete proof" that the ads are German in origin (look for the Munich street sign in the "3 Second Car Jacking" ad), complete jingle lyrics, and minutiae delivered with the cool detachment of academia: "The shape of a Mentos candy is disklike, with an elliptical bulge in the middle. They measure 3/4" in diameter and at their largest point, 6/16" tall." Site visitors have written in to announce such undertakings as "hammering out a 'freshness defense' for criminal acts committed under the influence of Mentos." Cheerfully obsessive! Fresh!

The PIX Page
http://www.kpix.com/

A mega-site for San Francisco's Westinghouse-owned TV and radio station KPIX, The PIX Page sets a standard that most other TV station sites should shoot for. This site will be especially helpful if you're in the Bay Area. News, weather and local info abound. PIX's traffic reports are up to the minute, believe it or not. Of course, you probably won't be surfing the Web as you're toodling down I-880. Another fascinating section of the site is its video page, using the VDOLive player (a Netscape plug-in). And you thought real-time audio was way cool. Try video with no download time. The catch—it's still rather crude if you have less than an ultra-fast connection. At 28.8 the video looks more like a slide show.

Trains, Planes, and Automobiles

Airlines of the Web
http://www.itn.net/airlines

If it's a Net site associated with one of the world's commercial airlines, webmaster Marc-David Seidel intends to have it hyper-indexed on this page. The list of such sites is already long, with categories ranging from Passenger Carriers (even those no longer in service) to Frequent Flier Programs, Airline Stock Quotes and beyond. Yeah, you can get to Northwest Airlines' homepage from here, but also Castle Air (U.K. aerial filming charters), Zurich-based JetClub (probably not modeled after People's Express) and C&C Aviation—for flight tours of the Mt. St. Helens volcano. And that's not to mention the heli-copters and biplanes. A pleasant interface and brief annotations enhance this excellent aviation industry bookmark page.

AutoSite
http://www.autosite.com/

AutoSite is your Web key to "everything automotive..." (Whoever said the age of making distinctions is long past?) ...and that includes access to more than 30,000 pages of car related info. Sounds too good to be free? You're right, as nominal subscriber's fees are required for, say, new car dealer invoice prices, model specs, reviews, and on. But wait! It won't cost you a thing to browse the troubleshooting diagnosis and repair guide ("Can you smell rotten eggs when you start your car?"), auto club links, consumer advisory articles, used car

resources, and tons more worthwhile features. A pleasing graphic interface enhances this excellent clearinghouse for "best buy"
and other auto related info.

Edmund's Automobile Buyer's Guides
http://www.edmunds.com/

This site is filled with enough inside info to turn a callow
buyer into the shrewdest of new and used car negotiators. On
virtually all models and makes, Edmund's guides and CD-ROM
products "take the side of the consumer," providing (mostly in
gopher format) a state-by-state "favored dealer" index, mean
strategies for "How to Win at the Dealer's Game," invoice
prices, ratings, reviews, and lots more! Check out Tire Kicking
Today, suggesting, among other things, that the 1995 Ford
Escort's "well-behaved four-speed automatic transmission does
not detract from the car's joyful nature." And after you use
Edmund's to get that great deal, you can tell your success story
here.

Landings
http://www.landings.com/aviation.html

A look around this virtual air-strip should erase all but the most
biased skepticism about it's being "the best Aviation directory/
infosource on-line." The original Webmaster, Dr. Guenther
Eichhorn of the Smithsonian Astrophysical Observatory, collab-
orates with a Web design specialist, among others, such that
Landings is not only exhaustive in its scope, but a rather spiffy
take-off point to boot. Try to think of a flying related Web site
not accessible from here! One, you say, offering products to
help avoid those mid-air collisions, or for use in the event of
wing loss? Try "Aero Break & Spares." (Ahem!) A link to Belfast
International? It's here... and Tulsa, too. Simply an excellent
index, covering virtually every manner in which humans take
to (and fall from) the skies.

Travel & Culture

Conde Nast Traveler
http://www.cntraveler.com/

"The insider's guide to the outside world" comes to the Web—
and it's teeming with the same sumptuous photographs and
well-penned articles that make the print version of Conde Nast
Traveler a jet-set essential. An interactive atlas (and searchable
database) will have globetrotters clicking for hours while one
vacation paradise after another appears onscreen. "Readers'
Choice" ranks each destination according to environment,
accommodations, activities, and people. And an on-site
"Arcade" houses diversions like a "Seven Characters in Search
of an Island" game, by which visitors are dispatched to the
most appropriate island locale based on personality type.
(Sophisticates should beach it on Necker Island, while the
young and disco-inclined should stick to St. Barts.) This is a
good-time site for good-time travelers.

Foreign Languages for Travelers
http://www.travlang.com/languages/

Sprechen sie Deutsch? Yeah, we know: "Just a little." If you've
already booked that flight to Frankfurt or Budapest, this page
offers a quick lesson in the language of your choice. The site is
adorned with foreign words and national flags—click on the
one that corresponds with the language you wish to practice,
and you're on your way. Maintained by physicist Michael
Martin of Long Island, NY, the site helps shaky travelers learn
to check into their room, find the toilet ("Gde zdes tualet?"
in Russian), and avoid embarrassment when ordering dinner
("Aceptati credit cards?" is a useful Romanian phrase). Sound
bytes accompany many lessons, so you can actually hear how
bad your pronunciation is. Pointers to other pages of topical
information are also included, from a Japanese-English dictionary to the Serbian Language Page.

Roadside on the Web

http://www1.usa1.com/~roadside/

Hold the mayo! This e-version of the funky northeast road food quarterly Roadside is as great looking as it is stick-to-your-ribs filling, with its boomerang background and EAT HERE graphics. And once you've settled down for a byte of countertop culture, you're in for a treat: real diner stuff abounds, from the Find-a-Diner page that lets you hunt for eateries in the northeast, to Napkin Notes, featuring road trip tidbits. Reviews and reports on American diners are the focus of Diner to Diner, though you won't find any dirt dished on these greasy spoons: Roadside's "Prime editorial policy is if we can't say anything nice, we won't say anything at all." That is, unless a wayward owner plans to remodel a classic diner; in that case, the Countertop editorial may urge readers to protest at public hearings. Roadside sees itself as the standard bearing publication of classic diner heritage—and cooking. Every issues features a piping hot diner recipe, with all the trimmings. Yummm. And after you've had your fill, hit the road again with a great collection of travelin' links.

TASOL: Travel at the Speed of Light

http://vanbc.wimsey.com/~ayoung/travel.shtml

Climb aboard T.A.S.O.L. (Travel at the Speed of Light) for a kaleidoscopically cavalier romp through the world of adventure and travel. T.A.S.O.L.'s eclectic collections of articles and essays fall into areas such as ecotourism, adventure, strange tales, and women's tourism (that last, Tips from A Broad, is penned by Suzy Young, a globe-trotting TV producer). Each area has its own offbeat sensibilities, but they share an out-there verve. Whether taking you along for a ride on the Nile Train through Egypt (in Adventures), or sharing with you the shock of eating weird foreign foods (Strange Tales), the pieces are uniformly fresh and different. Produced by Canadians Adrian and Stuart Young (there's an Australian edition, too), T.A.S.O.L.'s graphics are as bright and eye-popping as the reporting; together, they form a memorable journey at the speed of light reading.

'Zines

The Consortium
http://www.delve.com/consort.html

Investigative reporter Robert Parry, the brains behind this muckraking new e-zine, was way ahead of everyone on the Iran-Contra story. In his book "Trick or Treason" he also pushed the "October Surprise," the story that in 1980, candidate Ronald Reagan made a secret and (to put it mildly) illegal deal with Iran to free the U.S. hostages. The theory was "debunked" by Congress, but Parry revisits the story here, bringing to light some unsettling new information: an explosive document hidden deep in FBI archives. "A real life X-Files," says Parry. As if juicy info wasn't enough, The Consortium's classy design makes reading a breeze for the eyes.

The Fortean Times
http://www.forteantimes.com/

Now this "Journal of Strange Phenomena" is monthly, and that's good news to fans of weird stories. While the other media cover mundane mass murders and serial killer cannibals, *The Fortean Times* covers the really juicy stories: strange creature sightings, psychic experiments and men who live like fish. What you get here are sample stories from the 'zine, but the samples are ample and the design is divine (sorry). Sensitive souls should beware the morbidly gross amid the weird.

It
http://www.itzine.com/elevators/

"It," the hip, well-designed webzine, promises to "re-define itself with each issue," by delving "into wackiness with a startling degree of depth. Each month we will explore a totally new subject, but in a familiar way." The topic for June? Elevators. Click on It's Hot, and peruse pieces on the most popular elevator in New York City (the one(s) in the Empire State Building) and the trauma of being trapped in one. At Have Fun With It, you're given the opportunity to participate in this month's interactive challenge: "You are in the Sears

Tower...You've got five minutes before the Observation Deck closes on the 100th floor...if you don't make it, you'll go insane and hurtle down the elevator shaft to your violent end." Also fun is the elevator deviant alert. (Deviants "do things like stare at you in the elevator and fart loudly.")

Salon

http://www.salon1999.com/

Backed by Apple and Adobe, this bi-weekly literary Webzine is a truly terrific "online magazine of books, arts, and ideas." The last time we visited the Borders Books & Music-sponsored site, author Amy Tan, the subject of the *Salon* interview, talked about her new novel, "The Hundred Secret Senses," and admitted to taking the drug Zoloft to ward off serious bouts of depression. The immense issue also included a Q&A with John le Carré; Armistead Maupin's valentine to his poodle, Willie; and Talking Trash, which gave Camille Paglia the opportunity to use TV talk shows as an excuse to bust the chops of political conservatives.

Government and Politics

Indexes and Information

Australian Legal Information Index
http://www.spirit.net.au/~dan/law/

Think you've seen the king of specialty indexes? Daniel Austin has you beat with eleven sites specializing in Australian Aboriginal law and another six under the heading "Defamation." And those are just two of 42 subject indexes located at this gargantuan (and at times unwieldy) site. Austin and a host of Aussies have constructed a searchable database of ftp sites, journals, even other indexes. This place also has an e-mail list and a free service that sends you a message if a particular site changes. Search by topic or keyword and you'll likely find a host of resources for that particular legal question from Down Under. An essential Australian legal resource.

Government Resources on the Web
http://www.lib.umich.edu/libhome/
Documents.center/govweb.html

Thanks to the wonderful folks at the University of Michigan library for this extensive listing of U.S. government sites. If you're looking for something produced by or relating to the federal government, you can find the link here. We discovered the Internet version of the Green Book, the fact book on federal entitlement programs, federal tax forms and policy committees for U.S. representatives. But it doesn't end there. Foreign and international governments from Bangladesh to the United Arab Emirates are available. Happy hunting!

Political Leaders 1945–1996
http://www.lg.ehu.es/~ziaorarr/00index.htm

It's tough keeping up with world leaders these days. Since more countries have adopted the electoral system there have been more presidents and prime ministers to deal with. Consider Italy: since 1987 nine different leaders have been prime minister. Lucky for you Roberto Ortiz de Zarate (not a world leader) has this handy list. Not only do you get a list of leaders for just about every nation on Earth, but you also can look through a database of former heads of state who have passed on in the last six years and the ever-useful "rulers dead in violent circumstances since 1945." The lists are fairly easy to navigate and Roberto does his best to point out interesting tidbits: Bhumibol Adulyadej, king of Thailand, has held that post since 1946, making him the longest-running act in world politics.

Virtual Policy & Administration Community
http://superior.carleton.ca/vpac/

You don't hear heated discussions of Canadian policy too often. But if you had to participate, we'd suggest a visit to this clearinghouse of public affairs information and links. While this forum is international in scope, it's decidedly Canadian in influence and subject. Besides offering several listservs for wonkish chatter, VPAC connects you to some great resources via the Virtual Policy Shop, including accountants' analysis of the federal budget and a bunch of cool economic studies sites. And they're all serious pages with statistics and reports to back up what they say. That's good, especially if you were planning to debate the Canadian deficit armed with a 15-year-old's illogical rantings.

International Government

Australasian Legal Information Institute

`http://www.austlii.edu.au/`

This site is a phenomenal Web resource for researchers trying to suss out the Australian legal system. A database of Australian High Court decisions stretches back to 1947. AustLII is also the Web home for the Council for Aboriginal Reconciliation and a large collection of documents on aboriginal issues—including numerous volumes of reports of the Royal Commission on Aboriginal Deaths in Custody. The Privacy Committee of New South Wales will be of interest to technophiles (and phobes), documenting use of Orwellian technologies such as "smart cards" and video surveillance in the workplace. For its chosen subjects, this site is near-definitive.

European Union

`http://www.chemie.fu-berlin.de/adressen/`
`eu.html`

Just as music has the Artist Formerly Known As Prince, the globe has this group formerly known as the European Community. This comprehensive information station offers links to all 15 members of the E.U. Each link leads to a central home page of the particular country, and each page is a clickable map of the various Internet resources available in that country. You can consider it a self-directed tour of the European side of the Internet—some of these links will take you to places you probably didn't even know had Web sites. Some of the pages have more than just the usual—Luxembourg's full-color map, for example, provides a visual listing of sites that provide tourist information, as well as the official Luxembourgian (Luxembourgish?) Web sites. Deep.

The Fourth World Documentation Project

http://www.halcyon.com/FWDP/fwdp.html

This massive (and fascinating) project studies the "Fourth World"—small nations of indigenous populations that aren't recognized by the big countries, but with cultural or ethnic identities of their own. Examples: natives of Tibet, or Australia's Maori people. Organized by geographical region, the site tries to make available a wide range of information on the tribal governments, politics, and cultural environments of these nations: for instance, how the coca industry is impacting Andean cultural traditions, or why Indonesia is conspiring to cut off West Papuan defense havens. Some info is available only via FTP. Thorough pointers to publications and other indigenous resources.

NomadNet (Somalia)

http://www.users.interport.net/~mmaren/
index.html

Wow. Michael Maren is the author of this astonishing page, collecting information on the embattled nation of Somalia. And he's plenty angry, reproducing articles like the Washington Post's "The Italian Connection: How Rome Helped Ruin Somalia." Maren also holds Western journalists somewhat responsible for Somalia's troubles because of their demand for action. "Somalia," he says," is the story of how the media fed a famine—with tragic results." However, he's not just media-bashing: a striking article by Ali Musa Abdi, a Somali journalist who wrote this piece several months before his arrest in September 1995, tells the bleak story of how third-world journalists often risk their lives to report the news. Excellent photos, behind-the-scenes info, and powerful letters from Somalis.

Law

American Bar Association

http://www.abanet.org/

This is a can't-miss bookmark for any legal pro. The American Bar Association is the primary association of attorneys in the

United States, so it's fitting that this site includes just about any information one could want about the legal profession, from notices about ABA meetings to a catalog of ABA publications. Detail is deep but can be deadly dull: the ABA is made of over 2,200 entities, which "includes 22 sections, five divisions and more than 80 commissions, standing and special committees, forums and task forces." Those who are so inclined can check the products and services of the Standing Committee on Legal Aid and Indigent Defendants. And for the layman, it includes a Legal Help Center to answer questions or help locate an attorney.

Child Quest International
http://www.childquest.org/

At the same time one of the most important sites on the Web and one of the most depressing, Child Quest is an inventory of missing children with photos, descriptions, and online forms for reporting sightings (and new cases). It's important for obvious reasons, depressing because there are so many missing kids. And these are just "the most current open cases." A database of cases in which an alleged abductor is named are also here. In a large number of those cases the suspect is a "non-custodial" parent. The occasional case of "stranger abduction" features a suspect, but for the most part, strangers are strangers. This site is worth periodic checks by anyone and everyone, just in case.

First Amendment Cyber-Tribune (FACT)
http://w3.trib.com/FACT/

The First Amendment is perhaps the most-discussed part of the United States Constitution, and Charles Levendosky has created this fantastic guide to it. Most useful here is First Amendment Alert!, which includes weekly updates on the topic as it appears in state legislatures, courts, and Congress. If your timing is right, you can catch the page on Banned Books Week (generally the last week of September), which lists all books challenged in or banned from libraries around the U.S.A. (Some will leave you guessing—like the removal of the American Heritage Dictionary from classrooms in Washoe County, Nevada.) You'll also find Supreme Court decisions and a Q&A section where Mr. Levendosky or another scholar answers visitor questions. An amazing site.

The Legal List

    http://www.lcp.com/The-Legal-List/
    TLL-home.html

An absolutely mind-boggling resource for Internet legal eagles, this online "book" by Erik J. Heels offers a briefcase full of law-related government, educational and corporate links. Legal resources in all 50 states, plus an amazing variety of resources from Jewish law professors to Kansas attorneys. Not incredibly exciting, mind you; just relentlessly complete.

Military

AirForceLINK

    http://www.af.mil/

Although it holds plenty of spec sheets for aircraft, this official page of the U.S. Air Force is not just for fighter buffs. Probably the best of the defense force Web pages, Air Force LINK has very cool graphics (much cooler than you'd probably expect from the military), and lots of general interest information. For example, most people know a sonic boom is caused by air compression in front of a plane going faster than the speed of sound, but here, you can get all the technical info you'd ever need (or possibly want). Links are "faster than an F-16," too. You may even have fun (we read about how goats have interfered with radio transmissions in Utah). Aircraft facts, air show pictures, and good links around the world.

The Gulf War

    http://www.pbs.org/wgbh/pages/frontline/gulf/
    index.html

U.S. Air Force Colonel David W. Eberly spent six weeks as a captive in Baghdad. British soldier Andy McNab was the only one of his eight-person unit dropped behind enemy lines to survive. Lt. John Peters was shot down on his first low-flying mission in Iraq. Visitors can read their stories in this thoroughly constructed re-telling of the 1991 Gulf War. This special PBS production, taken from a "Frontline" special, has it all: timelines, maps, and audio files from the top decision-makers from Colin Powell to Tariq Aziz. Like a good textbook, this site doesn't just give you the facts—it gives you a story, one that is fascinating and horrifying all at once.

Military City
http://www.militarycity.com/

Lost touch with that Army buddy? Just found out you've been transferred to an Alaskan Air Force base? Visit this extremely handy guide. The publishers of several military-related products, including Defense News, now have this spot, which is a companion to a popular AOL forum. At Military City, visitors can find out about bases around the nation (2,851 folks are stationed at Fort Richardson in Alaska, where it cautions readers that "wildlife is abundant and should be avoided"). But here's the goldmine: a searchable Dept. of Defense listing of active U.S. military personnel and reservists. Happy hunting!

Peace and Security
http://www.cfcsc.dnd.ca/

There may be more than six Internet sites on the Philippine-American War at the turn of the 20th century, but we're betting that this index of military sites has found the best ones. An astounding array of historical tales and current defense links greet visitors to this simple Canadian page (in French and English). Choose from articles about the current Eritrea-Yemen conflict (what? didn't know there was a conflict?) or International Peacekeeping News, a British journal. If you don't like lost lists of links, try the maps or timelines in place here. Nearly any topic you might think of—maritime law, for instance—is well-covered. A definitive military site.

Politics

FECInfo
http://www.tray.com/fecinfo/

We're not going to be the ones to say working for the federal government can be restrictive, but consider the case of Tony

Raymond and Robyn Jimeson. They both left the Federal
Election Commission—and the general public is much better
off—because there's more info on federal campaign contributions here than at the FEC's fine site. Try searching for
"tobacco" and you'll get the list of contributions made by,
among others, Brown & Williamson. Perhaps you'd like to see
the financial reports of North Dakota's Congressional candidates
—no problem there, either. This is staggeringly easy—and staggeringly informative for anyone chasing the money trail.

The Jefferson Project
http://www.voxpop.org/jefferson/

This is easily one of the best political resources on the Net. The
authors not-so-humbly claim that this is "the most complete
archive of political resources in existence today." Essentially just
a list of links, the Jefferson Project hooks up to political candidates for nearly every kind of state or national office, from the
Texas Agriculture Commissioner to four unofficial Phil Gramm
for President pages (the official one is here, too). Nearly every
political perspective from the liberal Left On! to the Anarchy
Home Page can be found here.

League Of Women Voters of Iowa
http://lwvia.cornell-iowa.edu/

Currently celebrating its 75th anniversary, the League of
Women Voters has been a non-partisan player in American
politics since the Woodrow Wilson administration. Here the
League's Iowa branch dissects Iowa politics every which way
it can: excellent maps break the state down by county, congressional, and state senate districts, and legislative calendars,
background pages, and links abound. With Iowa a key presidential election state, this page could be a favorite of 1996
strategists from both parties. Bonus points for the electronic
recreation of a Civil War tribute book called "Battle Flag Day,"
a fascinating time capsule on the Net.

Politics Now
http://www.politicsnow.com/

Political junkies, say goodbye to free time. Take PoliticsUSA,
that encyclopedia of politics and policy, and combine it with

ElectionLine, the ABC/Washington Post's foray into Web news, and you've got . . . one really big site. The best of both worlds is preserved here—the Almanac of American Politics, the SoapBox, and Congress Alert—and while the transition may not be ultra-smooth, we're guessing the final result will be one slick package. The best of the new stuff is Hypertext, a feature that posts entire documents online, like a government-financed investigation of the Rose Law Firm by a GOP attorney—that turned up nothing. And it's all brought to you by (take a deep breath): the Post, ABC, Newsweek, the LA Times, the National Journal, Steven Spielberg, and Donald Trump (well, we're not too sure about those last two).

U.S. Government

Constitution for the United States of America
http://Constitution.by.net/Constitution.html

"We the people . . . " yeah, yeah, yeah, the boring old U.S. Constitution, right? Guess again: this site puts a new spin on the old girl. For one thing, author Mike Goldman has provided an index. You want to get right to the passages about fugitive slaves or declaration of war? The handy index will point you right to Article IV, Section 2, Paragraph 3, and Article I, Section 8, Paragraph 11, respectively. Netscape users will enjoy the parchment-like background (nice touch). Another nice touch: this uses the original language—and spelling—of the document's authors. Thus, when you read that "The Senate shall chuse their other Officers," don't panic—our founding fathers just spoke a different language. A simple, useful site.

The Federal Web Locator
http://www.law.vill.edu/FedAgency/
fedwebloc.html

The Federal Web Locator from the Villanova Center for Information Law & Policy wants to be your one-stop shopping center for federal government information on the World Wide Web. (It's a similar function to that offered by the Department of Commerce's FedWorld site.) Even though the VCILP is not a federal agency, it gets the job done very nicely. Hunting for the Naval Undersea Warfare Center? You can turn it up here. Or check under "Federal Government Consortium and Quasi-Official Agencies," and you'll find Web sites like the National Consortium for High Performance Computing, and the Smithsonian Institution. Plus the World Bank, Congressional Quarterly, and much more.

Government Printing Office Access—UCSD
http://www.gpo.ucop.edu/

Like its counterpart at Purdue University, this site allows users to search through Congressional bills, the Federal Register and plenty of other enormous federal documents. The advantage of this site is that it has deeper data, including House and Senate calendars, economic indicators and Congressional reports. Want to find out what Newt Gingrich really said on the House floor? How did that parakeet tariff bill become law? It's all here, with a simple search mechanism, too. If the Purdue site deserves a medal (and it does), the GPO deserves an even shinier one. A great, great site!

Thomas: Legislative Information on the Internet
http://thomas.loc.gov/

If you believe in freewheeling democracy, the Thomas archive of the Library of Congress will fascinate you. Named after Thomas Jefferson, this text-only site delivers on a simple, elegant concept: take the Congressional Record of the U.S. and every pending bill before Congress and put it in a bazillion-gigabyte Web server. Good Netizens can research bills, follow the actions of bills sponsored by their own representatives, or just filibuster around. The home page includes a short section of Hot Bills, a weekly-updated listing of "major bills receiving floor action . . . as selected by legislative analysts in the Congressional Research Service." An excellent public-participation tool.

Health and Medicine

Alternative Medicine

HealthCraze!
http://www.newhope.com/hcz/

Looking for an herbal headache cure or the latest nutrient news? HealthCraze! has it all wrapped up in a selection of areas devoted to alternative health care and treatments. The site, from New Hope Communications (publishers of Delicious! Magazine), covers a healthy range of subjects, from organics and sustainable agriculture to homeopathic treatments. The info is in-depth and abundant—at the Nutrition Advisor, for instance, you'll find write-ups on topics such as Fad Diets, Kids & Tofu, Low-Fat Living, and Cancer Fighting Vegetables. And at the VitaMan section, you can supplement your knowledge of the impact of vitamins and minerals on Depression, Fertility, Healthy Hair, Skin & Nails, Immunity, and Longevity.

HerbNET
http://www.herbnet.com/

Calling itself the "most comprehensive site on the Web for those seeking information on herbs, herb products and remedies, [and] herb publications," HerbNET, from the Herb Growing and Marketing Network, offers a homegrown collection of resóurces and info. Check out the HerbNET Magazine for updates on herbal news and happenings, as well as recipes and other goodies. April's issue celebrated the "Herb of the Year"—Monarda/Bee Balm, and so the 'zine was abuzz with concoctions such as Pineapple-Bee Balm Punch. The site also features an Herb Potpourri page with links to intertwined Web sites and mailing lists, the Herb Associations page, with lengthy listings for various orgs, and the HerbNET Calendar of upcoming classes, tours, and conventions. Since HerbNET had just sprouted when we strolled through, some of its pages—including the Herb Superb online catalog and the Herb Gardens page for enthusiasts—were still being planted. Butherbalists or those just curious about the powers of plants will be impressed by the resources, recipes and references that have already taken root at HerbNET.

Living in Victoria: The Magazine of Health and Healing

http://www.islandnet.com/living

From acupuncture to spiritualism, Living in Victoria is an online advocate for alternative and up-and-coming healthstyles. The magazine was designed to keep the populace of Victoria, B.C. in the pink with articles, links and practitioner lists relating to alternative and wellness treatments. Unless you live in Victoria, the local wellness listings aren't of much help; but the articles are worthwhile reading regardless of geography. Visit the Eastern Healing Arts pages, for instance, for articles such as Elaine Murphy's "Acupuncture Treatment for Substance Abuse." The Family & Parenting pages feature helpful pieces on family health and happiness, including Joyce Irvine's "Family Rules," about how families constrict and construct their own codes for living. "Out of limited perceptions and communication skills, we form our limiting beliefs and rules that separate us from ourselves and from other people."

University of Washington Medicinal Herb Garden

http://www.nnlm.nlm.nih.gov/pnr/uwmhg/

Wander the fragrant and health-giving paths of the Seattle Campus of the University of Washington's Medicinal Herb Garden at this hypertour site. You can check out some winter views (things look pretty dead) or take a virtual stroll through the garden in its livelier state, as it looked in August, 1995. For a closer look at these leafy healers, the site features gorgeous individual plant GIFs, indexed by botanical and common name. You won't find anything about the plants' medicinal uses here (a disclaimer advises visitors to seek professional medical advice on using herbs)—but at least the next time you're wandering through the woods, you'll know that Arctium minus (a.k.a. Beggar's Buttons) when you see it.

Family Medicine

Cyberspace Hospital
`http://CH.nus.sg/CH/ch.html`

Patients and practitioners alike will want to admit themselves to the Cyberspace Hospital to browse its collection of worldwide health links and resources. Created by the National University of Singapore, the site resembles a hospital structure. You can almost hear the elevator "ding" as you ascend to Level 2 (Hospital Services), home of the cafeteria, shopping mall, and emergency services; then to Level 3 (Specialists Departments), with everything from anatomy to medical microbiology; and at last to Level 4, with more specialized departments in areas such as Travel Medicine and Geriatrics. Each area has links to sites in that field: Visit ICU (Level 3), for instance, and you'll find the Australian and New Zealand Intensive Care Society. You may not leave Cyberspace Hospital with a cure, but you'll be discharged with a dose of healthful resources.

Go Ask Alice
`http://www.columbia.edu/cu/healthwise/`

We can't say enough good things about this general health and wellness site from the Columbia University Health Service. Colleges face a special public health challenge, serving people who are living on their own for the first time and who may suffer from medical ignorance (or bad judgment). Students (and Internauts) can turn to Go Ask Alice, where students can anonymously ask questions about anything from snoring to sex to watchband irritation. Alice's answers are archived, and it's easy to get hooked on browsing these very honest questions and forthright responses, organized into general sections like "Fitness and Nutrition," or "Sexual Health and Relationships." (You're likely to find a few you might have written yourself.) Though aimed at Columbia students, this is a great spot for anyone with a health or nutrition question.

Healthwise
http://www.columbia.edu/cu/healthwise/

Healthwise, "The Health Education and Wellness Program of Columbia University Health Services," lives up to both its title and subtitle. The star here is the renowned Go Ask Alice! Q & A service, which archives answers on every little (or big) health question, with topics ranging from sexually transmitted diseases to mental health. Alice aside, Healthwise has some other worthwhile features—notably the Healthwise Newsletter highlights page, with excerpts from the campus health newsletter. It's a trove of smartly written stories and tips. A recent article on sleep deprivation included a wide-awake analysis of insomnia and other sleep disorders, and offered suggestions for coping with a chronic lack of zzzzs: "Power nap if you can't increase your nightly sleep sessions. Even napping for a few minutes can temporarily boost mental and physical functioning."

Wellness Web
http://www.wellweb.com/

The Wellness Web, subtitled The Patient's Network, views medical and health care from the other side of the desk. Created by and for patients, its refreshingly honest and basic offerings include areas such as a Smoker's Clinic (info and sites to help you quit), Grassroots (organizations involved in health advocacy) and Medical Centers (with links to individual medical center resources). And since they say laughter is the best medicine, there's even a Be Happy Be Well area, with links to games, newspapers, and other fun sites to take your mind off your ills. The concept of wellness is a large part of this site, though it's not only about preventive healthcare but also about maintaining and restoring wellness to those sometimes lost in the quagmire of medical lingo and information.

Illnesses and Disorders

The Diabetes Homepage
http://www.nd.edu/~hhowisen/diabetes.html

This is the single best spot for diabetes information on the Web. Not only does it have detailed information for the layperson (like a careful explanation of insulin, or what "juvenile onset" means), but it's presented in an entertaining (if jarring) graphical format. The offbeat tone takes a little getting used to (diabetics are initially referred to as "those whose Pancrei have opted for early retirement"), but the well-organized links to the world's major diabetes sites are worth hunting for. (Many of the links are gopher sites.) What's really strange (and interesting) about this site is the Virtual Diabetic game, where you try to get Derwood the Diabetic through one adventure-packed day without ending up in the hospital. (It's hard!) This comprehensive site even offers links to data on diabetes in cats.

MedicineNet
http://www.medicinenet.com/

The more medical science advances, the more frequently we can feel left in the dust—but MedicineNet has the cure: It offers comprehensive, easy-to-understand information on everything from common ailments to prescription drugs. It's kinda like having a plain-speak Doc in your box. Click on Diseases and Treatments for an A-Z (actually, A-W when we checked) listing of hundreds of health problems and solutions, from "Acne" to "Warts, Genital," each described in detail, with key points outlined right up top. Sometimes the articles (written by physicians) offer a little too much info, but don't despair: The site includes an online Medical Dictionary that explains the lingo for you. Once you understand the ailment, you can learn more about its medications at the Pharmacy pages, which includes backgrounds on brand-name and prescription drugs. And if you take too many, the site even includes a truly useful listing of certified Poison Control Centers nationwide, including their emergency hotline numbers and addresses. You'll still need to see your doctor, but MedicineNet can help answer basic healthcare questions quickly and painlessly.

Online Mendelian Inheritance in Man
http://www3.ncbi.nlm.nih.gov/Omim/

This is an online version of Dr. Victor McKusick's landmark genetics book, "Mendelian Inheritance in Man." If you haven't heard of it or aren't interested in genetic disorders, this site isn't for you. But for interested parties (and for those with involuntary interest, like medical students), this highly technical catalog is a goldmine on how genetic differences cause illnesses, deformities and changes among species. If you understand the following, you're a shoo-in: "All pseudogenes of the ANT gene family seem to lack introns."

The Progress of Nations 1996
http://www.unicef.org/pon96/

The good news: Smallpox has been erased. Measles and Polio could be next, and the nations of the world could save lives and money in the process. The bad news, according to this "state of the world" report from UNICEF: the leading cause of death in children under 5 in the developing world is malnutrition. This wide-ranging document covers everything from teen birth rates in Japan (they're the lowest ever) to the shocking statistic that 65 women die each day in the Americas due to pregnancy or childbirth problems. Issued every year, the Progress of Nations is both a social and medical scorecard and a compendium of odd facts and stats (example: Finland has the heaviest percentage of 15-year-olds who smoke).

Mental Health

David Baldwin's Trauma Info Pages
http://gladstone.uoregon.edu/~dvb/trauma.htm

Psychologist David Baldwin has compiled a fascinating guide to the subject of emotional trauma. Baldwin says his particular interests include finding out what biological processes are set in motion by trauma, whether that be an individual traumatic experience or a large-scale disaster. You'll read that animal studies have suggested severe or chronic trauma may actually cause physical damage to parts of the brain. What psychologists do know, we are told, is that traumatic experiences "shake the foundations of our beliefs about safety, and shatter our assumptions of trust." It's not surprising, then, that we should be concerned about how best to treat those suffering from the impact of such trauma. Baldwin's pages are aimed at clinicians and researchers, but victims and their families will also find support information, including links to other Web sources, such as Nate's Traumatology Page and North Carolina State University's Disaster Info for Families.

Mental Health Net
`http://www.cmhcsys.com/mhn.htm`

John Grohol is at it again. The founder of Psych Central set his sights on a bigger target: the world of online mental health resources. The result is this index totaling more than 3,500 individual resources, including the Self-Help Sourcebook, a gopher site describing the types of headaches and tips on beating shyness. We found out the men's brains shrink as they get older (hardly a revelation to some of us) and an enormous database of mental health conferences and programs. All of this just makes us wonder: what kind of social life can Grohol have when he seems to spend all his time building great sites?

PsychLink
`http://www.psychlink.com/`

From alcohol abuse to an online psychiatry magazine, this index of mental health site offers a wealth of articles, lists, and resources for the layperson and professional. Insiders will appreciate the links to academic journals and the "Industry News" while the general public can find links on specific psychological and behavioral disorders. This is just a bunch of links; you won't find original material here. But since the field of mental health encompasses dozens of topics, it's a good one-stop resource.

Shuffle Brain
`http://ezinfo.ucs.indiana.edu/~pietsch/`

This deeply-thought-provoking Web site from Indiana University professor Paul Pietsch presents a number of well-written (and sometimes out-there) articles from scientists who wonder about, and experiment on, the nature of intelligence, perception, and how the brain stores the mind. Yes, we're talking brain transplants (on salamanders), which the boys in the white coats call brain-shuffling. The holographic concept—in which a fragment of a hologram contains the whole image—

gets a lot of play here, but none of these eggheads claims to particularly understand the brain. These are serious researchers, but their writing is accessible and engaging, like the funny interview with the fictitious (and cranky) Dr. Zook.

Nutrition and Wellness

Arbor Communications—Guide to Nutrition Resources
http://arborcom.com/

This comprehensive directory of Net nutrition resources comes courtesy of Australia's Arbor Communications. The site features listings organized into two main categories—Applied Nutrition (clinical nutrition, dietetics, nutrition journals and multimedia) and Food ("for resources concerning food composition, food science and food safety.") Each has a virtual groaning board of good-for-you sites, from FATFREE: The Low Fat Vegetarian Archive to The Health Inspector's Home Page, a "Private guy's home page with his set of well-annotated links on food safety and the food industry." And if you still can't find what you want, the Search page lists search engines, indices, and institutional and university food science sites.

Center for Food Safety and Applied Nutrition
http://vm.cfsan.fda.gov/list.html

The CFSAN, part of the Food and Drug Administration, offers a huge buffet of data on edibles. The consumer advice is particularly strong, with help on everything from mercury in fish to handling eggs safely (store below 40 degrees, cook above 140 degrees, don't put all in one basket). A lot of the data is aimed at the food industry, but it's still interesting to sniff around. Why, you may wonder, does the FDA restrict levels of benzene hexachloride to 0.05 parts per million in most foods, but let 0.3 ppm slip by in frog legs and carrots? Are fat substitutes safe? How do they taste? You'll even find flashes of humor: the page on pathogenic bacteria and parasitic protozoa is called the Bad

Bug Book. Highly useful guide for both professionals and the general public.

International Food Information Council

http://ificinfo.health.org/

The nonprofit IFIC Foundation is on a mission to tell the world about healthy eating. It describes this Web site as "the source on food-related issues." The text here comes mainly from Foundation brochures, conveniently broken down by area of interest: consumers, reporters and health professionals are all offered different topic lists. The newsletter "Food Insight" is also included—one article describes how astronauts can forego the pastes and gelatin cubes of space flights in the past by selecting from a list of specially prepared "regular" foods. Note that this site seems generally slanted towards food manufacturers. The food additive section, for example, is pretty interesting, but implies that all food additives are completely safe. And the discussion of "Food Biotechnology" is an unrestrained paean to genetically-engineered crops.

Wellness Web

http://www.wellweb.com/

The Wellness Web, subtitled The Patient's Network, views medical and health care from the other side of the desk. Created by and for patients, its refreshingly honest and basic offerings include areas such as a Smoker's Clinic (info and sites to help you quit), Grassroots (organizations involved in health advocacy) and Medical Centers (with links to individual medical center resources). And since they say laughter is the best medicine, there's even a Be Happy Be Well area, with links to games, newspapers, and other fun sites to take your mind off your ills. The concept of wellness is a large part of this site, though it's not only about preventive healthcare but also about maintaining and restoring wellness to those sometimes lost in the quagmire of medical lingo and information.

Parenting

Children and Adults with Attention Deficit Disorders

http://www.chadd.org/

Attention Deficit Disorder, once thought to affect only kids, remains with 70 percent of patients as they continue into adulthood. That's the word from this home of ADD advocates, which covers political, medical, and social issues of the disease. One of the best resources here is the list of local chapters nationwide, with meeting times and contact numbers and addresses. CHADD keeps tabs on legislation that would affect its members and ADD patients and responds to media stories about the disorder, including a blistering critique of a PBS show. Selected articles from Attention!, CHADD's magazine, also can be read online. CHADD's dedication to patients and its members is easily visible here.

Divorce Home Page

http://www.primenet.com/~dean/

Dean Hughson, a divorced dad, has created this page to help others going through a painful separation. Whether you started the split or were an unwilling participant, you'll probably find a resource here. Hughson's own "Steps Toward Recovery" include links to pages that provide help on sleeping well, eating well, and regaining a sense of humor. (A page called Dumping Your Lover Electronically "makes me laugh even though it didn't sound so funny when I was dumped," he notes.) This site provides a broad array of self-help guides like The Newly Divorced Book of Protocol: How to be Civil When You Hate Their Guts, as well as info on support groups and other organizations. Most of Hughson's own advice is anecdotal; he offers a telephone hotlist for professional help.

The SACC Project at Wellesley College
http://www.wellesley.edu/Cheever/saccp.html

Wellesley College's Center for Research on Women is home to the renowned School-Age Child Care Project, and this page offers Internet users the benefits of its resources. The project examines issues such as day care licensing, child care subsidies and school preparedness, and publishes numerous reports and studies, many of which are outlined online (you can also buy them here). Child care professionals and parents alike will also find the site's Fact Sheet on School-Age Children helpful if chilling: It notes that "Children spend more of their out-of-school time watching television than in any other single activity. Children's television viewing has been associated with lower reading achievement, behavior problems, and increased aggression."

Thomas Clark King's CyberNursery
http://www.flash.net/~cyberkid

Young Thomas Clark King's parents devote this page to him not only because they're proud of him, but because they want to share their experience with Tommy's very premature birth (he was born at 25 weeks gestation instead of the usual 40 weeks, and weighed only 1 pound 10 ounces). Clark King narrates the painful story of his son's long hospitalization in a Neonatal Intensive Care Unit, and Tommy's slow progression from what King calls "the smallest and most sickly baby I had seen in my life" to "a perfect little ten month old" (last we checked). The site also includes links to other sites with information about premature babies, and lots of general parenting info as well. An excellent resource for parents of preemies.

Professional Medicine

The Global Health Network
http://www.pitt.edu/HOME/GHNet/GHNet.html

The Global Health Network is an ambitious attempt to prevent disease by linking health care professionals around the planet.

This Web site presents their slightly breathless vision: instantaneous access to massive amounts of medical data, advances ranging from telemedicine (consultations with remote doctors) to disease prediction in large populations (by monitoring and forecasting diseases much the same way we do with weather). Already this site has gathered world-wide health links and resources, from the World Health Organization to BIREME, a Latin American health center, to U.S. State Department Travel Advisories. The number and variety of resources and contacts here is very large. Not to be missed by those seeking the widest range of health information.

Heart Preview Gallery
http://sln2.fi.edu/biosci/preview/
heartpreview.html

The human heart beats two and a half million times in an average lifetime (more than that for you coffee drinkers). The Franklin Institute's "virtual heart" presentation is a good way to spend a few dozen of those beats. This is real scientific stuff, not a kiddie trip, though it is presented as a tour. Learn about blood types—a person with Type AB blood can receive a blood transfusion from any type donor, for instance—or compare x-rays of a normal-sized and enlarged heart. The whole interactive enchilada is here: movies, audio segments (they call the two heart sounds "lub" and "dub") and pictures decorated with lavish descriptions and explanations. You can actually watch a movie of the exchange of oxygen and carbon dioxide between the capillaries and arteries. Your fascination here "will lead to understanding and respect."

Online Mendelian Inheritance in Man
http://www3.ncbi.nlm.nih.gov/Omim/

This is an online version of Dr. Victor McKusick's landmark genetics book, "Mendelian Inheritance in Man." If you haven't heard of it or aren't interested in genetic disorders, this site isn't for you. But for interested parties (and for those with involuntary interest, like medical students), this highly technical catalog is a goldmine on how genetic differences cause illnesses, deformities and changes among species. If you understand the following, you're a shoo-in: "All pseudogenes of the ANT gene family seem to lack introns."

World Wide Web Virtual Library: Biosciences—Medicine

http://golgi.harvard.edu/biopages/medicine.html

If it's a biology or medicine-related Net site, you can get there from here. We're talking major medical: schools from the U. of Aberdeen to Yale, the "Web of Addictions," "Rethinking AIDS," and so much more! The pros can really use this online almanac, but sore layfolk (you know who you are) will benefit from the repetitive strain injury primer and its many cousins here. Even old Bowser isn't left out: the Budapest U. of Veterinary Science is here, too. And those with fast computers won't want to miss General Electric's now-legendary multimedia Colon Fly Through. Getting the picture? This virtual library gives one a sense of the Net's awesome potential, for better or worse, as a huge informational warehouse.

Public Policy Issues

Dana Foundation

http://www.dana.org/

The Dana Foundation wants to understand what's going on inside your head. That's why it tracks the progress of brain research in reports and bulletins year-round. This New York-based charity awards grants and prizes for medical education and research, but its Acrobat files are the real strength here. Readers receive updates on Congressional funding for research and issue briefs on schizophrenia and other disorders. A good site for brain specialists and researchers.

HCFA Home Page

http://www.hcfa.gov

OK, the Health Care Financing Administration is a site for policy wonks. But at least this site provides the actual numbers behind the huge health care debate. We learned, for instance, that 37 percent of Alabama women not enrolled in HMOs have had Medicare-subsidized mammograms. (Now that we know that, what do we do?) The HCFA directory can also tell you who to call at Medicare or Medicaid. An important feature here is the inclusion of file sizes with the descriptions. When you're dealing with statistics, that's good to know.

Mary Shelley Resource Page
`http://www.netaxs.com/~kwbridge/maryshel.html`

Mary Shelley, author of the gothic classic "Frankenstein," gets an examined life and legacy at Kim Woodbridge's Mary Shelley Resource Page. Set to mood music (your Netscape browser will be giving you lots of warnings), Woodbridge stitches together a beastly good site, with bio pages of Shelley and her gang (notably her parents, and husband and poet, Percy Bysshe Shelley, and friend and poet Lord Byron); she also includes pages exploring "Frankenstein" and its inspiration. Perhaps most fascinating is the Summer of 1816 page, which tells of a tumultuous season shared at Lake Geneva by the Shelleys, Byron and a pack of other romantics—a hypnotic time when the group dared each other to write tales of horror, staying up late at night to share their work. The lasting result of this devilish endeavor was Mary Shelley's monstrous masterpiece, which she completed in May, 1817 and published the following year.

Office of Human Radiation Experiments
`http://www.ohre.doe.gov/`

While we may have learned a lot about the Cold War, one topic was jealously guarded in secrecy for years: the American government's biological tests on its own people. Although you might not approve of the Department of Energy's pace in releasing information about these tests, it's good that we're finding out something. Visitors can search the 250,000-page archives or read through recently declassified documents (like a Dec. 5, 1945 letter from Robert M. Fink detailing the result of "lethal dose experiments"). It's all a bit unnerving, but researchers and students of the Cold War won't be disappointed by the information here.

Internet

Access Providers

Delphi Internet
http://www.tvguide.com/

One of the largest U.S. consumer online services struts its entertainment-oriented stuff here. Delphi Internet, or MCI/NewsCorp as it's called here, is owned by the one-and-only Rupert Murdoch, who just happens to own the Fox Network, 20th Century Fox, and TV Guide, and probably the souls of millions, for all we know. So expect a lot of TV and movie info here, from current movie releases to the official "X-Files" page. At our last perusal, Delphi was serving up pictures and clips from the Power Rangers movie and Strange Days. Sports, fashion, and Net oriented news make the standard splash here, big and slick and . . . well, like watching TV.

How To Select an Internet Service Provider
http://www.cnam.fr/Network/
Internet-access/how_to_select.html

This guide to finding the right internet service provider (ISP) reads like a Consumer Reports guide to buying the right car—it gives you tips on "looking under the hood" of prospective providers. It's written by Rick Adams, president of UUNet, so you can be pretty sure he knows what he's talking about. Of course, all his tips probably point you towards his company, but it's not a veiled advertisement for his service—there's a lot of good information here often overlooked by Common Man, like network topologies, customer base, and the provider's internal network link speeds. Probably above your head if you're just trying to get e-mail accounts for your kids, but almost required reading if you're connecting your company to the Internet for the first time.

The List
http://thelist.internet.com/

The List is a database of more than 1000 Internet access providers around the globe. Almost all the listings have delightful piles of information: connection fees, customer service numbers, email addresses, and the like. You can pull listings by area code or by country, and you can also search by the provider's business name. The majority of the sites are in the USA, but more than 60 other countries are listed—so if you're in Belarus, Kazakhstan, or Zambia, you might not be totally out of luck. Neat feature: if your provider is listed (and it probably is), you can rate its service and provide notes. And if it isn't listed, submit the doggone thing! User support is one reason why these listings are so extensive and reliable—the Internet community knows the benefit of finding a good provider.

Telecom Information Resources
http://www.spp.umich.edu/telecom/
telecom-info.html

The problem with the term "telecommunications" is that it covers such a broad area of stuff. Here's how to wade through the muck to get what you want. This index lists more than 600 Internet access providers, telecom companies from the United States to Germany and a list of Internet business directories. Pretty much anything that has to do with cable, wireless technology, and any other form of telecommunication is grouped into neat categories. These are the best of the best, and the list is updated regularly to keep it that way.

Associations and Organizations

The Association for History and Computing
http://grid.let.rug.nl/ahc/welcome.html

One thing we have learned from history is that there's an association or organization for everything, including the study of history using computers. Much of this site, directed toward working historians and educators, involves the rather academic issues that surround standardization and practice, as well as the exchange of historical information and documents in cyberspace. Well, somebody has to do it. Besides this academic shoptalk, the site contains one of the best resources for hunting down historical info on the Web, their "WWW Services for Historians."

The Blue Ribbon Campaign
http://www.eff.org/blueribbon.html

POW/MIA activists have the yellow ribbon, AIDS activists have the red ribbon. Now the Internet anti-censorship movement— and free speech in general—has the blue ribbon, courtesy of the Electronic Frontier Foundation. The non-profit's promotional site provides news about the battle against the hated Communications Decency Act of 1996, and the reasoning behind the bitter opposition of government regulation of content on the Internet. Expect lots of black backgrounds, links to Net-freedom resources, and strong opinions about the subject.

CERNET
http://www.cernet.edu.cn/

CERNET, or the China Education Resource Network, is the "nation-wide (cyber)backbone" established to provide Chinese regional networks (e.g. institutes, communities) with Internet access. Also available in English, their home page features a project overview, a clickable province-by-province resource map, and an exhaustive list of links to Chinese universities. Thus, you can virtually explore the vast nation from Inner Mongolia to Hainan (not to mention points between), as well as find out what's cooking on the Guangzhou University of Technology campus. One should be prepared for that "server does not have a DNS entry" message via more than a few of the pointers here (it's a developing project after all), and yet this is already a powerful Web tool for anyone seeking information on China.

The Computer History Association of California

http://www.chac.org/chac/index.html

As it all goes whizzing past, these guys out in California are trying to capture the history of computers. That's what this "grass roots" organization is all about—preserving the details of one of the great technological changes in human history. Their newsletter, "The Analytical Engine," features interviews with early players, oral histories of the guys who were building circuit boards in their garages in the '60s. They're just as concerned with the artifacts of computer history, and have some on display (with a special role for their prized SDS 930, "the last known, complete, running SDS computer in the world"). For techies this is like getting back to your roots, man.

Browsers and Interfaces

Cyberdog

http://cyberdog.apple.com/

A new Web browser for the Mac normally wouldn't garner much attention, but when Apple's name is on it, it's probably worth a look. The project is called Cyberdog, and while the software was still unreleased at last check, it's clearly going to be an interesting alternative to Netscape. Based on Apple's OpenDoc technology for sharing information between applications, Cyberdog is a one-stop Internet package clearly meant to beat Netscape at it's own game. Instead of needing helper applications, multimedia viewers are built in. Mail and newsgroup access are also seamlessly embedded. It remains to be seen if Apple is too late coming to the table with this, but the legions of Apple users will at least want to check it out.

Intercon

http://www.intercon.com/

Intercon was one of the first software companies to develop commercial Mac and PC software for TCP/IP connection to the Net. Now it's part of PSI, an up-and-coming Net access provider. So expect a lot of changes at this site, which offers free demos of TCP Connect II for both Mac and PC. At our

last stop, we found a new tech support area and news of
the new WebShark browsing software. Best suited for large
corporate computer systems requiring extra support for terminal emulation; for fun, don't miss the 101 Cool Links page.

Tribal Voice
http://www.tribal.com/

Tribal Voice is base camp for users of software called PowWow
that lets up to seven people chat, exchange files, and cruise
the Web as a group. The Tribal Voice people call such groups
"cybertribes," and that's why this site is one part native
American folklore and two parts Dungeons and Dragons role-
playing. It's all half-baked, but full of fun. Visitors can check out
the best PowWow-user home pages, like Bill Godwin-Austen's
Billigan's Island, or pay homage to Tribal Voice's self-professed
False Prophet, Marty Burke, who says: "It isn't lying that you
should concern yourself with. It's inaccuracy."

Virtual Society on the Web
http://sonypic.com/vs/

Sony's programmers in Japan have big plans to usher in the
next wave of human communication via virtual reality. The
ideas here are grandiose, but the underlying concept isn't so
wild. Until the rest of the world catches up to them, the programmers offer CyberPassage, a Web-based VRML (Virtual
Reality Markup Language) package that adds some non-
standard extensions to VRML like sounds and interactive
objects. (Sound familiar, Netscape users?) They're also offering
CyberPassage Conductor, which lets you build your own
VRML worlds. Both packages are free, but even if you don't
imbibe the software, there's a nifty VRML gallery that works
with most VR browsers.

Converse/Communicate

Dan Kegel's ISDN Page
http://alumni.caltech.edu/~dank/isdn/

ISDN (Integrated Services Digital Network) is an all-digital
telecommunications service that allows (among other things)

voice and data calls on the same phone line. And Dan Kegel is wild about ISDN, faithfully gathering every scrap of information he can find to promote its development as a worldwide standard. Judging by the volumes of material Kegel has gathered, it's safe to say ISDN has reached prime time. As if the FAQ provided weren't already a wealth of information, the site also provides specifics, such as how to get an ISDN connection in your area, and what software/hardware you need (an ISDN "terminal adapter," for one). Still, we recommend a modicum of computer expertise to understand all of that phone company gibberish.

Global Village Communication
http://www.globalvillage.com/

This modem company comes across with a site that is "warm" (in Marshall McLuhan-speak), since it welcomes new Net users with cute small town graphics and invites them to tour the Net. You'll find plenty of information on Global Village's broad range of modem models, and extra perks include a library of Internet Software to help beginners get launched on the Net. The Customer Support Center goes to great lengths to support both the hardware and software dilemmas that can often make users feel like the Village Idiot. In a world where some computer hardware vendors have adopted the approach of Orwell's 1984, this village is indeed a pleasant escape.

Pacific Bell
http://www.pacbell.com/

Use this "slick information site" to study up on our digital future. Pacific Bell leads the way in ISDN service, a new digital phone standard that could make your Net connection 5-10 times faster. (Even if some say it stands for "It Still Does Nothing.") Get informed at the ISDN Overview page, and if you're a PacBell customer, find out how to order. If you're out of this Baby Bell's territory, then just check in to see how the other half lives. Snappy graphics, useful text.

Telecom Information Resources
    http://www.spp.umich.edu/telecom/
    telecom-info.html

The problem with the term "telecommunications" is that it covers such a broad area of stuff. Here's how to wade through the muck to get what you want. This index lists more than 600 Internet access providers, telecom companies from the United States to Germany and a list of Internet business directories. Pretty much anything that has to do with cable, wireless technology, and any other form of telecommunication is grouped into neat categories. These are the best of the best, and the list is updated regularly to keep it that way.

Indexes and How-to-Guides

Alta Vista
    http://www.altavista.digital.com/

A latecomer to the Web indexing field, Digital's Alta Vista is a strong competitor to Lycos (Point's sister company) and the other leaders. Along with the expected keyword searches of the millions of Web documents out there, Digital has added a similar search mechanism for Usenet postings. The databases can be searched using single keywords or using more complicated Boolean queries. Either way, searches are quick and generally turn up more hits than anyone would care to read. It's a crowded field, but Digital obviously wants its piece of the virtual pie.

The Classical MIDI Archives
    http://www.prs.net/midi.html

Of the many MIDI (Musical Instrument Digital Interface) sites, this is the granddaddy archive of (western) classical music samples to capture and use. This extensive library, with its vast sampling of works, should have MIDI tinkerers hunched over their computers and synthesizers for hours. From the fifteen century to the twentieth, the selection of mostly public domain classical works is a great source for MIDI users to tap.

Definitely for the initiated, but a newcomer could still benefit, thanks to the open-door policy of the site.

Globalprint
http://www.globalprint.nl/

These folks bill themselves as "The online information service for the world of graphic arts," and they very well may be right. After you choose your language from the four options on the home page, you enter the heart of the site, at the top of which is the "Suppliers" listings, which may be the most impressive thing here: the single-line name listing of all the suppliers for which they have contact information can take two minutes to load on the fastest modem connection. You can also register as a supplier or user, to offer or request products and services, sell your used graphic equipment, or just catch up on industry news.

HTML: Working and Background Materials
http://www.w3.org/pub/WWW/MarkUp/MarkUp.html

Our reporters call this the Strunk and White style guide to HTML and a must for anyone who is designing their own home page. Yes, you get all the whys and wherefores of HyperText Markup Language—the Swahili that makes the WorldWide Web possible. Or, as the intro to the site says, Here we discuss the HTML language, i.e. its syntax and semantics, including information on the history of the language, status of the standard, and development issues. In other words, not for the faint of heart. Edited by Web vet Daniel Connolly (who has a monster vita, by the way), this site is complete, informative, and dense—pack a lunch. See Also: HTML Design Notebook.

Internet News

Global Network Navigator
http://gnn.com/gnn/gnn.html

If the Internet were an airline, this would be O'Hare Airport. (There are tons of gates, it's easy to get lost, and like it or not you'll probably spend a lot of time here.) The Global Network Navigator (owned by America Online) has something for nearly everyone, offering guides to new sites, business listings, and the well-known "Whole Internet Catalog." It will also be the centerpiece of America Online's new Internet service, featuring its unique GNNWorks software. For what it does, it does a great job—giving you directions, moving you around efficiently, and reminding you just how vast the Internet can be. It even has some useful online magazines covering sports, finance, and travel.

Steve Jackson Games vs. the Secret Service
`http://www.io.com/SS/`

Steve Jackson was writing a book about credit card fraud in the future that didn't include the Secret Service. So they injected themselves into the picture, touching off a lengthy legal battle over privacy and the Internet. This site meticulously retells the tale, from a March 1990 raid on Steve Jackson Games (seeking evidence of computer crimes) to the ruling against the Secret Service by a Texas judge three years later. It's a fascinating tale, with the actual affidavits, opinions and analyses by the people involved. Sure, the Secret Service doesn't have much of a voice here, but they lost the case. A great primer on why policing the Internet could be the biggest problem in the Information Age.

webreference.com
`http://www.webreference.com/`

This catch-all site covers so much ground it should appeal to starry-eyed newbies Web users and haggard Webmasters alike. While the links to outside documents and tutorials are uninspiring, the real meat of the site is found in the original articles. On the low end, casual Web users will appreciate the beginners' guides, but more experienced users and professional Webheads will want to check out articles like "A Day In the Life of a Webmeister." Both recycled and original content are presented equally well—so well it's not always clear which is which. For anyone who fears falling behind trying to keep up with the Joneses (or at least Jones.com), this is a handy all-around tool.

Web Toolz Magazine
http://www.webdeveloper.com/

We don't learn much about the publishers of Web Toolz (weekly), but accomplished and would-be Webmeisters will love its excellent assortment of Net related newz, articlez, and reviewz—not to mention those toolz, and pertinent linkz. It's good for, say, the scoop on Netscape's newest browser version, or a download pointer to the Java-friendly version of Microsoft Internet Explorer. Click regular features such as "Advanced HTML" in the left frame, and in the middle appears the likes of Drasko Marcovic's tutorial on "using tables to simulate desktop publishing layouts." Get access to VRML editors and browsers, hot plug-ins, and all sorts of other good stuff. A comprehensive, elegantly designed, and most generous resource.

Standards and Security

Intellectual Property
http://www.ipmag.com/

It's not every magazine that will call for Internet Service Providers to become copyright police. But that's just what Intellectual Property did in one article by William J. Cook. IP is sort of the legalistic "Yes, but . . ." answer to the wide-open electronic world. While celebrating the information age, this mag also turns its attention to digital security and resolving online disputes (one story points out that "even with a rudimentary search of the Web, you will probably find a number of persons using your trademark as a generic term"). A certain level of lawyer-speak comes into play here, but mostly it presents critical questions and offers some solutions that may not be wildly popular—yet.

Internet Request for Comments (RFC)
http://www.cis.ohio-state.edu/hypertext/
information/rfc.html

This page gives access to the Internet RFCs. "The Request for Comments documents (RFCs) are working notes of the Internet research and development community," says RFC1206;

in other words, consider this a high-powered Internet FAQ list, with notes and comments about a wide variety of Web construction issues. There are "new user" RFCs, but many are like RFC1819: "Internet Stream Protocol Version 2 (ST2) Protocol Specification—Version ST2+." (Got that?) There are search functions available here, but we wish they were more readily obvious.

RSA Data Security, Inc.
http://www.rsa.com/

If you're afraid some 15-year old kid will break into your zillion-dollar corporate computers and steal trade secrets (or worse, read your private e-mail), a visit here may help you sleep better at night. Learn all about data security, firewalls, cryptography, and the like. You probably won't understand a word you read, but the complexity may help you feel safer. One of the most comprehensive (if not comprehensible) security sites we've seen.

TakeDown
http://www.takedown.com/

Computer security expert and flowing-haired ski bum Tsutomu Shimomura not only helped the FBI catch feared "darkside" hacker Kevin Mitnick but in so doing became the first genuine sex symbol of the cyber epoch. (Sandra Bullock doesn't count.) His book *Takedown*, written with *New York Times* reporter John Markoff, is his first person account of this sort of cyberspace French Connection. Given the topic and personalities involved, one would expect an ultraslick Web site to support the book. No disappointment here. Using extensive hypertext and Netscape 2.0's frames, the site gives an easy and exciting step-by-step account of the chase—and a staggering set of links to sites for just about everyone and everything mentioned in any context in Shimomura's account. Just about the only aspect of the adventure not online is info about the various other books about the Shimomura-Mitnick affair—most notably Jonathan Littman's *The Fugitive Game*.

Web Gadgets and Oddities

CyberTown

http://www.cybertown.com/

CyberTown is a huge shopping and services center that sprawls over the entire galaxy and across several centuries. Or perhaps it just seems to sprawl that far. The creators hope that CyberTown will become a central point for Web access and a sort of self-contained virtual village. By the look of things, they're well on their way. The graphic theme is space-age (the town is set in "the latter half of the 21st century"); so far most of the in-house stuff is shop storefronts, where you can in fact order things. But the site is linked "back in time" to our modern Earth and history resources, and plans are in the works for several interactive gizmos, like CyberHood, a virtual walk through the seedier side of CyberTown.

Dr. Fellowbug's Laboratory of Fun & Horror

http://www.dtd.com/fellowbug/

Dr. Fellowbug's Lab is a collection of weird and funny items, only a part of GigaBox, the local content created by the Web design firm Downtown Digital. Offerings in this morbidly-themed dungeon include the goulish Letter R.I.P. (a hangman-style puzzle with a twist), and The Skulls of Fate, a fortune-telling device made twisted by its cute-little-girl graphics. You'll also find a surprise or two: clicking a balloon tied to a rat's tail leads you into a little comic strip involving the rat and an executive. The artwork is terrific, if you have a fast connection, or if you're patient enough. You have to like a company that pours this much energy into just horsing around.

Sun Angel Productions

http://www.sun-angel.com/welcome.html

This Web mall makes available many New Age products and services, but with all the other stuff on here, you don't get the feeling they're just trying to take your money—the whole package seems geared towards helping you develop your inner self. There's an interesting array of things to buy, there's no doubt—at Star Water Press, for example, "Anubel" will use a picture of you to paint your aura. But there's also an enlightening collection of articles and art online, along with some "InnerActive Fun", like a module that allows you to "create" the perfect planet. Sometimes strange, but always friendly.

Wordbot

http://www.cs.washington.edu/homes/kgolden/
wordbot.html

The ultimate linguistics tool, Wordbot lets you load any page through its filter and then does to it what you will—need it translated into English from a major language? Done. Want hypertext links to dictionary definitions or thesaurus terms? Done—in a big way: every word will be linked to the Web reference tool (or even search engine) of your choice. If you get annoyed by seeing every frigging word underlined, you can switch off the link underlines (and the Frames as well) so you won't go completely mad. A wiggly arrow identifies existing links so you don't get a list of synonyms when you were trying to swim upstream. The homepage walks you through the Wordbot process and explains its functions; less precise is the answer to the question "How does it work?": "Magic."

Web Publishing and HTML

HTML Validation Service

http://www.webtechs.com/html-val-svc/

If you're writing Web pages and you want to check that it's up to HTML specifications, run it through the Validation Service. Give your URL, hit a button, and it retrieves the source of your document and tells you what's wrong. And it'll probably find something—this baby doesn't pull its punches. You can check for HTML 2.0 or (the experimental) 3.0, for Netscape and Java extensions, and at a "strict" level that catches a lot of

HTML niceties often ignored. There's also a text box where you can type in a few lines and check them "on the fly." Good way to find out if you really have your HTML down.

Photodisc, Inc.
http://www.phetodisc.com/index.asp

Photodisc, Inc. is a supplier of stock photography on CD-ROM. This new home page allows you to purchase their stock images right over the Web. With its graphic interface, the Web is a natural for this—one look at the site and you'll be amazed no one thought of this sooner. Before you can buy anything, you'll have to register by phone, but once you do, you can browse their entire collection and buy one picture at a time, rather than whole CDs. Even those not interested in the photos should visit Design Mind, a hefty section with advice on design, Web creation, and other tidbits.

Pixelsight
http://www.pixelsight.com/

Pixelsight's online graphics tools make it easy to create 3-D logos and text for aspiring Web publishers and anyone who needs some spiffy images to spruce up their life. What's most impressive is that all the tools are free. A design firm with some great artistic and programming talent, Keith Ohlfs' Pixelsight is both a company and a great Web resource. The real meat of the site is a tool that let's anyone design and create beveled, 3-D, slick-looking custom images for their own use—all with just a standard Web browser and no additional software. Also check out the huge clip art library which has dozens of free, professional-looking images for personal use. This is a great tool for those who can't afford the likes of PhotoShop.

WAIS, Inc.
http://www.wais.com/

Tour the company that "pioneered online publishing" with its popular search software called WAIS (rhymes with "chase"). The company now belongs to America Online, but its WAISserver software for Web searches will keep its name and live on as a major player in Net publishing. As you might expect, you use the search software to find information on the site. As a bonus, the database links you to WAIS databases across the Web, giving you a shot at searching for reams of valuable information on a broad range of topics. For example, by entering the keyword "congress," you get a list of WAIS database covering the latest bills in Congress. And for potential Web publishers (especially those considering using a WAIS database), this is one of the richest archives of technical information we've found.

Just For Kids

Children's Resources

CyberKids
http://www.cyberkids.com/

CyberKids is a quarterly online magazine by kids and for kids. It offers fiction, art, and news articles like "The First African-American Woman in Space" by correspondents aged 7 to 16. The writing and art, both impressive, are the products of a series of contests sponsored by Mountain Lake Software and Turner Home Entertainment; on our last visit, we found a story about a time-traveler who accidentally altered history by preventing the attack on skater Nancy Kerrigan. Besides the thrill of being published on the Web, contest entrants can vie for software, books and cash prizes. CyberKids is put together with wit and what seems like very little adult meddling. (The comments section is full of every possible variation on the words "this page is cool.") This should be a popular destination for preteens and early adolescents.

Cyberschool Magazine
http://www.infoshare.ca/csm/index.htm

Ring the bells and clap the erasers: Cyberschool Magazine is in session, and kids are likely to learn a lot from this fun educational 'zine. Each issue includes departments with articles covering science (Nuclear Newton), the arts (Bionic Bard), history (The Time Machine) and other curricular standards. A recent issue included features on stuff like the government's SETI (Search for ExtraTerrestrial Intelligence) programs and student life in the Middle Ages. And if you're ready to link out on your own, the Surfin' Librarian features hundreds of great sites worth exploring. Cyberschool Magazine makes the grade as a full-service e-ed zone, and one worth bookmarking for return visits.

Kids' Space
http://www.kids-space.org

This totally cool interactive site is home page to thousands of kids around the world. In the Kids' Gallery you can see artwork from Kaitong Ariel in Hong Kong or Nicholas in New York ("Spaceships!"). Make new cyber friends online—on our last visit, kids from Russia, Israel, and Italy were looking for pen pals (so were lots of American kids). Groove to music at the On Air Concert, or read some flights of literary fancy at the Story Book (cookie jars and rubber duckies were some common motifs on our last visit). Best of all, you can share your own artwork, music, stories, and personal home pages with other kids on the Net! If you need inspiration, the Beanstalk project lets you write a story for someone else's drawing, or draw a picture from someone else's story. Great fun!

The Page at Pooh Corner
http://www.public.iastate.edu/~jmilne/
pooh.html

Children's lit lovers of all ages will aaah and oooh over this cute, cuddly, and comprehensive Winnie the Pooh site. It's the work of James Milne (who insists that as far as he knows, he's not related to Pooh author A.A. Milne), and you could hunt throughout the 100 Acre Woods and not find a fonder tribute. This Pooh page covers all things about Winnie, including an article on how he got his name: Milne borrowed it from a black bear named Winnie (the fellow who named the bear was from Winnipeg) he saw at the zoo. You'll also find the lyrics to Kenny Loggins's treacly tune "The House at Pooh Corner," and a thoroughly researched page on the life of A.A. Milne. The site is a visual charmer, with its classic Pooh background and Disney images, and is so deep with links and pages that you're liable to wander these woods with Christopher Robin and his friends for quite a while.

News and Reference

Daily News

CNN Interactive
http://www.cnn.com/

It took a while for CNN to burst on to the Web scene, but this picture-rich site makes the wait worthwhile. CNN's home page covers breaking news, sports, health and showbiz stories, each nearly always including pictures grabbed from CNN's video cameras. It also offers a few limited video clips, still too time-consuming for most users to download but clearly a sign of what's to come as Net connections speed up. We especially liked the blazing-fast search feature that quickly calls up stories on a topic of your choice. Can you survive without the reassuring voice of a news anchor? Sure, but just to feel more at home, you may want to try your best imitation of James Earl Jones intoning "This . . . is CNN."

Federal News Service
http://www.fnsg.com

Think of the Federal News Service as an electronic version of C-SPAN. The private company provides transcripts of speeches, Congressional hearings, United Nations sessions and more. Of course, it costs money—the service is billed on a pay-per-view basis for web users (A transcript of one of President Clinton's speeches cost $6). But FNS provides a whole lot of information, including Latin American and Russian news, and can tailor their products to your needs. Four years of Washington D.C. and Moscow news are available on CD-ROM, and corporate clients can make use of their Russian law service, which electronically delivers the translated text of laws and decrees from Russia's Parliament. You'll pay, but you get a lot for it.

The Wall Street Journal
http://wsj.com/

The newspaper for investments just made a big one itself. Taking the copy-for-money plunge is one of the nation's biggest and most-respected newspapers, *The Wall Street Journal*. While access to this site remains free until August 31 for anyone who registered before July 31 (guess they like the end of the month), it will cost money after. Is it worth it? If you like the Journal it is. You'll find just about every story in the printed edition plus updates throughout the day—those classic center-column front-page tales and the aggressive editorials. And it even looks like the Journal. Articles from the Asian and European versions are included—along with the best business reporting you're likely to find. A fabulous read—even on a monitor.

WWW Virtual Library: Electronic Journals
http://www.edoc.com/ejournal/

You just know journals like Annals of Saudi Medicine are available online, but finding them is tricky. Here's a good place to look. Just the section on peer-reviewed academic journals is loaded with publications that are obscure, to say the least: Journal of Approximation Theory, Tree Physiology, etc. Students wishing to get their papers published somewhere can probably find the proper outlet here (the Richmond Journal of Law & Technology is one student-edited journal published exclusively online). Other journal topics include politics, collegiate publications and email newsletters.

Magazines

Boston Review
http://www-polisci.mit.edu/BostonReview/

Every now and again, one stumbles into a Web site that seems almost too good to be true. It might be a "bimonthly magazine of culture and politics with a broadly progressive outlook," yielding full text of current and past issues, including articles and commentary by Noam Chomsky, Ralph Nader, Sissela Bok . . . It might be efficiently designed, with texts accessible via an author index, for instance. Who knows? Open letters published here (e.g. "On the Responsibility of Intellectuals in the Age of Crack") might even spawn forums at places like Harvard's Kennedy School. There might be a generous supply of literary criticism, as well as first-run poetry and short stories. It might be a not-for-profit enterprise, offering print subscriptions at an extremely reasonable rate, or gently encouraging contributions from satisfied Web readers. Given all that, and more, such a site is Boston Review.

Elle
http://www.ELLEMag.com/

The latest fashions, runway images, and "a touch of spiritual direction" are featured in Elle magazine's elegant online entry. If you can get past the incredible hype ("Vibrant and visceral, passionate and provocative, diverse and distinctly innovative . . .") you'll find the likes of Christy Turlington wearing industrial-strength latex, or Isabella Rossellini in a "menagerie of animal prints just tame enough for city life." Many photos come with shopping links for those who dare to try such apparel themselves. The interface is stylish, the photos are slick, and rather than endless subscription appeals, this site concentrates on delivering the goods. Because of the many photos, you'll enjoy this most if your modem is as powerful as your fashion sense.

HotWired
http://www.hotwired.com/frontdoor/97/22/nc_splash1a.html

More than just an electronic version of Wired magazine, this outpost is the product of a full-time staff dedicated to keeping it fresh. The effort shows in slick neon graphics and intentionally unpredictable content: instead of assigning typical section names, Wired divides itself into categories like Signal (news of the wired) and World Beat (travel). HotWired adds flavor from its remarkably thoughtful discussion areas, and variety with plenty of pictures and sounds in its Renaissance (Art and Entertainment) section. There's more than a little self-serving digital snobbery here; the editors have no patience with those who don't share their Utopian visions of a wired world. But stirring up discussion and controversy is precisely what Wired does best, and for that, it shouldn't be missed.

Pathfinder

```
http://www.pathfinder.com/@@0xr8CAUAHcp7ewOj/
welcome/
```

Time Warner makes brilliant use of the Web with this online content machine, combining the best in information from the growing conglomerate's varied sources. You can read a review of new CD-ROMs, check the quotes on the New York Stock Exchange, or visit a "virtual garden" for tips on choosing the right perennials. This is both huge and continuously freshened; it's really about 50 to 100 Web sites in one, yet allows you to move between its sub-sites seamlessly. Why such a web within the Web? Pathfinder wants to become the advertising-sponsored heartbeat of the Web, and to build revenues, bigger is better. For now, Web consumers are the real winners, since they can get essentially all of the articles from magazines like Sports Illustrated, Time, and People in fresh daily editions.

Reference Information

The CIA World Factbook

```
http://www.odci.gov/cia/publications/94fact/
fb94toc/fb94toc.html
```

The Central Intelligence Agency receives billions of dollars to keep tabs on other nations. The factbook at this site is one grand example of that work, with political, social, and economic information on places you didn't even know existed—for instance, the Ashmore and Cartier Islands, located between Australia and Indonesia. Together, the factbook says, they are about the size of the Washington DC mall. (Not bad research, considering that the isles have no permanent residents.) And if you know nothing about, say, Botswana (hello students!), this would be a very good place to start looking. The title is slightly misleading: you won't find classified information here. But you will find a lot of everything else.

DejaNews Research Service
http://www.dejanews.com/

Usenet, the Internet free-for-all that encompasses thousands of newsgroups, can be a mess. So how can you find your way to newsgroup postings on, say, kangaroos (and there are plenty out there)? This service makes trying to find something a little bit easier, especially for newcomers. When we searched for "Richard Nixon," for instance, we found postings on such diverse newsgroups as rec.pets (Checkers, no doubt) and sci.space.policy. Searching for "orangutan" yielded 86 hits. Searches can be for whole words, phrases and even words with similar beginnings. And you can write to the author of the posts you find, too. The search menus are easy to use, making this both useful and a great way to pass the time.

GPO Access on the Web
http://thorplus.lib.purdue.edu:8100/gpo/

Purdue University ought to get a medal for this site, which allows users to search through over a dozen Government Printing Office databases, including the Congressional Record, the Federal Register, and much more. For instance: the General Accounting Office, the research arm of Congress, produces hundreds of "blue book" reports a year on major legislative issues like health care and federal funding of education, and visitors can find them here. The page takes some time to figure out, and then searches can take some time because of the sheer amount of material the computer has to wade through. Still, a magnificent resource.

Telecom Information Resources
http://www.spp.umich.edu/telecom/
telecom-info.html

The problem with the term "telecommunications" is that it covers such a broad area of stuff. Here's how to wade through the muck to get what you want. This index lists more than 600 Internet access providers, telecom companies from the United States to Germany and a list of Internet business directories.

Pretty much anything that has to do with cable, wireless technology, and any other form of telecommunication is grouped into neat categories. These are the best of the best, and the list is updated regularly to keep it that way.

Roads Less Traveled

Conspiracies and Hoaxes

60 Greatest Conspiracies of All Time
`http://www.webcom.com:80/~conspire/`

At last: an online 'zine that shows just how entertaining
conspiracy theories can be! This page is kind of a Noam
Chomsky-David Letterman hybrid: the authors provide the
grain (sometimes chunk) of salt required to digest some mighty
wacky theories—without calling anyone a liar (exactly).
Hardcore fans of conspiracies can still get their JFK-UFO-
Vince Foster fix here—they don't mess with tradition, and the
layout is slick enough to have come from a CIA photolab! The
true spirit of 50GCAT, however, lies in Lyndon LaRouch
explaining why British intelligence "grew" the Grateful Dead
out of mind control experiments, and stories like "Jonestown:
Population Zero," complete with Mr. Koolaid icon (sensitive
types beware!). Every month new features are "brought to light"
with an irreverent, cynical, and funny edge at this glossy site.

The Consortium
`http://www.delve.com/consort.html`

Investigative reporter Robert Parry, the brains behind this
muckraking new e-zine, was way ahead of everyone on the
Iran-Contra story. In his book "Trick or Treason" he also
pushed the "October Surprise," the story that in 1980, candidate Ronald Reagan made a secret and (to put it mildly)
illegal deal with Iran to free the U.S. hostages. The theory was
"debunked" by Congress, but Parry revisits the story here,
bringing to light some unsettling new information: an explosive

document hidden deep in FBI archives. "A real life X-Files," says Parry. As if juicy info wasn't enough, The Consortium's classy design makes reading a breeze for the eyes.

NameBase
http://www.pir.org/

An extremely helpful—sometimes frighteningly so—resource, and not just for conspiracy theorists. Reporter Daniel Brandt has assembled this database of books and magazines, focusing on hard-hitting investigative journalism. We're talking the CIA, religious cults, terrorism, Nazis—the whole charming cast of characters that populates the penumbra of politics gets the sunshine treatment. The essence of NameBase is a name search. Enter a name, preferably of a suspected spy or high-level conspirator, and NameBase presents you with a list of books and magazines in which that name appears. Equally valuable to armchair spook-spotters, Brandt and crew write short reviews of a couple hundred books sorted into categories from "Assassinations/JFK" to "Vietnam War/CIA." And as if that wasn't enough, the NameBase gang contributes an anthology of essays and reports including such titillators as "Mind Control and the Secret State," "Cold Warriors Woo Generation X," and "Organized Crime Threatens the New World."

The Nizkor Project
http://www2.ca.nizkor.org/index.html

Here's an incredible, all-encompassing research library devoted to combating one of the darker elements of the Net: the prevalence of Holocaust "revisionism." Canada-based archivist Ken McVay doesn't want to censor anti-Semites and neo-Nazis who flood the Usenet with Holocaust-never-happened spams. Instead, he wants to refute their every claim. The heart and soul of his site is the Shofar FTP Archive—something like 4,000 text documents rebutting, exposing and ridiculing every possible permutation of the revisionist theory. Nizkor is also home to the nascent HWEB Project, a volunteer effort to put the entire collection into HTML.

Crystal Ball

Esther & Son Daily Astrological Currents

http://www.teleport.com/~esson/

This one-size-fits-all astrology page (from a mother-son team in Portland, Oregon) offers a daily forecast based not on individual Zodiac signs, but on where the sun is positioned in relation to planet Earth. No muss, no fuss, no need to call mom for your exact time of birth. Think of it as an astrological weather forecast—it announces the directions life in general is supposed to be heading, rather than portents for each specific sign. Believers can find out when to "send signals wildly into the atmosphere," and when to lay low, and then pass this universal advice on to friends and business associates. (Or not.) You can have the daily Currents report sent to you automatically via e-mail, or even via postal mail. Or you can pay extra for the full treatment.

Ignatius Donnelly and the End of the World

http://www-leland.stanford.edu/~meehan/
donnelly/index.html

Ignatius Donnelly was a congressman from the last century, a failed "visionary" who serves as the voice of this compelling page of science, love, and religion. This isn't about Donnelly, who can loosely be placed with Catastrophism. Most of it is about the Great Flood, or as one section says, "What on earth happened in 3,200 B.C.?" The ensuing investigation includes lots of science (climate data, archeology, and geology), mixed with prehistoric myths from around the world (Celtic especially) and the spark and curiosity of the human spirit. One visitor wrote to say this was good science, but seemed disappointed at the "superstition." We think it's the superstition angle that keeps this from being just another entry in the "What If . . ." catalog.

Prophe-Zine
http://www.prophezine.com/index.shtml

This biblical prophesy magazine encompasses world events and politics in its eschatological discussions, based of course on literal Bible interpretation. One highlight is the editorial policy of "equal time to other biblically based doctrines." Contributing authors often have varied opinions as to what exactly signifies the end of the world. Believers will certainly find it informative and good reading, although when the discussion turns purely political (always very right-wing, to the point of castigating even Rush Limbaugh) the logic gets fuzzy and contradictions flourish. The site isn't particularly pretty, relying heavily on text, but it's bi-weekly format keeps things up-to-date (especially good is the "News Bites" section in each issue); don't miss the lively story in Issue #4 about the discovery of the Ark of the Covenant.

Used Karma
http://www.speakeasy.org/usedkarma/index.html

This unique astrological page offers a bundle of general information on planetary movements and lunar influences with a refreshingly broad stroke. Rather than simply looking up what your horoscope is ("Relationships central to your decision making; knees will appear wrinkled around midday"), Webmaster and astrologist Deek hopes to give you a perspective that will allow contextual interpretations of astrological trends. For newcomers, that means lots of education by way of Deek's Astrological Weather Map and Used Karma's Daily and Monthly Overviews or "forecasts." Also featured are articles on all manner of astrologically-tinted topics, from the future of a cashless society to how to look at the upside of Mercury in retrograde. While it's true that the charts here of Bill Clinton and Bob Dole seem like kooky diversions, even non-believers may stick around to read this level-headed approach to the Zodiac.

Death

Crisis, Grief and Healing
http://www.webhealing.com/

Washington, D.C. therapist Tom Golden has created the Crisis, Grief and Healing site to allow others to share their experiences, and also to promote lectures and workshops he gives, and a collection of booklets he's written. Though death is the primary focus of the site's related pages, at the home page Golden notes that grief also can be experienced over divorce and the loss of a job. This site's strengths are its coping and sharing pages—such as the Suggestions Page from alt.support.grief about helping someone in mourning, including Dale Monahan's list of things not to say to a bereaved parent, such as "Well, you still have _____." Those struggling with grief will find many useful areas here, including a discussion area and lists of other sites and resources. And though it's painful to read, *A Place to Honor Grief* offers a chance for the bereaved to share the experiences of loss. Reading the entries is often heartbreaking, especially those by parents who've lost their children. But for those experiencing this ultimate grief, the postings are a tender tribute to the bittersweet reality that no one suffers alone.

DeathNet
http://www.IslandNet.com:80/~deathnet/

The Right to Die Society of Canada doesn't mince words on its titles, does it? Here they offer a virtual library of resources on human mortality. Asserting its respect "for every point of view," the society has assembled here an impressive collection of info on its chosen topic: articles like "Then it was Birth Control, Now it's Euthanasia," a complete toxicology and poisons database from the University of Singapore, or the official transcripts from Canada's Senate Special Committee on Euthanasia and Assisted Suicide. It's not all doom and gloom: there's some mild whimsy here, like an audio clip of a bell tolling. Overall, it's an exhaustive look at the Last Roundup.

The Internet Crime Archives
http://www.mayhem.net/Crime/archives.html

For those with a macabre sense of humor, this site features lists and photographs of serial killers, mass murderers (yes, Virginia, there is a difference) and killer cults. This hall of shame features big-named killers and their death tallies, with brief reports whose flippancy may offend sensitive visitors. Besides Manson, Bundy, and Dahmer, these lists are disturbingly long and include run-of-the-mill killers like Leo Held (killed 6 people who had irked him) alongside the likes of Pedro Lopez, the "Monster of the Andes," credited with at least 300 murders. A "Group Portrait of Evil" displays photos of the killers featured.

Widow Net
http://www.fortnet.org/~goshorn/

Widow Net is Michael Goshorn's collection of kind and helpful resources to help widowed individuals through the grieving and healing processes. Visitors will find online resources for reaching out to other widowed people, and annotated bibliographies of recommended books on bereavement. The site also includes some nuts-and-bolts offerings, such as a FAQ about reducing junk mail (Publisher's Clearinghouse will continue to announce that the dearly departed may be its next $10 million dollar winner unless notified of the death) and a link to the Social Security Administration benefits handbook. Those who've lost a loved one will find the resources here meaningful and timely.

The Mind

Altered States of Consciousness
http://www.utu.fi/~jounsmed/asc/asc.html

Under the umbrella of "altered states" lie tales of out-of-body experiences (OBEs), lucid dreaming and tests for personality typing. The strongest section of this site, however, is devoted to hypnosis. Although techniques for self-hypnosis are implicit in the discussion, most of this is about putting others in a trance: how to do it and what to do once you've done it, going so far as to list possible "skits" for those in a trance, such as the suggestion, "there are dozens of ants all over your food and all over you." (Seems like a rather cruel joke, actually.) Of course, before each in-depth example of hypnosis induction techniques it says, "for informational use only, absolutely not for hypnotizing others." Hmm.

Neo-Tech's Profound Honesty
http://www.neo-tech.com/prosperity/

Be ready to trash that talisman and toss the rosary in the rubbish as the minds behind Neo-Tech publishing try to convince you to join their movement of neo-Objectivism. Taking Aristotle and Ayn Rand as their noble heroes, these guys want to expose "neocheaters" who want to destroy "value-producing" heroes like Bill Gates. Beyond whatever belief system they're busy selling, there's the up-coming book "Flame-War Justice," which promises to continue what seems to be somebody's obsession with retribution over Usenet posts. Somewhere in this mixed up 'zine (that promises to "push the limits of scorn and hostility") there is, in fact, a new way of looking at the Universe. Remember, it's all metaphorical (except the footnotes, which look real enough).

PSYCHE
http://psyche.cs.monash.edu.au/

This interdisciplinary e-journal offers complete research articles on the nature of consciousness. Those include Richard E. Cytowic's "Synesthesia: Phenomenoloy and Neuropsychology" describing a peculiar condition predominate among "females and non-right-handers" in which "the stimulation of one sensory modality reliably causes a perception in one or more different senses." (See if you don't think that text tastes great!) This is high-minded stuff, so to speak. Submissions welcome, too.

Psycoloquy
http://www.princeton.edu/~harnad/psyc.html

The American Psychological Association (APA) sponsors the publication of Psycoloquy, a deadly serious journal publishing "target articles and peer commentary in all areas of psychology as well as cognitive science, neuroscience, behavioral biology, artificial intelligence, robotics/vision, linguistics and philosophy." Whew! The current issue is online, and a huge searchable archive contains articles on subjects ranging from robotic consciousness and thought evolution to pattern recognition and modular neural networks. Definitely not for those who seek slick graphics and facile pronouncements, but a heavy hitter for the pros.

Miscellaneous Marvels

Ferndale
http://www.ferndale.com/

Here's an online soap opera that makes *The Spot* look like a bad B movie. The concept behind Ferndale: it's an experiment in therapy for troubled souls at a secluded retreat. The experimental part is that they're in a "digital glass house"—all of their journal entries, transcripts, meetings, and more are made available to the Internet public, so we all get to follow along. And what a multimedia experience: it's in text, picture, movie, and RealAudio formats that make it what General Hospital could never dream to be. Surprising lack of copy editing in places (they can't work out a common spelling for "titillator", and Candice Bergen might be upset at her name's misspelling), but otherwise, you can expect to sink hours of your day soaking it all in.

The Fortean Times
http://www.forteantimes.com/

Now this "Journal of Strange Phenomena" is monthly, and that's good news to fans of weird stories. While the other media cover mundane mass murders and serial killer cannibals, *The Fortean Times* covers the really juicy stories: strange creature sightings, psychic experiments and men who live like fish. What you get here are sample stories from the 'zine, but the samples are ample and the design is divine (sorry). Sensitive souls should beware the morbidly gross amid the weird.

The Kooks Museum
http://www.teleport.com/~dkossy/

Can the book be as fun as this museum? Kooks are respected as sincere weirdos in this splashy tribute, whether it's because they are just plain mental, or because they have PROOF that Jimmy Carter is Bill Clinton's biological father. With graphics that are slightly disturbing in their own right, we are directed to several of the Museum's wings: in the Hall of Hate hang the details of the Society to Cut Up Men (yes, that's "SCUM"); in the Schizophrenic Wing you'll hear voices like that of Dan "Am I Insane?" Ashwander. Elsewhere you'll learn about goat gland science, the demons of rock music, salvation by spaceship, and even scientific proof that Satan created dinosaurs just to irk God. Lovely to look at, delightful to know, and absolutely chubby with weird stuff.

Psychedelic Tabby Cabal
http://www.paranoia.com:80/~fraterk/index.html

Whispering an invocation to "Goddess Chaos," this page is a guaranteed gateway to the realm of "fringe" ideas. What sets this apart from similar sites is its slick interface and the quality of the suggested sites. Links to like-minded sites are, in fact, the bulk of the page, but it's a very good, quick catch-all stop to feed your hunger for weirdness, whether it's Timothy Leary or Buckminster "Bucky" Fuller. Good collection of conspiracy links, too. The name is never really clearly explained; it's bound to attract a certain number of confused cat fanciers, but even they may dig the psychedelic graphics that are a signature here.

Spirituality & Mysticism

COGWEB—The Covenant of the Goddess
http://www.cog.org/cog/

This page is home to international Wiccan congregations and sole practitioners around the globe. Wicca, an offshoot of

Neo-Paganism, claims to be one of the fastest growing religions in the U.S., and the discussions here of witchcraft as a "life-affirming, nature-oriented religion" run contrary to the cauldron-boiling, spell-casting bunch traditionally thought of at Halloween. ("Most Witches consider their practice a priest/esshood," the authors say.) Anyone worried about catching a hex should consider COG's Code of Ethics, which state, "An ye harm none, do as ye will." (Translation: no harm, no foul.) Those intrigued by the practice can study criteria for forming a coven and applying for membership with the National Council. It's different, all right, but it's engrossing reading.

Motherheart
http://www.afn.org/~mother/

This resource which "encourages nurturing in all aspects of life" is a massive index to Internet sites dealing with community, health, wholeness, spirituality, and more. Visitors can search for their ideal co-op in the Intentional Communities Database; on our last visit we found a pointer to Dancing Rabbit, a Berkeley, California co-op that hopes to eventually form its own self-sustaining town. If you're a fledgling clairvoyant, harness that spiritual energy with a quick lesson in channeling and learn to ground and clear chakras (it has nothing to do with that back 40 we've been meaning to plow). Expectant parents can link to an online "birth center" for info on midwifery and healthy birthing, or try the Alternative Medicine Home Page for advice on "unconventional, unorthodox, unproven . . . alternative, complementary, innovative, integrative therapies" for a winter cold.

The New Age Web Works
http://www.newageinfo.com/

More than 450 links to New Age related resources give this page from California (where else?) a warm inner glow. The services index can help you organize that next big drumming circle, or arrange for a little transformational travel. Or, tune in to Lisa Theil's goddess music and join the Pagan Poets Circle to read the latest musings on "Man's Milk." (Don't ask.) On the lighter side, you can explore the power of chaos with a tarot reading and learn how Larry, Moe & Curly have contributed to your good fortune today. Find out where the 32nd Annual National UFO Conference is being held, and leave your calendar open for the Crone Oracles Workshop. Druidism, astrology, magic spelled with a "k"—it's all cheerfully presented here.

Unification Home Page
http://www.cais.com/unification/

This "personal ministry" of Webmaster Damian Anderson offers an account of the life, teachings, and public work of Sun Myung Moon and his wife Hak Ja Han Moon. They're co-leaders of the Holy Spirit Association for the Unification of World Christianity (HSA-UWC)—a.k.a. the Unification Church, a.k.a. (can we say it?) the Moonies. It's a forum for news and events, like the 3.6 Million Couples Holy Wedding planned for November of 1997 in Washington, D.C. (No word yet on who's springing for the reception.) Prominent Moon sermons and speeches are accessible, with such treatises as True Love and Forbidden Love—An Investigation into the Cause of Immorality and Suffering, its Historical Origin and its Solution, by Jesús González Losada. Enthusiasts can also find their way to networking opportunities here.

UFOs & Mysterious Creatures
The Alberta UFO Research Association
http://ume.med.ucalgary.ca/~watanabe/ufo.html

This site from the Canadian UFO research group, the centerpiece of which is the AUFORA Journal, not only details UFO sightings from around the world (and you can report yours here with a handy form), but also tries to follow up on the sightings with international government agencies. The regularly updated "News" section reports on unusual sightings and occurrences across the globe: UFOs, crop circles, and even the more puzzling recent cat mutilations in British Columbia (cleanly severed, exsanguinated half-cats, "hauntingly similar" to 1970s' cattle mutilations). The Journal is skeptic-friendly, and it's clear that AUFORA is serious in its attempt to gain respect world-wide, making full use of the Web to gather and distribute information on this increasingly mainstream topic.

Hastings UFO Society
http://hufos.sonic.net/hufos/

Flash! "Possible UFO Abductee assaults Rural Deputy with her Bosoms!" (The distinctive gray color of the deputy's uniform was consistent with alien skin color; who knew?). Following in the footsteps of the Firesign Theater, these students from Hastings College will peddle no hoax before its time. The time has come for this all-audio probe into the unidentified realms of the universe. Saucer fans can plug into Psychic CB Channel 22 for the latest bulletins on possible alien births (followed by a cover-up in Albania), or tips on avoiding impact with the Giant Space Blob, "the fastest moving bulk of matter ever detected in the galaxy." No, that's not another Orson Welles reference. You may be downloading for hours, but where else can you hear "The Mystery of Blackie the Chicken"?

Psychospy: Guide to Knowledge
http://www.ufomind.com/

Groom Lake (or Area 51) is the Mecca for UFO-ologists, and resident expert Glenn Campbell keeps a wild eye (and a cocked eyebrow) on the "secret" goings on at this off-limits military base. This site covers the Nevada desert area and more, with an extraordinary set of links and features on sightings, crashes and abductions. The jewel in the crown is the "Desert Rat" news-letter, with more news stories and features than you would think possible about a small, inaccessible strip of dry land. Reports include President Clinton's order exempting Groom Lake from releasing environmental reports, on-going debates about crash study feasibility and a list of who's who in UFO-ology. This site is so comprehensive it makes us wonder when they have time to pester the Groom Lake guards!

Spotlight

`http://members.aol.com/iufog/index.html`

This is a great introduction to a very complicated subject: the world of UFOs and the people who research them. Zac Elston has reprinted several articles that explain the modern history of UFO research, including lists of the most credible experiences and a "who's who" (and "what's what") of the UFO world. Initial articles lay out the internal squabbles between those with different theories and experiences. Follow-ups include pieces on UFOs as a modern mythology, how to act if an encounter should happen ("stay calm!"), and detailed ways to file Freedom of Information Act requests of the U.S. government without letting them know what you are really after.

Science and Technology

Agriculture

Alternative Farming Systems Information Center

    http://www.inform.umd.edu/EdRes/Topic/AgrEnv/
    AltFarm/

This is a must-visit motherlode for anyone interested in regenerative, biodynamic or organic farming. Sponsored by the USDA, the site helps you find and order publications with titles like "Green Manures and Cover Crops" and "Wind Energy for Agriculture." Although this site could do with a few visuals, their logo is nifty and the bibliography unbeatable.

GrainGenes

    http://wheat.pw.usda.gov/graingenes.html

This plant genome database is sponsored by the U.S. Department of Agriculture and run from various servers, like one at Cornell University in Ithaca, N.Y. It lets you search for genes, traits, and alleles for wheat, barley, rye, and related grains—the information here deals basically with the seeds, not the end products of the grain. (We didn't find anything about beer, for instance.) As you may have guessed, this page isn't really for Joe Average. But it's a delight for agricultural scientists!

Infomine

    http://lib-www.ucr.edu/govpub/

Oh, no, not another government index site. Wait 'til you see this one at the University of California at Riverside. Take a look at the "S" resources—more than 100 are here—and then render your judgment. Ours? This site, searchable by keyword, really deserves its title. Federal government links are standard, yes, but what about direct links to school district data profiles, America's Job Bank, and U.S. crop statistics from Cornell? This is for the surfer who knows exactly what (s)he wants. Infomine also caters to California users with state and local government sites, but it's worth at least a visit from anywhere. You'll be surprised what you can find.

University of Florida—Institute of Agricultural Sciences
http://www.ifas.ufl.edu/

Did you know that agriculture is one of Florida's top three sources of revenue? All those oranges, don't you know. (And you thought the economy would collapse without Disney World.) From citrus to sugar, the Sunshine State's land yields a lot of produce. To get all the facts, point your browser to the University of Florida's Institute of Agricultural Sciences, and discover why Florida ranks 8th in the nation for farming productivity. IFAS is the king of outreach programs; it has offices in all 67 counties and does research on the Everglades and bugs, too. We also liked the National Food Safety Database, which teaches readers ways to prevent illnesses spread through food (can you say "salmonella?"). Top-notch interactive maps lead you through a geographic array of beans, cabbage, carrots, tomatoes . . . whew!

Anthropology

ArchNet
http://www.lib.uconn.edu/ArchNet/

There are any number of jokes to be made here about skeletons and Neanderthals, but why stoop so low? (Oops.) ArchNet is a terrific index to archaeology and anthropology sites on the Web, from Italian museums to rain forest researchers in Central America. Lovely graphics and well-organized categories make this a great help to professionals, students, or anyone who wants to bone up (oops!) on the subject. And it's a broad subject indeed, covering specialties like Ethnohistory, Lithics, and Mapping. Its best-kept secret is an excellent listing of museum sites on the Net, offering fine starting points for amateurs.

A firm pat on the back to the U. of Connecticut anthropology department for this top-notch site.

Office of Population Research
http://opr.princeton.edu/

Princeton University is the home of this gentle-looking site (although the building pictured here has a rather large cannon in front of it). The OPR is filled with people who love demographics (you know, like how many left-handed people over 30 live in Akron, Ohio). One major work: fertility studies which chart the growth of American families since the 1950s. The OPR's data archive contains the results of these and other studies, which can be downloaded by other researchers for their own use. You'll also find information on the school's programs and professors, but the main stuff is the data, which could fuel several lengthy dissertations.

Perseus Project Home Page
http://www.perseus.tufts.edu/

The classics department at Tufts University has put together this "evolving digital library on ancient Greece." An outgrowth of a CD-ROM project, this big and still-growing site has plenty of online texts. The plays of Aristophanes, for example are available both in Greek and in translation, with searchable online Greek lexicons to help navigate any difficulties or find specific references. (The word arachnion, Greek for "web," crops up twice in Homer's "Odyssey," as it happens.) Perseus the software provides quite an anthropological dig: it contains images and descriptions of "523 coins, 1420 vases, 366 sculptures, 179 sites, and 381 buildings," which are gradually being put up on Perseus the Web site. Who'd have thought such interactivity would spring from the minds of classicists?

Primate Handedness and Brain Lateralization
http://www.indiana.edu/~primate/index.html

Okay, admit it . . . just reading that title made you drowsy, didn't it? Well snap out of it! This is the well-designed site of

Dr. M.K. Holder, an anthropologist who's been doing research into handedness. True, it won't shake the world of most of us, but his research has potentially far-reaching implications. And what's best, he explains it in ways to interest us mere mortals—what do we mean by "handedness," anyway? The hand you write with? Catch with? Swing an axe with? You can help his research by taking a (huge) survey, and view pictures and hear sounds of the primates he's studied at various research stations in Africa.

Archaeology

Greek & Roman Cities of Western Turkey
http://rubens.anu.edu.au/turkeybook/toc1.html

This is actually a book on archaeology in Turkey, complete with chapters and handy search capabilities. This site will not win any awards for versatility. But for thoroughness and purpose, it is a phenomenal examination of excavations in present-day Turkey. Visitors will learn, among other things, that ancient grave sites often are in good condition (relatively speaking) because they were placed in non-livable areas. The page also offers excellent info on ancient religions and societies.

Maya Adventure
http://www.sci.mus.mn.us/

The educational Maya Adventure of the Science Museum of Minnesota is aimed at youths, but it's a fascinating journey for any Web surfer. The starting point is a map of what is now southern Mexico and Guatemala. Students are encouraged to take notes in their "log books" as they visit the highlighted sites illustrating Mayan civilization past and present. (The log books are the students' own papers, but online is a spiffy illustrated cover page they can download to dress up their reports.) Visitors will find plenty of photographs of ancient temples (we didn't like the sound of that "Altar de Sacrificios!") and city ruins. A highlight is a description of Mayan culture today as demonstrated by the Chiapas Maya, who still view their woven brocade work as a sacred duty ordained by the gods.

MSARP Virtual Slide Show
http://www.ucalgary.ca/UofC/faculties/SS/ARKY/
show/showintro.html

This visual tour of a high-Arctic archaeological research project
is exactly the kind of thing your mom hopes you're looking at
when you're browsing the Web. And not only is the McDougall
Sound Archaeological Research Project slide show good for
you, it's a beauty to behold. If your Web browser (like
Netscape) supports server-push animation, the entire show is
automated: just sit back and watch as the team lead by Drs.
James Helmer and Genevieve LeMoine uncover the remains of
the Late Dorset period civilization that populated the area on
Little Cornwallis Island between 500 and 1000 AD. You can
even download a howling Arctic-wind sound bite that's guaranteed to make you reach for your parka. Over the past four
years, the team has been uncovering, photographing, and cataloging evidence of sod-banked tents framed by wale ribs, ivory
carvings of polar bears, and spear points made of copper and
stone.

The Museum of Antiquities
on the WWW
http://www.ncl.ac.uk/~nantiq/index.html

On a recent visit to this online archaeological museum we
walked through an exhibit on the Stone Age, led by a virtual
shaman. As guides go, he was a bit of a dud, but the resident
archaeologist wasn't. Thanks to his notes it's possible to understand a little more about life in the United Kingdom back
when they were using stones and flints to prove a point instead
of electric guitars. And guess what . . . back then they weren't
simply clubbing each other over the head. They had specific rit-
uals and dances, THEN they clubbed each other over the head.
Anyway, this is a good place to visit—a few cheesy cartoons but
a wealth of information.

Biology and Botany

Chez Marco Thuispagina
http://www.euronet.nl/users/mbleeker/

This page for plant lovers comes from Marco Bleeker, a Dutch botany buff. He's especially keen on Surinam, and has put together a terrific collection of botanic and cultural data on the plants, people and species of its tropical rainforests. The flowers, with names like Heliconia psittacorum, are prettier than they sound, and you'll find them worth the brief load times. The plants of Holland and Northern Europe are also covered briefly, as are typical house and greenhouse plants. A virtual green dream.

Global Entomology Agriculture Research Server: GEARS
http://gears.tucson.ars.ag.gov/

This multimedia wonderland developed at Arizona's Carl Hayden Bee Research Center may have you dressing up like a beekeeper to hunt the elusive virgin queen (bee, that is). Learn why nasty Varroa mites are threatening the US bee industry, and find out how to handle swarming African honey bees, a.k.a. the dreaded "killer" bees. (Step one: remain calm.) The Sound Room features "the year's best insect-related sounds," like a "stridulating" desert harvest ant (that's insect talk for "ant scaring off an attacker") and a piping queen bee. Before you go, don't forget to stop by the trivia hive for a fast game of "Tribeeal Pursuits." Quite simply one of the best ento-sites around.

MendelWeb
http://www.netspace.org/MendelWeb/

This site celebrates the work of that pea-pickin' monk, Gregor Mendel. Mendel's 19th-century paper on "Experiments in Plant Hybridization" is considered to be one of the foundations of classical genetics; his work kicked off the study of plant cross-breeding, and by extension, biological genetics. Mendel's entire paper is here, in its original German and translated English, and is extensively hyperlinked to itself and an online glossary. Those with an interest in the paper can hit the Collaborative Hypertext page, where they can view and add annotations on Mendel's original.

Whole Frog Project

```
http://george.lbl.gov/ITG.hm.pg.docs/
Whole.Frog/Whole.Frog.html
```

The first goal of this project was to provide high school biology students with a 3-D imaging tool to use in studying frog anatomy. But it's so much more! Even non-science types will thrill to the tibio-fibula of the skeletal system, the detailed heart and lungs, and the rotating, transparent frog movie. (The authors say, "Ultimately we intend to be able to enter the heart and fly down blood vessels, poking our head out at any point to see the structure of the surrounding anatomy." Woo!) Among the advantages cited here are the ability to view more than one anatomical angle at once, and the nifty trick of "undissection"—plus, you don't have to "pith" your little green lab partner to do any of this. This is fun, unusual, and darned educational.

Chemistry

Chemistry Resources

```
http://www.rpi.edu/dept/chem/cheminfo/
chemres.html
```

Another resource site—long on lists, short on graphics. But this collection goes beyond other home pages—it lists gophers, online services and databases. Teaching resources, in particular, are well-represented here. From ChemCAI, for instance, teachers can find software sites to help better illustrate chemical principles. The site is also mirrored for non-American users.

Journal of Biological Chemistry

```
http://www.jbc.org/
```

This highly technical chemistry journal is one of the easier-to-use online science publications. It allows searching for the current issue and many back issues as well as "Mini-Reviews," which can help you decide if you really want to read something called "Xenobiotic-inducible Transcription of Cytochrome P450 Genes." The authors provide a very helpful FAQ, which first-time users should read before looking around. The HTML versions of the papers presented here include e-mail links to the authors and the popular science reference "Medline." An honest—and honestly good—science site.

Poly-Links
    http://www.polymers.com/

The word "polymer" means "having many parts." This page, then, is a chemistry polymer, so to speak. Maybe it's a little strange for chemists to shamelessly promote themselves, but Poly-Links backs it up. Visitors to this vast resource of information and links about polymers are politely requested to tell other folks how great this site is. It does have plenty of unique resources—the resume creator and polymer want ads are two examples. Something for anybody interested in polymers.

The World Guide to Chemistry
    http://www.theworld.com/

Here's a huge wad of chemistry links. From Cornell University to the Geochemisches Institut (that's in Denmark), both well-known and unknown schools are present and accounted for. The fare is mostly for scholars; for instance, Emory University's Postdoctoral Clearinghouse lists academic opportunities for would-be scientists. And there's no need to fear outdated links; this server proudly announces that updates are posted "daily."

Earth Science

Berkeley Earth Sciences & Map Libraries
    http://library.berkeley.edu/EART/

Plot a course to one of the Web's best sources of digitized maps at U.C. Berkeley's Earth Sciences and Map Libraries site. From its colorful global graphics to its growing collection of online maps, the site is as visually appealing as it is informatively browsable. The digital maps are organized into areas such as nautical charts, topographic maps, transportation and communications maps, facsimile maps and reproductions, and aerial photography. You'll also find research round-ups of fire insurance maps—invaluable historical, building-by-building cartographic community portraits. Though once used by insurance companies to assess risk, the site notes that "Today these maps are used by scholars and researchers in such fields as history, urban geography, architectural history and preservation, ethnic studies, and urban archaeology."

Environmental News Network
http://www.enn.com/

ENN's home page is a virtual environmental news clearinghouse, collecting info from sources as widespread as the Swedish government to U.S. green-beat reporters. The vast database is updated regularly to include breaking eco-news as it happens daily around the world. During the ruckus over French nuclear testing in the South Pacific, for instance, ENN fed continuous reports to its "Daily News" file, including an eyewitness account of a Tahitian riot and commentary from France's top political and environmental journalists. ENN also maintains an extensive library of resources: abstracts, articles and papers can be searched by topic or date. Access to ENN's complete files is not free; the cost of total access is roughly that of an annual magazine subscription. This is a hot spot for students and journalists.

Pacific & Yukon Green Lane
http://www.pwc.bc.doe.ca/

Sponsored by Environment Canada, this very green page links ecologists to Canadian environmental sites and offers a tour of "E-Town," an interactive graphical city filled with eco-facts and industry. Click on the school house, for instance, and discover a weather tutorial where budding meteorologists can soar through the virtual skies testing their knowledge of altocumulus and cumulonimbus clouds. The Science Lab is home to Canada's Pacific Environmental Science Centre, where ongoing biodiversity studies examine the health of Canada's soil, water, air and wildlife. Corporate watchdogs can stop by the Hall of Industry to find out how pollution prevention and abatement programs are providing incentives for industrial polluters to clean up their acts. Informative and entertaining.

Soil, Water and Climate Web Server
http://www.soils.umn.edu/

"Just another Stuckey's on the Information Superhighway," boasts this page from the University of Minnesota. Visitors can forage through the "Farmstead Assessment Decision Support System," and download a software program designed to evaluate how well farmsteading (as opposed to mega-corporate farming) protects our drinking water. (There's a great online tutorial, too.) If dirt's your thing, link to a garden of earthy delights at the Earth and Environmental Science page from the U.S. Geological Service, or jump to the famous UMN gopher to peruse articles on climatology, rhizosphere studies and "precision agriculture," a system designed to maximize soil-specific crop management for long-term environmental benefits. You'll also get the inside info on graduate programs at UMN and connections to other soddy sites around the country.

Engineering

Discovery Place
http://dp.worldweb.com/

The petroleum industry is huge—that much we know. It also turns out to have a nice Web site. Discovery Place, maintained by the oil industry in Alberta, Canada, is a global site for industry members or enthusiasts seeking information and links on the oil and gas business. An extensive list of resources is the most useful site for the lay person, offering everything from heavy construction equipment to rental geologists to emergency service provider Wild Fire International. In case you're a starving petroleum engineer (and who doesn't know one?), a few companies advertise job listings in the online career section. Or join a discussion on "finding reverse osmosis for glycol," if you dare. A well-structured site, which, considering the emphasis on engineers, isn't too surprising.

Electronic Engineering Times Interactive
http://techweb.cmp.com/eet/823/

This electronic version of Electronic Engineering Times delivers headline news on business and technology (daily!), plus feature articles like "The 1995 Worldwide Salary and Opinion Survey" ("How much is the engineer in the next cubicle making?"). The "CrossTalk Forum" is an interactive letters-to-the-editor column; readers are invited to submit their thoughts on topics like whether Microsoft is taking over the world. This "best-read publication in the engineering industry" is certainly worth a look in its online format, too.

The Farnsworth Chronicles
http://www.edge.net/noma/philo/index.html

Paul Schatzkin's lively site is a biography of Philo T. Farnsworth, the inventor of video. Here, you'll learn that as a 14-year-old Idaho farm boy, he sketched his idea of electronic video on a high-school blackboard. That was in 1922. Few know it, and Schatzkin wants that changed. He interviewed Farnsworth's survivors (he died in 1971), and now presents in melodramatic installments the whole story. Writes Schatzkin: "It seems appropriate to re-tell this story on the World Wide Web . . . (because it) is very analogous to the state of Farnsworth's invention during the 1920s and '30s. There is much that we can learn from his story." Agreed. So, can we blame Farnsworth for "American's Funniest Home Videos"?

The National Institute of Standards and Technology
http://www.nist.gov/

The NIST was established "to assist industry in the development of technology needed to improve product quality, to modernize manufacturing processes, to ensure product reliability . . . " Wow! No small task, and this is certainly no small Web site. You'll find everything NIST-related here, from the types of research grants the NIST awards, to the low-down on each of its main research laboratories. This may be dull reading for many people, but those who dig this sort of thing (and who wouldn't like to brush up on Isotopic Technologies for Environmental Pollutant Source Apportionment) will be happy as clams.

General Science

Frank Potter's Science Gems
http://www-sci.lib.uci.edu/SEP/SEP.html

Physicist Frank Potter and colleague Jim Martindale here feature links to over 2000 Web resources that are appropriate to math and science classrooms. It's selective and extremely well organized! Main categories such as Physical Science, Life Science, and Engineering are sub-divided into the likes of Biology of Viruses, Introduction to Quantum Mechanics, and Algebraic Geometry. Popular sites (e.g. Predator-Prey Simulation) are culled from the virtual stacks. Resources are also sorted by grade level, with annotations like: "Penguin images, hole in the ozone data, and links for teachers and students to ask scientists questions about Antarctica." This is an excellent K-16 math and science index!

New Scientist: Planet Science
http://www.newscientist.com/

With the possible exception of *Science*, the U.K.-based *New Scientist* is the world's leading popularized science newsweekly. *Planet Science*, a fruit of the New Scientist staff's labor, certainly ranks near the pinnacle of science on the Web. (It's free, but registration is required.) Pleasant to look at and easy to understand without resorting to "science lite," *Planet Science* posts the latest *New Scientist* plus material from the magazine's archives, arranged by category. The section that really jumps out is "strange science," with topics like "Why orange juice tastes terrible after brushing teeth," and "Why eating asparagus causes aromatic urine." There's plenty of more pertinent and timely science news, too, providing edification for both pro scientists and the merely curious.

NASA Information Services via World Wide Web
http://www.nasa.gov/

If you think space, you probably think NASA, and this is the gateway to the largest repository of space-related information on the Internet. For all of its problems and bureaucratic malaise, the accomplishments of this agency defy belief. NASA landed men on the moon who drove around in a buggy! Vehicles launched from the Kennedy Space Center have explored the surface of Mars. The Hubble Space Telescope has photographed the outer limits of our galaxy with unprecedented clarity and detail—even though HST has to wear glasses. Revolutionary advances in aeronautics, computer science and technology development can be directly attributed to NASA's programs. The Mission to Planet Earth alone has led to radical advances in environmental science, meteorology, geology, cartography, navigational systems and a host of applied and theoretical disciplines. NASA's Web presence is quite possibly the single largest entity on the Internet, and this gateway takes you to an incredible array of information, images and databases. Launch yourself into a galaxy of resources that encompass the whole of modern science and technology.

SciEd
http://www-hpcc.astro.washington.edu/scied/ science.html

Like it says here, no fancy graphics, but plenty of useful science links. The titles range from anthropology to pseudoscience, with math and science ethics thrown in for good measure. The Science Reference Shelf has all those figures scientists need handy—the mass of electrons, gravitational constant, and even a table of all known nuclides—who doesn't need that? The author takes pride in having no pictures here. He's right: they aren't needed.

Mathematics

The Chaos Network On-Line
http://www.prairienet.org/business/ptech/

This friendly home page belongs to People Technologies, a
company that attempts to apply modern chaos theory to business management. Sounds dull, but the jazzy fractal art grabs
your attention and the jargon-free tutorial about chaos theory
is lively and absorbing. (Chaos theory is reflected in the much-
discussed idea that a butterfly's wingbeat in Argentina might
affect tornadoes in Idaho). There's a great reading list, too.
Sample quote: "Complexity theory is causing most quantum
theorists to accept what Einstein rejected: that God probably
did play dice with the universe."

The Geometry Forum
http://forum.swarthmore.edu/

The Geometry Forum isn't just geometry—it has resources for
many math disciplines. The Teacher's Place is a wide collection
of math teaching resources on the Net, spanning Web sites, FTP
sites, and mailing lists. The Student Center consists of resources
of interest to the student. Included in these is Ask Dr. Math,
in which volunteers at Swarthmore University answer surfer
questions. These are organized by school level, and the college
queries will sail over most people's heads (What is an
Eigenvalue, anyway?). They sound like they know what
they're talking about.

Lawrence Livermore National Laboratory
http://www.llnl.gov/

Simply put, this is an awesome science site. This Department of
Energy lab does a staggering amount of research on everything
from plutonium to lasers. Visit the "National Ignition Facility,"
(which does not study cars) and learn how the U.S. is keeping
its nuclear arsenal "secure and reliable" without underground
testing. The lab also publishes a lot of its reports and several
journals, including Science & Technology Review, which details

the latest breakthroughs by lab staff (we read with interest a story about a zinc/air battery that weighs less and uses less electricity yet delivers the same power to vehicles). If you ever wanted to know what the U.S. government spends its scientific research budget on, here's an excellent place to start looking.

Richard Hawkins' Digital Archive
http://www.newciv.org/

Here Richard Hawkins displays dozens of geometric slides and animations related to Synergetics. See spinning interconnected spheres, a "buckeyball" (a sort of geodesic sphere named for R.B. Fuller), fantastical icosahedra (12 vertices and 20 equilateral triangular faces), and even those out-of-fashion octahedra. "TimeStar" animations get special attention, defined as a Mayan structure of "5 interpenetrating tetrahedra whose vertices lie on the 20 faces of an icosahedron." Is this somehow connected to a parallel universe? Who knows? Hawkins keeps the discussion pretty technical, not philosophical, and offers a delightful array of eye-popping images.

Meteorology

Road Conditions and Weather
http://www.pepperdine.edu/misc/weather.htm

You'll have to be in Southern California to make use of this page, but wait until you see the stuff here. The up-to-the-minute freeway speeds map tells you how fast you'll have to go to get on (or off) a highway like Interstate 405. Blue dots warn of accidents or "suspected incidents." Surfers can also get tide conditions for the LA region, or check the Southern California Swell Model, which charts how high waves have been getting. This is high-tech surfing, courtesy of Pepperdine University. Their nickname? The Waves, of course.

Soil, Water and Climate Web Server
http://www.soils.umn.edu/

"Just another Stuckey's on the Information Superhighway," boasts this page from the University of Minnesota. Visitors can forage through the "Farmstead Assessment Decision Support

System," and download a software program designed to evaluate
how well farmsteading (as opposed to mega-corporate farming)
protects our drinking water. (There's a great online tutorial,
too.) If dirt's your thing, link to a garden of earthy delights at
the Earth and Environmental Science page from the U.S.
Geological Service, or jump to the famous UMN gopher to
peruse articles on climatology, rhizosphere studies and "precision agriculture," a system designed to maximize soil-specific
crop management for long-term environmental benefits. You'll
also get the inside info on graduate programs at UMN and
connections to other soddy sites around the country.

Weather Information
http://atmos.es.mq.edu.au/weather/

Yes, it's another collection of weather links. But the truly
international scope of this site makes it unique. From an
English-language report on the conditions in Croatia to forecasts from South Africa, the international weather information
you need is right here. Plenty of the links have satellite images
behind them, although the main page is decidedly gray. Still, it's
hard to fault a site that has both Australian ski resort conditions
and Spanish-language forecasts from the University of Chile. If
you don't find what you're looking for, try searching the database of weather servers here.

Weather Processor
http://WXP.ATMS.PURDUE.EDU/

Here's a heavy-weather site for cumulo-nimbus junkies—just
the kind of high-tech, up-to-the-minute stuff that makes the
Internet so irresistible for the obsessive. Coming to you live
(well, hourly) from a GOES geostationary satellite orbiting
22,000 miles above the equator, Purdue University offers a
hailstorm of images and a flood of data from strangely-
named places like the European Center for Medium Range
Forecasting. Wind-chill factors! Water-vapor readings! Up-close
maps of Indiana! Still not satisfied? Then play dueling rainbows
by jumping to other university weather sites nationwide . . . if
you dare. But go lightly on the millibars, please.

Oceanography

The Aquatic Realm

```
http://www-personal.umd.umich.edu/~scubajl/
index.html
```

Something's fishy here ... in fact, just about everything is fishy in this sprawling tribute to underwater photography, pond building and aquaria (think fish tanks, not longhaired musicals). Submit your own fish tank info, or simply browse through others' and sometimes even see what they see. A visit to the Gallery of the Realm is a worthwhile slideshow of underwater photography from places such as Barbados, Mexico and the Florida Keys. The Pond's Edge will perhaps have more interest to water gardeners than to aquarium freaks (although it, too, has fish), and is a nifty site on its own. We highly recommend using the Express Menus offered at every turn, as our fingers were worn down to little nubbins from all the clicking required here.

Hydrographic Atlas of the Southern Ocean

```
http://www.awi-bremerhaven.de/Atlas/SO/
Deckblatt.html
```

Quality research on Antarctic oceans is hard to find, but this is one place to get it. Scientists from Germany and Russia have teamed to create a virtual atlas of their observatory work. Yes, this page has nice pictures—several of them. But the major portion is a report with plenty of data taken from 38,000 stations around Antarctica, with temperature and salinity readings and charts. This is not for the layperson; the sheer amount of data is enough to overwhelm anybody. Oceanographers will dig it, though.

Ocean Planet Homepage

```
http://seawifs.gsfc.nasa.gov/ocean_planet.html
```

This beautiful Smithsonian Institute project lets visitors explore the world's oceans with ease. Visitors can jump from room to virtual room, from "Sea People" in Sri Lanka to "Oceans in Peril," where we learned that the levels of toxic contaminants in our seas have reached unprecedented proportions. Audio files play back whale songs and seagull calls, a lonesome buoy and the turbulent winds of a hurricane. And what museum would be complete without a gift shop? This "sea store" is one of the best: it even clued us in on the hidden environmental costs that may be involved in producing and distributing ocean products. The page aims for a non-technical audience, with plenty of visuals, making it a great spot for kids to learn about the mysteries of the deep.

Satellite Oceanography Laboratory
http://satftp.soest.hawaii.edu/

This site provides "real-time data for meteorology and oceanography." True enough, but the pictures are even better. If you're wild about oceans, you'll find terrific satellite images, technical reports and access to mountains of data here. Some of the features are unique—one set of satellite shots tracks canoes from a Polynesian village society as they make their way across the water. Volcanoes are well-represented, along with regularly updated weather information from Maui. (Hey, you never get a bad forecast.) And you won't have to wait for the 11 o'clock news anymore to get your "Doppler radar" or "polar orbiting" movie fixes. They're all right here, captured in real time. Even for non-experts, this is a great site for poking around.

Physics

Brown High Energy Physics
http://www.het.brown.edu/

This isn't just regular old physics. We're talking about the top quark and other high-energy principles. Visitors to this site can find national and Brown University resources, including a great collection of pages with physics-related news from sources like the Drell Panel, which has studied the future of particle physics research in America. Browse through several lists of physics and astronomy laboratories around the United States. One big plus is the access to preprint archives—abstracts of previous physics papers.

The High Energy Weapons Archive
http://www.envirolink.org/issues/nuketesting/
hew/

Still doubt the wisdom of that "one nuclear bomb can ruin your whole day" bumper sticker? Melbourne University Ph.D. aspirant Gary Au proudly presents all of the atomic facts and figures you hoped you'd heard the last of when the Cold War went kaput. Gary's going for his degree in theoretical particle physics, so he knows whereof he speaks. Luckily, he's got a knack for digging up articles that will still be comprehensible even if your theoretical particle physics is a little rusty. An inventory of every nuclear bomb ever exploded is awe-inspiring, while an investigative report on the "Vela Flash" (an unexplained 1979 explosion off the coast of South Africa) is eerie. Not much eye-candy here, only an exemplary research archive on a, sadly, still-important subject.

NCSA Relativity Group
http://jean-luc.ncsa.uiuc.edu/

The National Center for Supercomputing Applications puts their mega-machines to work researching Einstein's General Theory of Relativity. This Web site brings relativity to the public. Here's where you can download simulations of two black holes smashing into each other, and of numerous other phenomena that, frankly, you just don't see every day. If your grasp of relativity is not what it should be, don't miss the "Space-Time Wrinkles" exhibit that explains Einstein's theories as clearly as possible—though they're still pretty baffling. The exhibit can also be viewed as a movie, but it's 12 megabytes. NCSA warns that it could take "several minutes" to download. Several minutes? We're not running supercomputers here, guys. At 28.8 baud it'll take half an hour. Also get info on the federally funded "Grand Challenge" project, "to develop numerical codes to solve the problem of the 3D spiraling coalescence of two black holes." Say, that does sound like a challenge.

Physics Around the World
http://www.physics.mcgill.ca/physics-services/
physics_services2.html

Physics Around the World offers links to science resources and information. This site is a "Physics Yellow Pages for the Web," with a great search engine (which we dearly wish our telephone book had). It's funny to enter non-physics words, like "cow," and see what pops out. Also interesting is the Internet Market Place for Physicists, where scientists can buy or sell used instruments. We found one ad searching for a "differential sputter gun" (it's a real physics tool, we checked). Other links can get you a job, provide free software for download, show basic (and not-so-basic) physics tables and information, and let you sniff around the world's leading physics departments.

Psychology

L.S.I. SCAN
http://www.getnet.com/~lsiscan/index.html

L.S.I. SCAN stands for "Laboratory for Scientific Investigation—Scientific Content Analysis." Dull stuff, right? Wrong! Anyone interested in the workings of the criminal mind, or for that matter, the human mind, should find this site absolutely fascinating. "Scientific Content Analysis" is the craft of analyzing people's words, particularly written words, to tell if they're lying or not. Note that SCAN doesn't compare words against outside facts, it analyzes them on their own merits. For example, an analysis of O.J. Simpson's book, *I Want to Tell You* reveals that the Juice never actually denies killing his ex-wife. Hmmm. The L.S.I. site explains some basic principles of SCAN, then applies them to some famous, recent criminal documents. For example, the L.S.I. analysts dissect Simpson's "suicide" note and Desiree Washington's accusations of rape against Mike Tyson. The results are sometimes surprising and unrelentingly provocative.

PSYCHE
http://psyche.cs.monash.edu.au/

This interdisciplinary e-journal offers complete research articles on the nature of consciousness. Those include Richard E. Cytowic's "Synesthesia: Phenomenoly and Neuropsychology" describing a peculiar condition predominate among "females and non-right-handers" in which "the stimulation of one sensory modality reliably causes a perception in one or more different senses." (See if you don't think that text tastes great!) This is high-minded stuff, so to speak. Submissions welcome, too.

The Psychology Web Pages
http://psy.ucsd.edu/otherpsy.html

These pages are an exhaustive index to psychology resources on the Web. Hosted by the Department of Psychology at the University of Southern California at San Diego, the list specializes in the Web sites of other university psychology departments. A section for resources outside academia includes entries such as the Danish Society for Humanethology. The odd thing here is that the site's main page is a rather cryptic index consisting entirely of hyperlinked letters of the alphabet, meaning you have to know that Swinburne University has a psychology department before you'd find it under "S." The thought that this obstacle might in fact be some kind of secret behavior test did cross our minds.

The Thinking Page
http://world.std.com/~thinking

Consultant Daniel Aronson spends a lot of time thinking about a topic that most of us don't usually think about: thinking. His Web site is set up to convey his thoughts about how we can all get better at thinking. Think about it. Is your physical and emotional environment helping or hurting your ability to think? And what about the way you think? Are you finding the best solutions to your problems in the most efficient way possible?

Aronson is an advocate of "systems thinking," which is, not surprisingly, a system of thinking developed at MIT. While originally "system dynamics" was designed to give academics in the social sciences the same sort of objective standards as their counterparts in the traditional sciences, its principles can be used by anyone. Unfortunately, our brains don't ship with a user's manual. This site is at least a rough draft of one.

Sociology

Coombsweb: ANU Social Sciences Server

`http://coombs.anu.edu.au/CoombsHome.html`

The Schools of Social Science & Pacific and Asian Studies at the Australian National University have assembled this massive resource, covering significant research in the social sciences, humanities and Asia-Pacific studies. Generally for pros and academics, the server offers links to its own Asian Studies Meta-Resources Center, an Aboriginal data archive and access to over 100 theses abstracts, like "Fertility in Ghana" by Tetteh Dugbaza. Good general Net resources on Netiquette and Web design strategies.

Demography & Population Studies from the Virtual Library

`http://coombs.anu.edu.au/ResFacilities/`
`DemographyPage.html`

This number-filled page has far-ranging links to demographic resources in places like Thailand and Norway. Visitors can browse abstracts from the Australian National University's demography program (with titles like "Growing up in Melbourne") or Princeton University's Office of Population Research. Data is the key word here; these sites have lots of it, or will tell you how to get it. As part of the World Wide Web Virtual Library, the site is well-organized and easy to use.

Progress of Nations, 1995:
A UNICEF Report
http://www.unicef.org/pon95/

UNICEF, the caretaker of the world's children, presents its annual report—The Progress of Nations—for the first time online. The goal is to rank the nations of the world "according to their achievements in child health, nutrition, education, family planning, and progress for women." Terrific statistics here for world-watchers on polio eradication (nine African countries earned failing grades this year), birth control (Gabon was nearly alone in seeing its birth-rate-per-woman actually rise to 1.3%), and other key issues. The report's bottom line: "The day will come when the progress of nations will be judged not by their military or economic strength ... but by the well-being of their peoples."

WWW research information locations
http://www.swin.edu.au/sgrs/
research-sites.html

A huge listing (more than 250 entries when we last checked) of research sites around the Internet. Need the page of Xerox Research? How about Japan's Kashima Space Research Center? Both are here with dozens more covering everything from wind tunnel studies to biodiversity. Basically, if you sat down at a computer and typed: "Find research," this probably is what you'd come up with. For scientists and engineers, it's a good way to keep tabs on what everybody is looking into around the world. A fantastic resource, if you know what you're looking for.

Space and Astronomy

The Astronomy Cafe
http://www2.ari.net/home/odenwald/cafe.html

Take an astronomy lesson ... please. Astrophysicist Sten Odenwald has put together a page of astronomy resources that is part lesson and part fun. You can find out what it's like to be an astronomer (from personal accounts by Dr. Odenwald and other scientists about projects like high-altitude balloon-based research). Or learn how to write a real research paper. You can even ask a question, which he may post—along with the response, of course. One such query: "If the sun is made of hydrogen and helium, why can't we see through it?" Hmm. Visitors can also read cool essays by Dr. Odenwald like "Hyperspace in Science Fiction," where he reviews how sci-fi writers have treated the topic of space travel.

Comet Shoemaker-Levy
http://newproducts.jpl.nasa.gov/s19/s19.html

Comet Shoemaker-Levy vs. the planet Jupiter is the most spectacular catastrophe since Godzilla vs. Tokyo. In July of 1994, 21 chunks of comet, some as big as two kilometers across, collided with Jupiter, and the effects on the Jovian atmosphere have been simply spectacular. All the greatest hits from the clash are here in gorgeous color, with more camera angles than Monday Night Football. In fact, nothing shows better why we spent all those tax dollars on the Hubble telescope—it's all here on the screen. There's even a scary section on comets striking the Earth. The visuals can be slow to load, but the wait is well worth it. Shoemaker-Levy is doomed in the end, of course, but it wreaks havoc on its way out. Godzilla would be proud.

The Nine Planets
http://seds.lpl.arizona.edu/nineplanets/
nineplanets/nineplanets.html

Perhaps you can name Santa's eight reindeer faster than the nine planets. If so, this page can help. It's an excellent guide both for newcomers and for folks who were sharp enough in school to learn about moons. Take Europa, one of Jupiter's satellites, for instance. This page showed us how big it is (3138 km in diameter) and how far it is from Jupiter (670,9000 km), then offered an amazingly close-up photo (it's sort of brown, with interesting lines) and the history behind its name. The full tour consists of some 60 pages and includes the whole solar system (including some really obscure Neptunian moons, like Larissa); an express version is available, too. For those romantic journeys, snippets of Gustav Holst's "The Planets" can be heard.

Space Movie Archive
http://www.univ-rennes1.fr/ASTRO/anim-e.html

This monster archive contains nearly 500 movies of space imagery, from comets smacking into Jupiter (there are dozens of these) to the creature from Alien (or even the lip-smacking Captain from "Star Trek"). Many of the animation or film sequences are VERY big (a starship Enterprise flyby is small, at 97 Kb, but most of them exceed 1 megabyte), but what a catalog! 11 days of the Mir-Atlantis encounter, a day-by-day account of other shuttle missions, and hundreds more films, including meteorological overheads of Europe and the great 1991 eclipse. We found cometary motion movies, an exploding Atlas booster, and old films from Lunar Ranger series of impact probes (space exploration's gotten a lot easier since then). The archive even includes a massive 14 Mb tour of the Enterprise quarters of "Star Trek: The Next Generation's" Deanna Troi.

Suns 'n' Roses
http://www.Stars.com/Roses/

"Why is there something instead of nothing?" "Where do the laws of physics come from?" Suns 'n' Roses is a jumble of metaphysical thought and speculation from astrophysicists and futurists, compiled by NASA systems whiz Alan Richmond, who provides his own perspective. After the introductory warning ("Reality under construction"), there's lots of very interesting talk about cosmology, quantum fluctuation, and Heisenberg's Uncertainty Principle, which "allows you to have a free lunch—as long as you eat it quickly enough." Quotes from notables like William Gibson, Carl Sagan, and even William Wordsworth are supplemented by color graphics of space, planets, and cool swirly abstract color-things. You can also link to places like Stanford's Metaphysics Research Lab. Not for the casual surfer (or for readers of Cosmo), but it will make you think.

Veterinary Science

Minnesota Zoo
http://www.wcco.com/community/mnzoo/

Feel like wandering through the tropics, gazing at exotic birds and beasts? At the Minnesota Zoo site you can hear the call of the wild from the comfort of your computer. The site features a series of virtual tours of visual adventure along the zoo's Tropics Trail, Beach Trail, Minnesota Trail, and Northern Trail. Each features gorgeous photos and nearly encyclopedic descriptions of the zoo's inhabitants and their habitats; the Tropics Trail, for instance, offers an adorable photo of rare Amur Leopard cubs, and notes that their natural diet includes "wild boar, roe, sika and musk deer, goral, badgers, raccoon dogs, and Manchurian hares." Maybe the zookeepers shop for those exotic treats at the nearby Mall of America.

NetVet
http://netvet.wustl.edu/

NetVet marks out its territory here with a colorful list of veterinary home pages. Vets and zoologists will frolic amidst these fields of links to colleges, labs, and animal-rights groups. The site features a Pick of the Litter (the best animal page of the week), and it's also the Web home of the USDA's Animal Welfare Information Center, which covers topics like "ruminant anesthesia problems." Pet owners who just want to know how much to feed a two-headed calf will have more trouble. Finding anything can be hard here, since the links are piled up behind complex categories like Informatics and Virtual Library. Still, veterinarian Dr. Ken Boschert deserves a scratch behind the ears for his hard work in compiling this site. Good boy!

Oklahoma State University Department of Animal Science
http://www.ansi.okstate.edu/

The star attraction of this site is the "Breeds of Livestock" file on horses, cattle, sheep, goats—even llamas. It's an online encyclopedia of various livestock breeds from around the world. You can browse it by breed or by region, then see photos and read about specific breeds. Some entries are of course more bare than others; some have fascinating stories as part of the breed history (try the American Morgan horse, for example). Still in the early stages, a "Breeds of Poultry" companion page is planned. The other section to mention is OSU's Virtual Library of animal resources, covering the turf from animal rights discussions to beef council Websites. The Animal Science Department has done a bang-up job here, giving us a useful and entertaining place to visit.

rec.pets.cats FAQ Homepage
http://WWW.Zmall.Com/pet_talk/cat-faqs/

Covering topics from finding a swell cat to how to treat skin infections to choosing the best cat litter, this site is a comprehensive bookmarkable cat resource. Here you can find articles on feline nutrition, the ins and outs of vaccinations, and the variety of everyday ailments which might plague your kitty, or you find out what to do if said kitty has a proclivity for climbing the chintz. Part of the Mall of Cyberspace, the site also leads you to other sites of feline interest.

Society and Community

Aging

ElderCare Help Page

http://www.mindspring.com/~eldrcare/
elderweb.htm

ElderCare is a financial management outfit "helping Baby
Boomers navigate the elder care maze." With some 50 million
Social Security recipients these days, and (hopefully) the matu-
ration of the post-WWII boomers, this is probably going to
end up being big business in just a few years. The ElderCare
Lady, Laura Beller, offers more than just a pitch for her
company here. Online you can participate in a forum for the
elderly and their caregivers, or get advice on things like
"Medical Self-Care for Healthy Aging" (the title of a book for
sale here). Although you don't get the entire Caregiver
Newsletter online, there's enough good sense here to be helpful
and comforting.

Elderhostel Home Page

http://www.elderhostel.org/

Because "the later years should be a time for new beginnings,
opportunities and challenges," Elderhostel, a non-profit educational organization, provides senior citizens with short-term
study opportunities at colleges, universities, and even marine
biology field stations throughout the world. Their home page
features searchable (seasonal) catalogs of international
Elderhostel programs, but especially those in the U.S. and
Canada. Click on Minnesota Summer of '96, for instance, and
up comes practically all you need to know about Bemidji State
U's "There's A Song In The Air: Elderhostel Choral Workshop."
Nova Scotia, on the other hand, offers one on "Agriculture In
The Annapolis Valley," among others. A great page for seniors in

search of learning adventures in an array of academic and cultural disciplines.

GeroWeb
http://www.iog.wayne.edu/GeroWeb.html

The Institute of Gerontology at Wayne State University supports this center for links and resources on aging. This is a very nice presentation, with annotated link lists separated into categories for universities, government agencies, private organizations for services and census data, and health and biomedical research sources. Whether you are a senior looking for activities or legal rights, or a researcher looking for updates and raw materials, GeroWeb is a good place to start.

Seniors-site
http://seniors-site.com/

The best thing about Seniors-site is that it doesn't have the feel of some big corporation telling everyone over 55 what they should be doing in their "golden years." No, this is surely more neighborly, and addresses just about all the seniors-related issues we'd ever heard of: Social Security, insurance and care-giving, frauds and scams and even jokes and pets. The text-only approach (we also went nearly click-crazy, bouncing around all the content-free title pages) seems a bit dry, but it IS informative, and sincere as all get-out. Seniors looking to connect with other seniors should get a kick out of the wide variety of forums, or the chance to share a (clean) joke or grandkid story. Things get a little more rowdy in the political forums, but the postings there are usually well-crafted compared to most bulletin boards. Seniors, family members and caregivers can all find something worthwhile here.

Consumer Information

101 Uses for your Old Shoes 'n Other Stuff
http://www.knosso.com/Shoes/index.html

This site presents a wide array of tips on how to recycle and reuse old things instead of tossing them in the trash. Based on the book, *101 Uses for your Old Shoes* (with illustrated pages of the whimsical booklet sprinkled throughout), it goes beyond second-hand footwear: more than a dozen categories have charity organizations and bureaus that can make use of things you don't want, and stores that will buy your used whatever. And of course, there are recycling tips, like cutting up old clothing into rags instead of throwing them away, and exchanging old toys with neighbors (so everybody's kids get "new" things to play with).

The Better Business Bureau Web Server
http://www.bbb.org/bbb/

The BBB is the place for information on everything from "work-at-home" schemes to complaint reports on businesses in your area. And the BBB's Internet presence is growing. Plans are in the works for individual bureaus to offer "reliability reports" on area businesses beginning in Boston at the end of 1995 and expanding after that. For now, you can find money-saving tips (like the fact that participating in foreign lotteries is not only costly but illegal) and advice on refinancing a mortgage loan. It's also a great place to find the nearest bureau. In any event, it's nice to have somebody looking out for you.

Consumer Prices and Price Indexes
http://stats.bls.gov/cpandpi.htm

The answer to the popular question, "What is a consumer price index?" can be found here. This site is chock-full of statistics—some available by gopher—on the prices of food, clothing, pretty much anything. And get this: the Bureau of Labor, which compiles the data, gets most of the info through personal interviews. Yet another labor-saving device for those of us who can be called "comparison shoppers."

Consumer World
http://www.consumerworld.org/

Ralph Nader didn't create this index, but his spirit fuels its pointers to "over 700 of the most useful consumer resources on the Internet." We're talking about all the sorts of info a buyer needs to make wise decisions in the post-modern marketplace, as well as the means for faulty business practice victims to fight back. Examples include an "All Things Automotive Directory" and "Computer Buyer's Guide and Price Cruncher," while a Best Bet tag was also attached to "Last Minute Travel and Cruise Specials." For fun, after consulting, say, The Better Business Bureau, an Internet Wonders section offers the chance to "peek in on people with spy cameras." All that's missing from Consumer World's vivid interface are audio clips of shysters muttering, "Curses, foiled again!" Thanks be to advocate/educator/attorney Edgar Dworsky for instituting this excellent consumer's index.

Gay and Lesbian Resources

GaySource
http://www.gaysource.com/

On our last visit to "Gay Source," the monthly online, "interactive general-interest magazine for the gay, lesbian, bisexual, and transgender community," there was an interesting update on the movement in Hawaii to legalize same-sex marriages. (In 1993 Hawaii's Supreme Court ruled that same-sex marriages would be "declared legal under the state's constitution unless the state could present 'compelling state's interest' for such discrimination in District Court.") Also included pieces on meeting Mr. or Ms. Right and where to see and be seen in cities like San Francisco, Miami, and Houston. Lots of links to AIDS service organizations, political sites, and activist groups.

Human Rights Campaign
http://www.hrcusa.org/

This site for the Human Rights Campaign promises visitors "the same information and resources our lobbying group uses to educate Members of Congress on lesbian and gay, AIDS and health issues." The "Issues Explained" include workplace discrimination, lesbian and gay parental rights, and HIV/AIDS research, prevention, and care. One impressive feature here is the list of "scorecard" ratings for senators and members of Congress. (And should you take umbrage at your representative's voting record, a click of the mouse will let you send him or her a form letter, a communiqué of your own composition, or a combination of the two.) HRC makes a pitch here for people to join up, and supporters can also shop online for items like National Coming Out Day T-shirts (with the official Keith Haring logo!).

Out.com
`http://www.planetout.com/`

"America's Best-Selling Gay and Lesbian Magazine" brings its glossy, gossipy style online at this site, an impressive translation that seems to include all the printed articles (and some of the ads, too). On our last visit, we found a long interview with k.d. lang, whose decision to come out "[freed] her up to titillate concert audiences with taunts like 'Yes, the rumors are all true. It's time I told you: I am a L-L-Lawrence Welk fan.'" The site also takes advantage of its electronic medium to present the News and Gossip of the Day: entertainment and political news ("Gay Activists in Europe Convene in Latvia") updated regularly—though not, it would seem, quite daily. And, finally, you'll find "our ever gratuitous Boy and Girl photos." Flippant and fun, but with plenty to say, too.

Qworld
`http://www.qworld.org/`

If it's gay or lesbian news and services you're after, look no further than Qworld. In addition to links to several little-known 'zines (including "A Dyke's World" and "Visibilities"), you'll find message boards, regional resources, and a QMall, complete with books, clothing, and jewelry. Especially interesting are the QFiles, which offer everything from health information to shareware. Click on Queer History here, and you'll find background on the rainbow flag, pink triangle, lambda symbol, and slogans. Lots of links to other gay-related pages, including entertainment, health, community, and youth sites.

Youth Action Online
   http://www.youth.org/

Youth Action Online is a volunteer organization with a mission to help gay, lesbian, and bisexual youth and to "provide young people with a safe space online to be themselves." Its content-rich monthly e-zine, *Oasis*, has featured advice from parents on coming out; poetry and stories written by gay and lesbian teens; and interviews with prominent activists like Mel White, author of "Stranger at the Gate: To Be Gay and Christian in America." The News and Reviews section has included an item on the censorship in some communities of a "Friends" episode, a description of a citizen lobby day in California "devoted solely to the issues of queer youth" and a rundown on "queer-core" bands. Newsy, informative, hip.

Minority Affairs

Afro Americ@
   http://www.afroam.org/

The Afro American Newspapers company of Baltimore has been publishing for 103 years, but no one can accuse them of not changing with the times. The publisher's extensive collection of African-Americana now finds an outlet in this well-written and beautifully designed site. Up-to-date technology doesn't obscure the paper's sense of history. A thoughtful and well-researched (and hyperlinked) Jackie Robinson retrospective is a joy. The contributions of the pioneer ballplayer who broke the Major League "color barrier" are often overlooked, as is his monumental personal ordeal. A section on Martin Luther King is even more comprehensive, covering King's eloquent opposition to the Vietnam war as well as his desegregation struggle. As a result, King emerges as an even greater humanitarian than he's usually considered, if that's possible.

Afronet
   http://www.afronet.com/

Whether you want to study the history of the North African country of Chad, or you're looking for "the 411" on

African-American politics and culture, Afronet provides stacks of enlightening writing. The graphic design's not too shabby either. Weekly news updates hit on such topics as vandalism of black churches and whether a CBS executive was quoted accurately when he (reportedly) said that blacks don't work and have short attention spans (this supposedly makes them a key late-night TV audience, according to the disputed quote). The recent film *Waiting to Exhale* gets its own mini-site, too. The occasional, annoying "under construction" tag popped up when we checked, but otherwise, Afronet appears poised to join the Web's elite echelon of African-American sites. Not to be confused with AfriNet.

Asian Week
http://www.asianweek.com/

Asian Week, which calls itself the only pan-ethnic English-language weekly for Asian Americans, doesn't put all of the material from its paper edition on the Web. But there's enough on this site to make the online version an important stop on any Web tour for Asian Americans concerned about their place in American politics and society. Top stories in the issue we pored over dealt with congressional moves to undo bilingual voting requirements and "The Legacy of Chinatown," a nicely written piece about San Francisco's most heavily Asian neighborhood. It's not all Chinese anymore, the article points out. In fact, the influx of immigrants from other Asian countries is credited with helping keep Chinatown culture thriving. Recent back issues remain online in the site's archives. Very slick, professional and enlightening.

The Womanist
http://www.uga.edu/~womanist/home.html

Emanating for the Institute for African-American Studies at the University of Georgia, this scholarly journal looks at issues in feminist theory from an African-American perspective. The Womanist began as a "newsletter" but after just two issues, the editors say that the response was so positive that the publication will morph into two broader projects: "Womanist Theory &

Research and the Womanist Studies Consortium." The editors don't say whether the new journal, "Womanist Theory & Research," will be posted on the Web, but they would like you to subscribe to a dead-tree version. However, the second and last edition of the newsletter covers such relevant topics as "Black Women's Sexual Sense of Self: Implications for AIDS Prevention," and "Examining Depression Among African-American Women." The term "womanist," by the way, was coined by *Color Purple* author Alice Walker in her 1983 book *In Search of Our Mothers' Gardens*.

Social Services

54 Ways to Help the Homeless
http://ecosys.drdr.virginia.edu/ways/54.html

This electronic book from Rabbi Charles A. Kroloff offers practical advice to individuals trying to cope with one of society's most overwhelming problems. (Kroloff knows about the homeless first-hand: the school in his Temple serves as their shelter at night.) The 54 steps outlined here include suggestions like carrying fast food gift certificates to offer to panhandlers. Kroloff's big on prevention, too: he recommends community housing projects like Habitat for Humanity as real long-term solutions. A pragmatic and optimistic site.

Child Quest International
http://www.childquest.org/

At the same time one of the most important sites on the Web and one of the most depressing, Child Quest is an inventory of missing children with photos, descriptions, and online forms for reporting sightings (and new cases). It's important for obvious reasons, depressing because there are so many missing kids. And these are just "the most current open cases." A database of cases in which an alleged abductor is named are also here. In a large number of those cases the suspect is a "non-custodial" parent. The occasional case of "stranger abduction" features a suspect, but for the most part, strangers are strangers. This site is worth periodic checks by anyone and everyone, just in case.

Queer Resources Directory
http://www.qrd.org/QRD/

Here's an extremely in-depth collection of info on everything from teenage homosexuality to queer media. The Gay TV This Week section, for instance, may tell you that a showing of Mrs. Doubtfire stars Harvey Fierstein and gay comic Scott Capurro as a couple who transform Robin Williams into an elderly woman. Or you can read the American Psychological Association statement that recent research suggests "that efforts to repair homosexuals are nothing more than social prejudice garbed in psychological accoutrements." Links aplenty, too. QRD is more full than Liberace's closet, and far more useful.

The Wounded Healer
http://idealist.com/wounded_healer/

Although this site's name seems to imply it's a sort of support group for therapists who themselves need help, it's much more. It's a resource which focuses on the needs of psychotherapists and people who have survived child abuse, and provides resources for victims of abuse in general. As the page describes, you can find "downloadable files, relevant news and point-of-view pieces, treatment resources and pointers to interesting people and places." If you don't have the time to check back frequently (and items are added often enough to make it necessary), there's a weekly e-mail service available to keep you updated.

Women's Resources

VOW World: Voices of Women
http://www.voiceofwoman.com/

This is the online version of VOW, a Chesapeake Bay area women's magazine and, according to this page, "the most comprehensive women's resource on the Internet." Using what they describe as "intermedia synergy," the editors hope electronic communications will put "a new set of power tools" into the hands of women. Some of these tools include articles like

"Talkin' About a Girl Revolution" and "The State vs.
Midwives: A Battle for Body and Soul," which challenges the
notion that the only "safe" birth is a "technological" birth.
VOW is compelling reading, but the page offers more than
journalism: it also sponsors an annual women's conference and
expo, details of which are available here, and a directory of
"woman-owned," "woman-friendly" businesses, from accounting and acupuncture to writing workshops and yoga.

Women's International Center
http://www.wic.org/

WIC is a non-profit foundation that honors and encourages
women who make positive contributions to humanity. This
page outlines their mission and projects, including the annual
Living Legacy Awards. Among the projects detailed here: schol-
arship assistance to older women reentering the work force;
medical studies scholarships; and "Operation Greentrees," an
ongoing donation of tree seedlings to organizations and
schools. Biographies, a "global town hall," and a terrific history
of women in America make this one of the better resources for
women on the Net.

Women's Sports Page
http://fiat.gslis.utexas.edu/~lewisa/
womsprt.html

This no-frills index offers a terrific collection of links to everything from women's soccer to gender equity discussions to
track and field. You'll also find plenty of rugby, karate,
weightlifting, and other formerly "unladylike" sports. Women's
hockey alone has 8 different links and women's volleyball has
more than a dozen. Compiled by citizen Amy Lewis (a self-
proclaimed "philosopher, athlete, subvert, aesthete, student and
gadfly on the Internet"), this is a great resource for anyone
excited to know that team handball isn't just for men anymore—and probably never was. Perhaps the greatest thing
about this list is that it contains so many things we didn't know
existed in the first place.

Women's Wire

http://www.women.com/

When Mom's line is busy and your best friend's on vacation, the sisters are "in" at Women's Wire. This sharp, politically savvy page from San Francisco has everything from headline news to a forum for "back talk," where women can share their opinions on controversial issues. "Question Authorities" provides women with opportunities to query experts in the fields of fashion, business, and sex (subtitled "carnal knowledge"). There's even advice for stargazers: asks Therese in California, "If my husband is an Aries and the oldest child and I'm a Pisces and youngest, do we have a marriage made in heaven? Or are we an accident waiting to happen?" (We'll keep the answer a surprise). And lest we forget those irksome (and ubiquitous) troubles with men, you may want to consult "eMale: The Gender Challenged."

Shopping

Apparel

Fashion Net
http://www.fashion.net/

Fashion Net is a non-profit "global meeting point" for amateur and professional style seekers. One half of the page is aimed at the general public, offering an index of magazines such as Beauty Online, a link to the Supermodel Homepage, shopping at 3 Suisses (in French), and lots more. The second half of the site is dedicated to business-to-business communications: make-up artist want ads, online portfolios, press releases ("Spain's Spring/Summer '96 International Collections"), and industry bulletin boards. This site can't offer all the flash bulbs and excitement of a seat beside the runway, but it's a stylish attempt to create an online home for an entire industry.

Global Shopping Network
http://www.gsn.com/

This shopping site is steeped in marine and outdoor gear for both amateurs and professionals. Visitors tend to cast out compliments like great graphics and awesome selection. No wonder: you can go to MarineNet for frog hooks or even fishing line—or look through the FishNet photo gallery, where an old woman holds a salmon as big as she is. Those with fat wallets can look into a champagne charter boat to Juneau, Alaska, or use the search engine (computer, not outboard) to buy a real schooner.

Lands' End
http://www.landsend.com/
spawn.cgi?ZEROPAGE&GRAPHIC&NULLPAGE&0

You'll come to shop for the button-down Oxford shirts and stay to browse the chatty reminiscences of the people behind Lands' End. Most of the material is reprinted from the company's engaging, seasonal catalogs, but it's still interesting to read founder and yachtsman Gary Comer's tale of the firm's early '60s beginning in a small Chicago loft above an all-night saloon. Using e-mail, you can contact a Lands' End Specialty Shopper advisor if you need help with such tasks as coordinating your wardrobe or choosing the perfect gift. And once you're ready to get down to business, the site offers a "shopping cart" function so you can load up before proffering your credit card at the checkout.

Levi's

http://www.levi.com/

This hip-as-can-be site for clothing manufacturer Levi's is a lot more than an on-line stop for purchasing jeans. Click on Fly Zone and peruse an array of graffiti-covered walls. (Bomb the Wall invites you to submit your own computer-generated graffiti for display at this site.) The Inner Seam takes you inside the company, where you'll get a closer look at how it does what it does, from the factory floor to advertising. (Don't miss the interview with hot young director Spike Jonze, whose commercials for Levi's led to his directing the Tri-Star feature film *Harold and the Purple Crayon*.) On our last visit, the Street, in a quest for the next big thing, took us to England's Portobello Road Market and South Africa's Durban City.

Autos

AutoSite

http://www.autosite.com/

AutoSite is your Web key to "everything automotive . . . " (Whoever said the age of making distinctions is long past?) . . . and that includes access to more than 30,000 pages of car related info. Sounds too good to be free? You're right, as nominal subscriber's fees are required for, say, new car dealer invoice prices, model specs, reviews, and on. But wait! It won't cost you a thing to browse the troubleshooting diagnosis and repair guide ("Can you smell rotten eggs when you start your car?"), auto club links, consumer advisory articles, used car resources, and tons more worthwhile features. A pleasing graphic interface enhances this excellent clearinghouse for "best buy" and other auto related info.

Classic Car Source
`http://www.classicar.com/`

Classic Car Source does a smashing job of backing up the claim that its classified ads and features are "the premier online source for Classic Vehicles, Automobilia, & Rare Parts." It's great whether you want to buy or sell, but have specific criteria in mind on the vehicles or accessories for which you want to search. Those looking for a good browse will find that here, too, including worldwide club and museum links, and an archive full of articles such as: "Torino Tales and Fairlane Fantasies." The bulletin board allows reaching out for help, say, if you're "looking for info. on a late 40's - early 50's German car called an Adler." There's stuff on motorcycles, racing, and kit cars, too. Exotic auto enthusiasts won't want to pass on this one!

Soundings
`http://www.gsn.com/bin/fishing.exe?/sports/`
`boating/soundings/soundings.htm&graphics&guest`

This searchable database is loaded with articles, classified ads, and other features from the monthly pleasure boating tabloid, Soundings. The print version focuses on the Eastern United States, yet this online edition aims for a broader appeal. Looking for a powerboat or sailboat? Simply type in your criteria (e.g. manufacturer, size, price . . .) for fast searches through thousands of watercraft classifieds. Waterfront real estate listings from Maine to the Caribbean are also accessible. Oh, yes, and the voluminous archive of back issues features JPEG photos, and full-text articles ranging from the literary (e.g. "They Cruised Just Like Bogey and Kate") to the issues oriented (e.g. "Government, Builders Fight Over Jet Bike Regs"), and on out to the horizon. An excellent site for pleasure boaters!

Toyota
`http://www.toyota.com/`

You'll get all the dope on Toyota vehicles here at its official U.S. home page. Marvel at the Camry's DOHC engine design and nod knowingly at the description of the Land Cruiser's four-speed ETC. (And if you don't know what DOHC and ETC are, the site's online glossary of terms like Double Over-Head Camshaft and Electrically Controlled Transmission will help you sound like a seasoned tire-kicker.) On top of the torque talk, Toyota also offers a truckload of content in the section it has labeled, automotively, The Hub. There visitors will find family travel suggestions (the canals of England was a recent tip) along with men's and women's pages in what Toyota calls a "lifestylish eye on the world." In a section titled "A Man's Life," a doctor answers questions from visitors. (That numbness in your arms at night may be carpal tunnel syndrome.) What's that got to do with cars? Well, nothing. But it's fun.

Books

Amazon.com Books

```
http://www.amazon.com/exec/obidos/subst/
index2.html/6586-3933723-574315
```

Billed as "Earth's biggest bookstore," Amazon.com Books features a database of one million titles. Proprietors aspire to the lofty goal of listing every book in print. A quick search for obscure titles leads us to believe they aren't kidding around, either. Ordering is quick and easy, and more than 20 categories can help ease the burden of browsing such a huge stack. The real achievement here is the free personal notification service. Subscribe and the folks at Amazon.com will notify you of new titles in your category (say, insect taxidermy), or tell you when a new book comes out by your favorite author. Perhaps most impressive is the speed of searching—nearly any combination of keywords brings a quick list of related titles. Sound impersonal? It may be, but a daily spotlight on favorite titles offers recommendations from the staff, capturing at least a little of the coziness of a small bookstore.

Book Stacks

```
http://www.books.com/scripts/news.exe
```

Book Stacks Unlimited, Inc., bills this page as "Your local bookstore. No matter where you live." They boast of more than

250,000 titles, searches by author, title, or ISBN number, and major browsing capabilities—all without the Dewey Decimal System! We searched—successfully—for a copy of Stendhal's *Scarlet and Black* ($5.95) by ISBN number, and for Ivana Trump's *Free to Love* ($6.50) by author. You must open an account to order.

BookWire
`http://www.bookwire.com/`

The Big Daddy of online book resources, BookWire is thick and heavy with information for readers, publishers and dealers. Publisher's Weekly and Boston Book Review run the show, so new titles are whisked to review desks, and the authors are promptly sat down and interviewed. The amount of options for visitors here is daunting, so we recommend using the site's Navigator page. From there, link to the "Reading Room," an amazing online library of books for download, mostly classics from Abbott to Wolff, with a particular strength in children's titles. Or skip to the BBR's page of essays and interviews with people like Camille Paglia and Art Spiegelman. Looking at books always seems to lead to spending money, and of course that's easy enough to do here, too.

Stacey's Professional Bookstore Homepage
`http://www.staceys.com/`

The strength of this large and well-established California bookstore is its huge storehouse of technical and professional books, and we can tell from their online presence that they aren't kidding around. Search the database or simply use their nifty "autobrowse" method, and get an idea of the catalog. If something sounds good, chances are you'll be able to read a good chunk of it online. The samples here are truly impressive (long and varied), and other juicy bits include sections on publishers and specific authors (including recommendations updated frequently). Although it is clearly still growing, this site already commands a high position among ALL online bookstores.

Entertainment

Criterion Collection
http://www.voyagerco.com/CC/gh/p.crit.html

It began with *Citizen Kane* in 1984, and since then the Criterion Collection has issued on laser disk the definitive versions of many of the world's finest films. Now, you can surf its smart (and credit-card secure) online catalog, which contains lengthy essays about and clips from the films. Here, you learn that its version of *Close Encounters of the Third Kind* includes two versions. You can download audio of Jodie Foster speaking on *The Silence of the Lambs*. And in a long, hyperlinked essay, you'll discover that Ingmar Bergman, as a boy, traded his set of lead soldiers for a "magic lantern." (So he wasn't a child prodigy, OK?) A cineaste's delight.

EMusic
http://www.emusic.com/

This shopping site, with more than 100,000 CD titles available, stakes a claim as the "fastest, easiest, and most enjoyable way to browse the world of music today!" This fun way to shop for CDs allows surfers to search for discs by song, year, album, or artist. A search of 1976 turned up 10 of that year's top-selling albums, including Marvin Gaye's "Greatest Hits" and the Eagles' "Hotel California." Then we searched for Led Zeppelin under "artist," and found 16 Zep albums, with color graphics of album covers. Visitors can also enter their own reviews for albums, and read the reviews of others. Rock on.

Jazz Online
http://www.jazzonln.com/

Like the music it covers, Jazz Online is exceedingly smooth. Beautiful graphics and stylish design make the site visually stunning, and strong writing and content keep it entertaining. Look for well-written feature articles (jazz great Oscar Brown, Jr. was featured on our last visit), live music calendars, album reviews, and a healthy dose of corporate tie-ins to pay the bills. The site's designers have used just about every HTML trick in the book, so don't expect the full effect without Netscape, and, sadly, those without some type of graphical browser are out of luck. Still, this is a site with unquestionable style.

Nuke
http://www.nuke.com/

Sendai Publishing presents more than 2000 pages of multimedia extravaganza here with a dense (yet lively) interface. It's meant to be the starting point for fans of video games, computer entertainment software, movies, television, comics and trading cards on the Net. It includes news, reviews, shopping, and much more. (And faced with this many options, you're likely to go reeling for the site's Frequently Asked Questions section for an orientation.) Past TVScape items have included an interview with Star Trek's Patrick Stewart ("What a pompous ass," he said of himself); on our last visit the computer game "Alien Virus" received respectable ratings from the Review Crew. And the Shelter will always sell you loads of PC software. The site continues to mushroom. Wow!

Flowers and Gifts

1-800-FLOWERS
http://www.shopping2000.com/

If you haven't heard of 1-800-FLOWERS yet, you probably also need to be told there's a Democrat in the White House. This company, created for people who forget their loved ones at crucial moments (Oops, is TOMORROW our 10th anniversary?), now lets you scan its merchandise online. Gourmet cheesecake and plants as well as roses can be sent to that special someone, though it can all be quite pricey: a half dozen mylar balloons will run you $34, a basket of apples and pears even more (not including shipping, tax, etc.). Special gift baskets are also available—but be forewarned, "Stuffed toy may vary."

Flower Stop
http://www.rmii.com:80/fstop/fstopmain.html

This online fresh-flower market offers next-day delivery (in the U.S.) of bouquets, vases, and that grand standby, the single long-stemmed rose. (The blooms come from Pikes Peak Greenhouses in Colorado Springs, in case you were wondering.) Shoppers can frolic among an "Enchanting Alstomeria Bouquet" or "Exotic Orchids"; if necessary, they can select a "nice" clear plastic vase or a nicer etched crystal one for delivery. The "Romance and Roses CD Set" features two centuries of the world's greatest love themes ("for lovers only!") to accompany your flower purchase. The prices are probably higher than your local florist, but this is still a nice example of online shopping. It's colorful, quick, and lets you see the product without provoking your allergies.

PC Flowers & Gifts
http://www.pcgifts.ibm.com/

There's no excuse not to have a gift for those special occasions now that it's this easy to order flowers online and select a personalized greeting card. PC Flowers, which has been handling electronic orders since 1989, serves up an attractive Web site in its incarnation as PC Flowers and Gifts on IBM's network. Some of the most popular items are right on the introductory page, so shoppers with a secure Web browser will be able to order a dozen roses or a gourmet-foods gift basket from Hickory Farms with a minimum of fuss. If you want to say it with more than just flowers, the site is integrated with a Web-based CreataCard kiosk from American Greetings. When you place flower orders, they're delivered by the FTD florist nearest your much-impressed recipient.

Trade Mission, Inc.
http://tayara.com/souk/

Houston's Trade Mission, Inc. world crafts store markets its collections in a beautifully wrapped package of cultural and experiential content. The site creates the feel of an Eastern marketplace with its "Souk," which you enter through an evocative page: "Inside the Great Souk tides of rainbow costumed natives sweep along eager and anxious, flowing in streams through passageways filled with treasures from the four corners of the earth." Within, you find Trade Mission's international art, crafts and accessories, including items such as stone sculptures from

Zimbabwe and costumed dolls from the hilltribes of Northern Thailand. Fascinating backgrounders on the cultures behind the crafts round out these worldly offerings. Trade Mission also hosts the Travelers Club, a refined online gathering place for travelers to share their stories and resources.

Food and Drink

Clambake Celebrations

http://www.netplaza.com/plaza/strfrnts/1004/storepg1.html

Clambake Celebrations will whisk a fresh Lobster-Clambake to your office party or home doorstep overnight—complete with claw-crackers, bibs and wetnaps. Get the mouthwatering details here, where ordering is as easy as a click . . . if you can get past the options. Choices range from a pot of soft-shell steamer clams to a seaweed-lined crustacean extravaganza. The company has been in business for 10 years and guarantees every lobster, clam, or mussel that hops on Federal Express has been hand-picked and quality checked. If you're a landlocked lover of seafood, you'll be happy as a clam with this site.

Salsa Express

http://www.stw.com/se/se.htm

This down-home, folksy online catalog bills itself as one-stop shopping for your salsa and hot sauce needs. The emphasis is on specialty salsa lovingly made by small companies. The family that runs Salsa Express in Albuquerque (be sure to check out their photo) has kept prices reasonable and the product info is hilarious and helpful. Includes the Hotter than Hell cookbook, and the note that hot sauce can make you go deaf for a brief time—that's right, you can't hear your own screams. Yowch!

Weight Watchers

http://www.weight-watchers.com/

Get the skinny on the heavy weight-loss champion of all time, Weight Watchers, at the organization's pretty-in-pink official home page. Curious about those new-and-improved programs

WW seems to announce every year or so? The latest offerings are outlined at How to Choose a Weight-loss Program, which also helps dieters figure out their personal needs and priorities. WW products, including foods and accessories, also are marketed at the home page. But the site does more than sell the program: It also promotes good eating habits in general at its Nutrition Facts & Tips page, which offers some basic info on diet-busters such as fat, sugar and dining out, and tips on how to increase your intake of such necessities as fiber and various nutrients. Since Weight Watchers is famous for its interaction between counselors and dieters, the Wellness News & Forum offers a little give and take. And if you think you know it all, click to the Facts & Quiz page to test your diet acumen. Go ahead—you've got nothing to lose.

A World of Tea
http://www.stashtea.com/

Steep a mellow bag of chamomile and settle in here for tales and trivia from the fascinating world of tea. Brought to you by the Stash Tea Company, an Oregon-based mail-order firm, this surprisingly entertaining sales site spins in some tea history ("Three great Zen priests restored tea to its original place in Japanese society") and news ("Animal studies suggest tea is a cancer-preventing agent"). Stash's online catalog makes it easy to order teas, gift packs, kettles, and mugs. Basically, you'll find everything here but the tea party, including tea quotes. "There is a subtle charm in the taste of tea which makes it irresistible," said Kakuzo Okakura in 1906. "It has not the arrogance of wine, the self-consciousness of coffee, nor the simpering innocence of cocoa."

Grab Bag

FringeWare, Inc.
http://www.fringeware.com/

FringeWare is a group of high-tech "fringe" entrepreneurs who compile, synthesize, and peddle twisted products and weird ideas. Need a set of Bondage Pig Earrings for that special someone? If these are too flashy, try the Wicked Hand Dangle Pendant. Cover that unsightly prom night pimple with the "life size" Alien Face Hugger Kit. Distributing weird ideas naturally translates into their online e-zine, TAZMEDIA, a grade-A work covering weirdness ranging from JFK to OKC. Catch also the text on Applied Memetics ("Memetics is to media as genetics is to biology"), which shows they're truly on the fringe: they know where Power lies and what tactics are required to get it. An inspiring link for those skirting the edge; a survival manual for those already over.

Smokin' Joes
http://www.smokinjoes.com/

For the North American tobacco connoisseur, Tennessee-based Smokin' Joes offers an impressive inventory of cigars, pipes, snuff, and other such stuff. Read up and electronically order 'em by the box, bundle, or sampler pack. Newbies get info on how to cut and light their smokes, while Joe offers old-timers a certified Masters Degree of Cigarology (well, a certificate, anyway). Amid other features, we learned that Whoopi Goldberg prefers to puff on a Macanudo Prince of Wales Cafe. Accessories galore include Zino Davidoff Humidors and (whew!) a full line of air purifiers.

Sun Angel Productions
http://www.sun-angel.com/welcome.html

This Web mall makes available many New Age products and services, but with all the other stuff on here, you don't get the feeling they're just trying to take your money—the whole package seems geared towards helping you develop your inner self. There's an interesting array of things to buy, there's no doubt—at Star Water Press, for example, "Anubel" will use a picture of you to paint your aura. But there's also an enlightening collection of articles and art online, along with some "InnerActive Fun", like a module that allows you to "create" the perfect planet. Sometimes strange, but always friendly.

Upscale Wholesale Page
http://www.upscale.com/

Upscale Wholesale is the name; cool, hard-to-find (even hard-to-imagine) gear is the game. Specialty and fun are top priorities at this virtual storefront, where prices are supposed to be 20 to 30 percent lower than they would be on retail tags—provided you could even find some of these gadgets. Affordable night vision equipment and audio/video surveillance goodies reflect a military inclination, but animal lovers could go for the Australian chew-proof trampoline dog bed. Channel-surfers with an itchy trigger finger should appreciate the "Gunvertor," a handgun-shaped remote control. And what kind of motorist could resist at least taking a peek at Granny's featured auto product? When you're done shopping, stop by the upscale offering of funky links, which run from supermodels to Al Gore.

Home

Carnivorous Plants Invade the Net!
http://cvp.onramp.net:80/feedme/

Peter Pauls Nurseries want you to know that flesh-eating plants are "exciting, educational and make a distinctive statement in any setting." ("Distinctive" is the operative word.) They're also hoping you'll buy a few bug-biting beauties (or at least seed packets) from this virtual greenhouse. We found the Butterwort a particularly virulent assassin (it oozes gooey slime to trap its victims), though the dependable carnage of Venus Flytrap is always a crowd-pleaser. And the prices ($4.95 for the venomous Cobra Lily) won't bury you, either. And if you've already been bitten by these verdant jaws, you'll really enjoy the site's offering of Carnivorous Plant Links, including a searchable database and a Carnivorous Plant Society Homepage.

Lindal Cedar Homes
http://www.lindal.com/

This site offers to help make "dreams of cedar" come true for those who want to design their own home. Founded in 1945, Sir Walter Lindal's company has put up a beautiful web page, featuring an all-day (for those with slow computers) home tour, plans, specifications, etc. Among other options, there are interior and exterior photographs of "Casa Islena," "Chalet," and "Pavilion"—all made with the "natural wonder" of cedar and instilled with "the Lindal difference." This is a first-rate Webvertisement.

Pacific Coast Feather Company
http://www.pacificcoast.com/cgi-bin/
nph-pcf-welcome

The Pacific Coast Feather Company—makers of what it says are the world's finest down comforters and bed pillows—may be the first company to hope that its Web site puts visitors to sleep. With lots of photos and detailed product specs, this site encourages you to cozy up to such luxurious-sounding items as the Silken Romance comforter, made from a blend of silk and Egyptian cotton and stuffed with goose down purchased from Hutterite colonies. Visitors can buy online or use the site's zip-code search engine to find the retail outlet nearest them. Once you buy your comforter, you should heed the site's maintenance tips and fluff it up regularly: the puffier your comforter is, the warmer you'll be. Even if you're not ready to buy, you'll find some interesting bedtime reading in the company's Ten Healthy Sleep Habits, one of which is: "Go for quality, not quantity. Six hours of good, solid sleep can make you feel more rested than eight hours of light sleep."

Price OnLine
http://www.priceline.com/

Brought to the Web by the shopping-club pros behind PriceCostco, Price OnLine lets visitors browse an electronic-department store and make purchases electronically or over the phone. Shoppers can go straight to specific departments—such as jewelry, sporting goods or housewares—or use a search feature to find the item they're looking for. Our search for a radio turned up a General Electric Spacemaker that mounts under a cabinet, but shopping will be more interesting when Price OnLine finally lists what it says is a line of 9,000 products and we can do more comparison shopping. Among the 300 products already online, our favorites were the Muhammad Ali Boxing Gloves ($169.99) and the Shaquille O'Neal Basketball ($154.99) in the sports memorabilia department.

Hobbies

Guncraft Sports, Inc.
http://www.usit.net/guncraft/

This Knoxville, Tenn. firearms and ammunition shop ("serving the shooting public since 1947") takes aim at the Internet and hits the bullseye. If you're into guns, you'll find the answers here. Order ammo by e-mail, or sign up for gun safety courses. Plenty of links to other gun sites on the Web. Odd on-site fact: 53 percent of the U.S. population lives within eight hours' drive of this store.

Infinite Illusions Juggling Supplies
http://infinite.pd.net/

Talk about exquisite toys! On our last visit, this splendid e-catalog featured devilsticks, Tom Kuhn yo-yo's (only 11 Silver Bullets left!), and "Maximum Hook" by Flight Stix ("If you have the arm for it, you need this boomerang"). The extensive inventory is presented against serene backdrops with photos, some of which move. How-tos including juggling three balls, wielding the likes of a Radical Fish Diablo, and making newspaper clubs enhance this boon for the young at heart.

Tried & True Trains
http://www.tttrains.com/

For model railroad enthusiasts worldwide, here's a fine online switching yard. Hobbyist engineers can browse the product manufacturers showcase, including "Garden Railroad Accessories and Miniature Carousel Components," as well as collected tips and wisdom in articles like "Backdrop Know-how." And innovators will especially appreciate resources on Digital Command Control, a new method for micro-processor control of model trains. No matter what scale you're into, it's likely to be informed by pictures and more via this virtual community—thanks in large part to Debbie Ames, who deserves a good hobby, having come to model railroading "after teaching art, raising a family, and directing a church school."

Where to Buy Model Railroad Supplies in the 1990s

http://www.tucson.com/concor/buy.html

In addition to being a "Where to" buyer's guide for the latest model railroading equipment, Con-Cor Models company offers helpful how-to information here, for anyone just venturing into this popular hobby. Veterans will want to scroll down (through so much home page text) to the link embedded graphic train, the engine of which will transport you to Grand Central Station. That's a gateway to all manner of other model train sites, including competing manufacturers, clubs, shows, and even real railroading pages, such as for Amtrak and Chicago's Metra commuter system. Then, if you're ready to buy, click on the boxcars for e-catalogs from Illinois based Con-Cor, featuring HO and N scale products, and assorted "Route 66 Vehicles," or their Arizona sister company, JMC, which has "over 15,000" model railroading products in stock. An excellent shopping and info site!

Kid's Stuff

Dragonfly Toy Company

http://www.magic.mb.ca/~dragon/

For children with special play needs, The Dragonfly Toy Company sells (and ships) toys worldwide. In categories such as Fine Motor Skills, Cognitive, and Sensory Stimulation, you can browse an inventory that includes Texture Dominos, a Sound Puzzle Box, and Curved Martian Canal—a semicircular sandbox on legs designed to fit around a wheelchair. Here as well is a selection of books, and a toy search service, in case you didn't find exactly what you had in mind. Real nice stuff!

FAO Schwarz

http://www.faoschwarz.com/

FAO Schwarz claims to be the oldest toy store in America. The store, opened in 1862 in Baltimore, has since branched out all over the country and now onto the Internet as well. If this site isn't as fun as being there, it's certainly pretty close. The

Ultimate Toy Catalogue is a good place to start browsing, and may save holiday shoppers some agony: why go out looking for Nintendo's Virtual Boy when you can mail-order it? Even if you're only screen-shopping, you'll likely get a kick out of specialty catalogues like Barbie at FAO Schwarz. (Don't miss Barbie and Ken as Scarlett O'Hara and Rhett Butler.) And the company information shouldn't be skipped: you can tour the trademark clocktowers of FAO Schwarz, or read about the construction of a 12-foot, 6,112-pound bronze teddy at the Boston store.

The Natural Baby Catalog
    http://www.parentsplace.com/shopping/
    naturalbaby/

This catalog is both a product push and proselytizing effort from the Natural Baby Company, a cottage industry begun by "Jane" and "Dan" to sell baby-related goods made of natural fibers. Jane intersperses chatty commentary on breast feeding and baby-bonding with pictures of blankets, clothes and booties. For the truly dedicated, there's a full selection of cloth diapers, plus instructions on how to wash them. The wood and cloth toys offered are appealing—you may want to get the kids a few of these before they start demanding plastic guns, bikini-clad dolls and CD players.

Toys "Я" Us
    http://www.tru.com/

You'll never suffer the embarrassment of buying an un-hip gift for a young friend if you monitor this site's list of best-selling items at Toys "Я" Us stores. The fact that we had never even heard of the number one-selling action figure (Spawn) just goes to show how vital this service is. And what's a toy store home page without something special for kids—like a game? Youngsters are encouraged to find the six stars hidden among the Toys "Я" Us pages in order to guide Geoffrey the Giraffe back from cyberspace. (Soon, astonishingly, they're likely to see most of the toys in the store.) Finally, the site's Store Spotter will help you find the Toys "Я" Us closest to you, no matter where you are. (That goes for Luxembourg, too.)

Office and Technology

Black Box On-Line Catalog
http://www.blackbox.com/bb/index.html/tig7915

One of the hardest things you can do with computers is to interconnect them, and the Black Box company has been helping out for 18 years. Now they've moved their comprehensive catalog of little black boxes to the Web, and they've implemented one of the best on-line shopping experiences anywhere in cyberspace. We admit that they're selling pretty dull stuff like modem cables, but they do so in a manner that's both outgoing and businesslike. There's also an excellent bit-head glossary (no, the ISDN D-channel has nothing to do with Disney), with friendly technical articles, all eminently searchable.

Cisco Systems, Inc.
http://www.cisco.com/

Here's a site the tech kids will love. This is the official site for Cisco Systems, Inc., one of the world's biggest suppliers to enterprise networks. If you need info on Cisco products, it's here: from serial cables to the component list for the latest Lightstream 2020 ATM switches. The CiscoPro section describes the company's tailored networking solutions packages, and tech support and upgrades are available online for registered Cisco customers. Impressive.

Egghead Software
http://www.egghead.com/

You can tell that Egghead Software is up on the Web game by looking at their finely crafted home page. Upon arrival, you will find an entry for "other browsers" and an entry for Netscape which takes you to Egghead's secure Netscape Server. From there you can enter the store and order items online. Each product has a special review button next to it which brings you information about that product from Ziff-Davis Publishing. Sections for corporate, government, and education customers as well as a discount club contribute to make this site one of the best stores on the Web.

Software.net
http://www.software.net/index.htm/
SK:doclihfbbeidablj

Software.net is one of the first to do online software sales and distribution for commercial software that's usually only available on disk. Shareware authors have offered online distribution for years, but only recently have the commercial packages followed suit. Most of the 16,000 software packages listed here are still shipped the old-fashioned way, but a surprising number of them can be downloaded immediately. With such a huge selection, Software.net's an excellent source for hard-to-find software. Just enter a keyword or two and you'll be able to complete the deal entirely online. Prices are competitive, and they've also thrown in software reviews from 16 magazines—a bonus you won't find at your corner Mom and Pop software store unless you lug 'em in yourself.

Real Estate

Homeowner's Finance Center
http://www.homeowners.com/in-yahoo.html

If you're clueless about covenants, appurtenances, and ARMS, this page can help you unravel the mysteries of the mortgage. First-time buyers will get a kick out the mortgage calculator, a clever device which instantly computes monthly outlay using the interest rate of your (or more likely, your lender's) choice. You even get daily updates on economic factors affecting home loan rates, including the latest juicy rumors from the Fed. (Did Alan Greenspan just sneeze? And if so, what does it mean?) Even pros will appreciate the loads of useful tips on buying and refinancing. These folks do a nice job of promoting their services, available in 24 states across the U.S., but don't forget to shop around.

International Real Estate Directory and News
http://www.ired.com/

The International Real Estate Directory and News (IRED) is not just a terrific jumpstation to some 5,000 real estate sites on the Web: it's also an online magazine jam-packed with articles that both buyers and sellers will find useful. Billed as "the independent source for real estate information on the Web," IRED keeps tabs on the industry's use of the Internet in articles such as "Apartment renters and building owners finding Web useful" and "AOL offers Bank of America home loan resources." On a recent visit, writer Dian Hymer was explaining how to overcome "Buyers' Remorse"—feelings of regret, fear, or anxiety many home buyers apparently experience during the course of a real estate transaction. Good research is the solution, Hymer writes, and IRED looks like a good source for that.

OnSight Real Estate Online
http://www.onsight.com/

OnSight Real Estate bills itself as the premier source for online real estate in the New York metropolitan area. If OnSight's service seems a little more mature than others of this genre, it's probably because the company was providing the information through a custom dial-up service even before setting up camp on the Web. The good-looking design is easy to navigate as you search for your favorite Central Park view, but the best part may be the detailed information available here on individual neighborhoods. After searching by zip code, we discovered that only six percent of the people in our target neighborhood drove to work, while 38 percent took the subway. So now we'll know to leave the Buick in Montana when it's time to move to the big city.

Visual Realty (Tulsa)
http://www.citysurf.com/

This online real estate listing service for the Tulsa, Oklahoma, area promises to take most of the stalking out of house hunting. Visual Realty lets you describe your dream home, then displays pictures and descriptions of likely candidates currently on the market. The site provides simple and sophisticated search engines. We chose the Power Search, because we insisted on a home with a mother-in-law suite, lots of trees and a hot tub (not necessarily in that order). There were several matches, which at least bodes well for mothers-in-law in Tulsa. Also online is a directory of area real estate agents. Clearly, the site is most interesting to those who in fact plan to buy a house in Tulsa. However, Visual Realty has an approach here that looks like it might travel well.

Travel

DeLorme: High Quality Maps for Every Need
http://www.delorme.com/

When a train derails in Massachusetts or a hurricane hits Florida, turn to the DeLorme map site for a cartographic view of the headline news. The Freeport, Maine, mapmaker has created a stunning commercial site to promote its products, including such high-tech offerings as the Street Atlas USA and Phone Search USA CD-ROMs. But it does more than sell merchandise here (yes, you can order online): it shows you its products in action. At the Maps in the News page, click on major stories for Street Atlas maps pinpointing the location of the event. Or, if you're planning a trip, have the interactive CyberRouter page plot your course—using DeLorme's Map'n'Go program, it spells out the fastest route point to point, with driving directions, time and mileage. DeLorme's site proves that online marketing works best when you let folks play with your toys before they buy them.

Internet Travel Network
http://www.itn.net/cgi/get?itn/index

Internet Travel Network is an "authorized World Wide Web interface to a national reservation system." That means by connecting to this site, you can research real time availability of airline seats or hotel rooms, and book your own reservation! Documentation and payment is then routed through a member travel agency in your area. Minimal on site registration is required, but there's no need for credit card numbers, and easy user directions are provided with hints on finding the lowest rates and fares (e.g. "Select '15 choices per leg'"). If nothing else, now you can confirm flight times and prices for yourself. We tried, and it works! At present, ITN is rather U.S. oriented, but they plan to expand. Check this out!

Walt Disney World
`http://www.disney.com/DisneyWorld/index.html`

Tomorrowland is here today at Disney World Online, Disney's official, sunny home page for the megalopolis theme park complex in Orlando, Florida. Those corporate elves know not all Web browsers can handle their intense colors, so the main graphics come to you in the black and white of a fresh coloring book. Click the "turn colors on" button to paint the picture in Technicolor. Kind of makes you feel like an animator. Oddly, though, there's no text-only version: If you can't view graphics, go home. If you can, the cute icons navigate you through the system: The snow globe takes you to park info pages, the guest book helps you make reservations at the park's hotels, the camera lets you download Quicktime VR movies of the parks, and the What's New clock guy tells you everything that's opened since your last visit. The icons are, we must admit, adorable little Disney characters themselves.

Virtual Mall

Branch Mall
`http://www.branchmall.com/`

One of the first malls on the Net, Branch has accumulated dozens of retailers but done little to beautify its digs: lots of gray space remains. Still, eight florists will sell you everything from orchids to miniature grapevines, while one hobby-department store offers personalized letters from Santa. E-mail your encrypted order, and you can buy Dolly Parton's autobiography. Or sign up for the Branch Mall mailing list, which announces special sales. Nostalgists may want to avoid The Fuller Brush company's slot, which announces that it's "cutting out the middle man." No Fuller Brush man?

Cybershop
`http://cybershop.com/`

This digital shopping mall injects an element that online shopping tends to lack: fun! (If you can make it through the elaborate-but-slow intro and registration process, that is.) Time spent registering here won't be wasted, as Cybershop puts your personal information to good use for a birthday greeting and reminders of your loved one's special days. The site promises "the ultimate shopping experience!" and we won't spend much time arguing with that. After browsing everywhere from home electronics to personal fitness, we nearly spent $2929 on Fischer-Price bedroom furniture—for kids we don't even have! Fortunately, the check-out point displays photos of and prices for everything—and a convenient, cart-emptying chicken exit. Cybershop may be more salesroom than playground, but it's well-organized, dazzlingly displayed, fully searchable, and extremely easy on the feet.

CyberTown
http://www.cybertown.com/

CyberTown is a huge shopping and services center that sprawls over the entire galaxy and across several centuries. Or perhaps it just seems to sprawl that far. The creators hope that CyberTown will become a central point for Web access and a sort of self-contained virtual village. By the look of things, they're well on their way. The graphic theme is space-age (the town is set in "the latter half of the 21st century"); so far most of the in-house stuff is shop storefronts, where you can in fact order things. But the site is linked "back in time" to our modern Earth and history resources, and plans are in the works for several interactive gizmos, like CyberHood, a virtual walk through the seedier side of CyberTown.

The Gigaplex!
http://www.gigaplex.com/

This "whopping 600-plus page Webmagazine devoted to arts and entertainment" definitely delivers the gigagoods: excellent coverage of film, music, food, theater, and photography, among other fields. The fabulous Filmplex offers Hollywood interviews galore with stars like Richard Gere (who tenderly reveals a moment when he and Jodie Foster watched the Oscars with friends, "lying on this bed . . . and throwing things at the screen"). Musicplex interviews Zubin Mehta and k.d. lang.

And the Theaterplex features excellent Q&A with movers and shakers of the stage like Terrence McNally and Anna Deveare Smith. There's even a YogaPlex! However subtly, some of these pages want to sell you something—A Hawaiian retreat, a photo-journalism book—which makes the Gigaplex part shopping mall, part magazine. And wholly entertaining.

Sports

Archery

Archery
http://www.stud.his.no/~morten-b/archery.html

This Norwegian site not only gives the basics of the bow and arrow sport, but a nice history of archery—including an overview of the Robin Hood legend. It would be a pretty big omission to skip history's most famous possibly fictional archer. The very fundamentals of the sport are here, too. There's more to bows and arrows than meets the eye. This rundown covers the three major types of bows, the latest in arrows (full carbon or aluminum-carbon compound—you be the judge) and other archery equipment. Yes, you do need more than a bow and arrow to be an archer these days. For those of a literary bent, the site includes a bibliography of archery books, magazines, and articles.

The Bowsite
http://www.netmart.com/plnet/bowsite/

The Bowsite claims to be the "largest and most comprehensive bowhunting site on the Web." We don't doubt it, even if the title is won almost by default. The main purpose of this site is to sell equipment and supplies for hunters who prefer to use a bow and arrow to fell their prey. Because this type of activity is fairly heavily regulated, Bowsite is packed with legislative information state-by-state, so you know you're not letting the arrows fly in violation of existing statute.

Kyudo: Japanese Archery
http://www.negia.net/~pdarden/

Japan's most ancient martial art? Not Karate. It's Kyudo, the Zen-influenced craft of shooting an arrow with a bow. This page, like Zen itself, has few frills. Basically one long download, it contains most everything a novice archer needs to know about this distinctly Japanese take on the sport. So Japanese that it is not really a sport. It's a spiritual quest using pure discipline—the object isn't to hit the target, but to see the target as a reflection of one's own mind. "When you release, you cut ego. You can see your own mind," says Japanese Master Kanjuro Shibata, quoted here. Enthralling stuff for Japanophiles perhaps even more than archers.

National Archery Association
http://www.USArchery.org/

If you're an American and you like to shoot bows and arrows—and what real American doesn't?—then you ought to consider signing up with the National Archery Association. Or at least checking out its Web site. This is the governing body of U.S. archery and their Web site is the best source on the Web for information and background on archery—a historical essay takes it back to the days of Mongol hordes—and what American wouldn't like to be taken back to the days of the Mongol hordes?—and up through the current Olympics. Also on the site, the NAA's two newsletters, "Nock-Nock" and, for kids, "The Edge." For non-archers there's a spectator's guide to the sport. Just stand behind the guy with the bow.

Associations and Organizations

IAAF—International Amateur Athletic Federation
http://www.iaaf.org/

Based in Monte Carlo, the IAAF governs the sport of athletics (track & field, road running, cross country, race walking) throughout the world. With an organization overview, their official home page serves up detailed news, events information, and athlete profiles. Find out who holds the Men's 800 meter world record (1:41.73 Sebastian Coe GBR 81), or compare the Top 10 women's half marathon marks this year and last. Training advances are detailed under "Science, Research, and Coaching," and don't miss the MPEG video of, for instance, triple jump technique tips from the great Jonathon Edwards.

Meanwhile, the Store promotes IAAF Magazine subscriptions with sample articles and photos. A fine athletics resource!

NCAA Online
http://www.ncaa.org/

While this official Web site of the (U.S.) National Collegiate Athletic Association serves up the requisite sort of bureaucratic and administrative stuff, their aim is to make it "one of your favorite stops for information about college athletics" in general. Coaches and member institution staff (serious fans, too) will appreciate an online edition of The NCAA News. Athletes can review eligibility and recruitment rules, or check to see how they stack up on the comprehensive statistics page. The NCAA Championships section is great for site and ticket information, or previews and results, say, of the Division III Women's Track & Field meet. Some areas were under construction on our last visit, but this promises to be an excellent resource on all levels of U.S. intercollegiate athletic competition.

NHRA Online
http://www.goracing.com/nhra/

The National Hot Rod Association (NHRA) is about drag racing. (It's also "the world's largest motorsports sanctioning body," for whatever that's worth.) With an organizational overview, their sporty Web site features news and results from the prominent Winston Cup Racing Series, access to the online edition of their National DRAGSTER magazine, and a multimedia gallery offering, for instance, hot rod video clips from the Atsco Nationals. Fans can also browse profiles of member race tracks, and top drivers like Cory McClenathan, Shelly Anderson, and Joe Amato. Worth visiting if you dig those top fuel dragsters, super stocks, alcohol funny cars, and such.

United States Swimming
http://www.usswim.org/

USS, Inc. is the sanctioned governing body for competitive swimming in the United States. For instance, they're in charge of determining and developing the U.S. Olympic men's and women's swim teams. In addition to a complete overview of the organization, their homepage is a wealth of swimming information, including a history of the sport ("The Assyrians showed an early breaststroke in their stone carvings"), diaries of U.S. Olympians, meet results, qualifying standards and lots more. There's a special Kid Pool here for the tadpoles, a searchable swim club listing, and (if you're really out of it) a primer on "What to Watch in a Swim Meet." Dominated by text, this is a good resource for athletes, coaches and parents.

Baseball

Akron Beacon Journal: Cleveland Indians

http://www.beaconjournal.com/

Forget news—Cleveland Indians' baseball is what's important. The entire Internet presence of the Akron Beacon Journal is devoted to coverage of the Tribe, baseball's long-forgotten stepchild. Visitors can find game stories, notes and photographs—some really good ones, by the way—along with a collection of columns by noted writer Terry Pluto. The coverage is the real thing, and some of the pictures are simply amazing. For the Cleveland faithful—especially outside Ohio—this is the site.

FASTBALL

http://www.fastball.com/

Major League Baseball junkies will love this page, featuring free access to the latest 1000 wire stories, "batter by batter" updated results, discussion areas for each team, and lots more. The site's creators, Cox Newspapers, Inc. assure us that "Fastball is entirely devoted to the off-season," so the site has plenty of photos, audio, and transaction news all year around. And no such archive would be as complete without a section on baseball wisdom, like Mike Lupica's theory that "October doesn't care what your name is" and relief pitcher Larry Anderson's existential query, "How come we drive on parkways and park on driveways?" This page has lots of hits and runs, few errors, and nobody left on base!

Japan Pro Yakyu This Week
http://www.towntv.co.jp/~westbay/

Michael Westbay's site is the best source on the Web for up-to-date Japanese pro baseball ("yakyu") news and statistics. Standings, batting and pitching leaders, play-by-play summaries of Japan Series games are all here. The most interesting stuff is Westbay's own writing, mainly derived from his translation of the national Japanese sports dailies (the country has seven). His six-part series on the short, troubled Japan career of Bobby Valentine, American manager of the Chiba Lotte Marines in 1995, is fascinating as much for what it reveals about the Japan-U.S. culture clash as about baseball. Westbay relies heavily on tables for his stats and standings, so those without table-capable browsers will have a hard time.

Skilton's Baseball Links
http://www.baseball-links.com/

Baseball fans will bookmark this page, created by fan John Skilton (holder of season tickets to the Wilmington Blue Rocks). The page itself is, of course, pinstriped. It's a solid collection of links to the national pastime on the Web: from ESPNet SportsZone to the Northern California Minor League Guide, to the Negro League Baseball Archive, to the Minnesota Twins and other individual franchises. Basically, if you don't want to bother with other sports, this is the place to come. This also is, mitts down, the best site for information on amateur baseball teams like the world-renowned Saugerties (N.Y.) Dutchmen. Merchandise, collectibles, and newsgroups round out the lineup. Grab a mouse and step up to the plate.

Basketball

College Basketball Page
http://www.onlysports.com/bball/

College hoop fans will find "the rock" at this page from Carnegie Mellon University computer science grad student Scott Reilley. Pizzazz here is inversely proportional to content; this site is not in the least fancy. From the Air Force "Falcons" to Wyoming's "Cowboys," dozens of men's and women's teams are included, with "The Prep Stars Recruiters Handbook," the NCAA Division III site (How about Capitol's lady "Crusaders?!?"), and more. We noted in recent rules changes that officials no longer have to raise one finger after a made free-throw. (We'd stop doing that too, if they'd only call a foul when the shooter gets hit!)

Kollege Sucks
http://www.kreft.net/home.html

This is the home page of Dan Kreft, an electrical engineering student at Northwestern University, and 7-foot member of the Wildcat basketball team. Dan claims that "disturbing people" is what he does best, but, if you can stand the Beavis and Butthead graphics, occasional condom-type jokes, and pictures of his shaved head, Kollege Sucks is really rather entertaining. Along with the usual sorts of personal favorite links and info, it features a candid, often satiric look at what it's like to play Big Ten hoops—click on the hypertext schedule for game by game diaries—and, if you've ever dreamed you have what it takes to play the game, don't miss "The Mouli Chronicles." If Dan Kreft is actually as deft with a basketball as he is with HTML, he'll be a force in the NBA!

NBA.com
http://www.nba.com/

Woo! The official NBA Web site is created by the Net-worthy Starwave Corporation, makers of ESPNET SportsZone, and we're here to tell you it's good. Newcomers can take a guided tour, running from the "Home Courts" (sanctioned pages of every team) to NBA Notebook ("a potpourri of league-wide notes and analysis"), through video highlights in the NBA Theater, and beyond. Here's also a fine Global Game section, featuring the likes of news in Spanish and French, Veltins Basketball Bundesliga standings, and NBA—FIBA rules comparisons. Meanwhile, Popeye Jones fans can review the exploits of their hero via NBA.com's complete individual player directory. A lively and generous resource for pro game enthusiasts.

On Hoops
`http://www.onhoops.com/`

Those who like their NBA updates in a humorous vein should proceed straight to this page, maintained by "Los Chucks," a couple of California guys with basketball joneses. News flashes such as "Terry Porter Joins Googs in Minnesota" are supplemented by "Stats, Stats, Stats!" (for the obvious and then some). Many other features include the Golden Chuck Awards (who'll be this year's "Bolted to the Floor" winner?), Dunks (open letters to Bernie Binkerstaff, etc.), and the Journeyman/Chump Register (Alan Ogg, Pete Meyers, and more). It's obvious the Chucks have lots of fun here, and so will other NBA fans.

Blading and Boarding

Flake
`http://users.aol.com/flakezine/fzine.html`

"Flake" calls itself the "world's only honest critique of advertising, marketing, and greed gone silly in the world of snowboarding." It also promises a monthly look at the "backstabbing, name-calling, and all-out-lack-of-talent that pervades the beast commonly known as the industry." Woo! On our last visit, the 'zine's Rant Fest section took aim at Olympic snowboarding in Park City, Utah ("Unless either the venue changes, or Park City begins allowing snowboarders at their resort, I will commence spreading as much negative publicity about the SLC Olympic snowboard events as possible"). Loads of links, as well as "Flake's" Snooze Paper, a regular roundup of new stories, press releases, and anything else found on the Net that's "remotely connected to snowboarding."

Hardcore Inline Skating
`http://www.aggressive.com/inline/`

As opposed to those satisfied by a leisurely Sunday roll, this page aims loads of info and images at aggro inline skaters. So naturally there's a detailed injuries section on everything from broken bone symptoms ("grating feelings/sounds") to care and prevention of rabies. Yet, on a positive note, skating trick how-tos are complemented by Quicktime videos of, say, "Arlo doing a half cab to farside soul on a rail." And along with reviews, professional info. Webmaster Justin Anderson failed a term paper to provide you with "Inline Flavored Prose, Poetry, and Other BS" (i.e. "Skategirls dodge floppy disks and fish heads on the streets . . . "). Good stuff for shredders and other extreme types.

Inline Online
http://bird.taponline.com/inline/

You could spend a long time at this site devoted to anything and everything having to do with inline skating, and probably not get to it all. The Tips section is filled with the wisdom of experienced skaters ("when I began attempting stairs backward, I found some shallow stairs—long, flat ones—about six steps deep, with a handrail . . . using the handrail for security saved my rear end repeatedly"). You'll also find links to an exhaustive list of the world's skateparks, inline magazines, organizations, and other Web sites. Don't miss the image of three Team Skydigger members catching air against a sunset.

New York City Inline Skating Guide
http://www.skatecity.com/NYC/

Well it's no secret they got plenty of pavement in the Big Apple, but where to rollerblade in Harlem? Riverbank State Park is not bad, suggests Robert B. Schmunk, maintainer of this comprehensive (if Manhattan-heavy) guide. It includes a legal section ($50 and a half day "sitting around in court" for skating the subway), info on rollerbasketball, JPEG maps, and the skate-hostility ratings of Greenwich Village cafes. Both newcomers and expert "bashers" will love this. Special bonus: Schmunk's Skating the Infobahn.

Cricket

CricInfo
http://www.cricket.org:8002/

Hey, the London Times said this site is "to Net Cricket as Project Gutenberg is to Net literature." They might get a little argument from The Wonderful World of Cricket, but with worldwide scores, stats, player profiles, and more presented through a tight graphic (or text) interface, CricInfo is certainly an excellent resource for fans, players, and officials. It features everything from statistical history to recent articles such as: "Apartheid Keeps on Batting Strongly" and "Hadlee—The Sultan Of Bowlers." A whole section is devoted to cricket humor (e.g. the ins and outs of "What is Cricket?"). The huge database is searchable, too.

Cricket World Monthly
http://www.cricketworld.com/

Easy for Americans to forget, if they ever knew in the first place, that cricket is one of the world's most popular sports. Hence, Cricket World, which sets out to cover the entire gamut of global cricketing, "from Punjab to Pudsey, Staten Island to Sutton, Brisbane to Bristol, Corfu to Catford." The current issue when we checked contained a section on "Continental cricket." Europe is not much more known for its cricketing prowess than is Staten Island, so Cricket World seems well on its way to fulfilling its wide-ranging promise. Features on various cricketers round out the magazine. On June 20, Cricket World even highlighted the first-ever live, online cricket interview, as India captain Mohammad Azharuddin gets his feet wet on IRC with reporters from Cricket World as his guides. The transcript of the interview remains on the site after the actual event, which took place during the Test at Lord's between England and India.

Ultra Cricket
http://diana.ecs.soton.ac.uk/~ta/uc_home.html

University of Reading chemist Tim Astley runs this fantasy cricket league which will expand to upwards of 250 teams in the coming season. Wow. To win this league, you really have to know your cricket. The refreshing aspect of Astley's play by e-mail league is that, though cricket is an esoteric sport outside of countries once ruled by Britain, Ultra Cricket doesn't appear to require an in-depth knowledge of cricket. Everything a cricketer from, say, the U.S. (which kicked out the British too early for the cricket craze to catch on) needs to know is right here on Astley's Ultra Cricket headquarters on the Web. So fill out your batting order, select your bowlers and start taking virtual wickets.

Wonderful World of Cricket
http://www.dcs.ed.ac.uk/home/sma/HTML/cricket.html

Expert batsmen, and strangers just wanting to know what the heck a wicket is, will find this cricket index worthwhile. Talk about a Spartan sport! "Thinker's Cricket Laws" state dispassionately that substitution is allowed "only for a player who satisfies the Umpires that he has become injured or ill during the match." (And we baseballers consider pitching a complete game a big deal.) In Rick Eyre's "Today In Cricket," we learned July 13th is the birthday of Ray "Candles" Bright, the legendary "slow-left armer" out of Australia. Or, to test whether you really know what this game is all about, see if the jokes in CricInfo set you to howling. Lots of links.

Cycling

Cyber Cyclery
http://cyclery.com/

"An Internet Bicycling Resource" is the subtitle of this site. Talk about understatement! It's a most excellent uber-index, serving up publications like Cycling Science, company pages, local bike shops from Kansas to Norway, you name it. Given a leisure readings section, maintenance tips, pointers to the likes of "Bicycle touring across Labrador," and on, the Activities Resources section alone would make a fine page. We can't say enough about what the rather anonymous Webmasters have assembled here, except check it out!

Mountain Biking
http://xenon.stanford.edu/~rsf/mtn-bike.html

For "Fat Tire Fotos," racing tips, club links, and the like, this is the place. Read trip reports from places like the Ho Chi Minh

Trail, where, "As an American in Lycra shorts and bright shirt on a fancy bike, you are constantly the center of attention." No doubt. Every month, this site features a different bike trail that includes riding directions and the kind of wildlife you'll see along the way (this is mountain biking, after all). The emphasis is on riding in the San Francisco Bay area, but you're not out of luck if you live in, for instance, Costa Rica. And those needing mechanical advice can "Ask Uncle Knobby" online. Be sure to check out "101 Tips That Don't Suck."

WOMBATS on the Web
http://www.wombats.org/

This WOMBAT is not a critter; it stands for WOmen's Mountain Bike And Tea Society. (Guess that sounded better than just WOMBS.) As the authors put it, "women have more obstacles than men to overcome when taking up the sport of cycling." Since 1984 this nationwide group (based in Fairfax, California) has been hitting the rugged trails; now they ride in cyberspace, too. Both informative and inspirational, this site provides plenty of know-how and support for women riders. Check the newsletter to see what's new with WOMBATS or visit a number of other links relating to women and cycling. This site has lots of great artwork (with speedy transfers), plus well-written think-pieces. And heck, the name WOMBATS itself is worth the visit.

The WWW Bicycle Lane
http://www.cs.purdue.edu/homes/dole/
bikelane.html

Purdue University graduate student Bryn Dole has assembled a fine index of Internet bicycling resources. Presented in frames, visitors can browse a seemingly exhaustive list of pointers via the middle frame, or, thanks to a clickable category outline on the left hand side, cut right to the chase. Speaking of categories, they include just about every one you could think of (e.g. magazines, companies, clubs, tours . . .), plus an especially strong list of advocacy groups, such as: "Bicycles—A Global Solution to

Local Problems" and "Bicycle Commuting, in the Bay Area."
Amid a number of extensive cycling indexes out there, this one
stands out for its efficiency, and should prove worthwhile,
whether you cycle competitively or simply for the fun of it.

Equestrian Sports

Cyberspace Racing Team (CRT)
http://207.137.115.250/

The Cyberspace Racing Team (CRT) could be a fantasy sports
league for horse race lovers—except that these folks actually
own the horses you learn about online. CRT is "a group of
over 30 internet users who are racing fans and aspiring owners
from all over the US and Canada who have formed a partnership." When last we checked, team members owned shares in
two Arizona-based racehorses, Snow Pack and Enliven Kleven,
and more horse purchases were in the offing. CRT's Web site is
a virtual racetrack, with photos and Quicktime clips of the
horses and their races, as well as audio bites of race calls.
Breeding background is covered on a pedigree page, while
those interested in joining the team can read a page by managing partner Toni Richardson with information for potential
investors. CRT partner Cindy Pierson created this site; she also
showcases her collection of racing postcards online at the
Racing Memorabilia Pages.

Hay.net
http://www.freerein.com/haynet/

Hay.net is a horse resource, of course, and one of the best on
the Web. Set up by Karen Pautz, who also edits the U.S.
Dressage Federation Web site, Hay.net delivers on its claim of
being "An Exhaustive List of Horse Sites on the Internet."
Subject listings include everything from Breeds and Associations
(for places such as the International Andalusian and Lusitano
Horse Association) to Veterinary Resources (for horse med sites
such as a Colorado State Bulletin on Collection and Transfer of
Equine Embryos). But Hay.net offers more than lists of links; it

also describes each area, so you know where your path is leading. Saddle-weary Web riders will want to bookmark Hay.net as a blue-ribbon index that offers useful needles of information along with its stacks of sites.

Racing Memorabilia Pages
http://www.wsnet.com/~sysclp/postcard.html

Cindy Pierson's Racing Memorabilia Pages are gloriously graphical collections of horse racing postcards and other memorabilia. The home page itself is pretty as a picture, with an antiqued background that begs you to scrawl "Wish You Were Here" all over it. Take "tours" of Pierson's postcards depicting famous horses, racetracks (many now gone) and horse farms, with background text such as this notation about racehorse Twenty Grand, "from Mrs. Payne Whitney's Greentree Farm, near Lexington, Kentucky, [who] came into first prominence in 1930 by setting a new mile record of 1 minute and 36 seconds. He won the Kentucky Derby in 1931. Soon after he went lame and never recovered. (postmarked 1943)." Pierson's Horse Racing Memorabilia Online Museum page, also at this site, showcases her other racing collectibles such as a Kentucky Derby clock and Preakness commemorative drinking glasses.

Thoroughbred Times On-Line
http://www.thoroughbredtimes.com/

This online version of the horse racing weekly Thoroughbred Times covers the racing world from nose to tail. Regular updates (daily and weekly) keep track of everything from stakes to sales reports; news and round-up pieces cover the stories big and small emanating from the racing world. Special features provide thematic coverage of major racing stories—"Racing to the Triple Crown," for instance, prances through its paces with pages on horses, breeders, jockeys, owners and other factors that tell the "story of the three-year-old Thoroughbred's tough road to racing's most coveted prize." The Connections page of links to other sites is a real winner, too, with resources on everything from Museums, such as Lexington's American Saddle Horse Museum, to Veterinary Resources.

Extreme Sports

PB's Triathlon Home Page
    http:// www.triclub.com

"PB" is Paul Wilson, an Australian ironman who intends for his site to be the Net's "biggest" triathlete's info source—a goal he may already have achieved. Whole sections are devoted to the Australian Triathlon Scene, Triathlons Abroad, and Ironman competitions. Training tips include a beginners zip file as well as John Walker's open water swimming guide. This lively index is also good for news, commercial resources like Quintana Roo (bike and wetsuit makers), plus individual triathlete page links.

Portland Marathon
    http://www.teleport.com/~pdxmar/

This complete and colorful electronic brochure provides a great overview of the Portland Marathon, which *Runner's World* called "the best people's marathon in the West(ern U.S.)." After previewing a graphic profile of the new "faster" course, visitors can download a registration form, check out a photo of the finishers' medals, for instance, and more. Beginners will appreciate info on the Portland Marathon Clinic, and, if 26 miles 385 yards isn't enough of a challenge for you, see the related events page for details on the "24 hour Ultra." Past results and other "Rose City" resources are also accessible.

Skydive Archive
    http://www.afn.org/skydive/

Here's a fine index of Web resources for those who would "slip the surly bonds of Earth." (Who wrote that darned "High Flight" poem, anyway?) With no duh! disclaimers such as: "The activities described on this page (VRW, Sitflying, Skysurfing) can be dangerous," you'll find John Leblanc's advice on "Flying and Landing High Performance Parachutes Safely," movies and pictures, a stolen gear list, and other neat stuff. Full text of the "relative work" classic "United We Fall" will inspire those who'd like to join hands up there. These links aren't presented with lots of flare, but site maintainer Bradley C. Spatz's discretionary time is probably better spent on packing his own canopy.

T@P Extreme Sports
http://www.xpcsports.com/

Part 'zine and part Web resource index, T@P Extreme Sports offers current and archived articles, plus links pertinent to skating, climbing, biking, ski and snowboarding. "Wendell's Edge" (column), for instance, is good for, say, a eulogy on "ski instructor, extreme freestyler, and friend Phil Gerard," while, in "Mountainbiking Winter Wimps," Joshua Fruhlinger discusses "the amazing studliness of East Coast riders." And for some exciting photos, check out the "Hairball Shot of the Week." Then, if you're inspired to great feats via pointers to the likes of Inline Online (skating 'zine), you can brag it up in the Extreme Chat forum.

Fantasy League

Fantasy Sports Interactive
http://www.cdmnet.com/fsi/home.html

So, you keep grousing that you can run a major league team better than the owners, eh? Well, time to put your money where your mouth is, bucko—Fantasy Sports Interactive takes the intellectual sport of fantasy sports leagues and raises it to the level of cash prizes. You can only enter before each sport's season, but you have five to choose from: football, baseball, hockey, basketball, and golf (yes, golf). After signing up and calling their 800 number to charge your entry fee (which can be hefty— $89 for the basketball league, for example), you can choose your teams and hope your players make it to the big time— and win yourself some big-time cash.

Nordic Dream League
http://www.fictionleague.no/

The craze for sports fantasy leagues is hardly confined to the U.S. Even Norwegian soccer fans get in on the act. Infinite A.S.

is Norway's first fantasy league company and they now take to the Web with a simulation based on the European Soccer championships (held in England in the summer of 1996). The catch: it costs money to play. About eight bucks in U.S. dollars. The upside: you can actually win money in this game. So, arm-chair managers, brush up on your soccer strategy and start counting that bankroll. Infinite A.S. plans to premier two new fantasy leagues once their Euro '96 simulation winds up—one based on the Italian League, another on the English Premier League.

Pro and Fantasy Football
http://www.best.com/~football/

Fantasy-league fanatics will enjoy frequently updated (free!) NFL statistics, injury lists, and more on this page. A complete draft list for 1995 included Steve McNair, Michael Timpson, Eddie Murray, and Walter Reeves—at the bottom of their respective positions. (Who's the QB, K, WR, and RB?) Features such as "Hot and Cold Players" will facilitate those shrewd midseason trades, and "The Way We Heard It . . . " offers the latest gossip from around the league, such as "that Bernie Parmalee will be the starting back for the Dolphins next Sunday." Links to other FFL and NFL sites as well.

TFL's Fantasy Football Report Service
http://www.tflreport.com/index.html

TFL claims to be "the strongest fantasy football information site available on the WWW," but a full subscription to their service will cost you money. Still, for free, we found NFL updates and rumors, such as this (from their department of redundancy department?): "49ers' second year man William Floyd apparently appears to be chiseled out of stone after reporting at 225-230 lbs. for this year's training camp." Steve Young and Dan Marino are #'s 1 and 2 respectively on TFL's Top 20 Fantasy League Draft list. Pay service includes weekly e-mail newsletters, injury reports, and the like.

Flying

Airship

http://spot.colorado.edu/~dziadeck/airship.html

We know you love blimps. Everybody does. And this page, which also hosts the Lighter-Than-Air Society, is just the place to find out anything you want to know about blimps, zeppelins, and other aerial creations. We all know about the Hindenburg accident in 1936 (you can hear a RealAudio recording of it if you don't), but did you realize that zeppelins had flown more than a million miles without one casualty before that episode? You'll find photos, history, even an incomplete schedule of locations where you can catch the Goodyear Blimp in action. The site isn't heavy on the graphics, but you can get them if you want. A lofty creation.

Sky Adventures

http://w3.ime.net/server/missing.shtml

Apparently, there are plenty of people out there who like hang-gliding and paragliding. Otherwise the list of sites here wouldn't be so big. Sky Adventures is a links page, but it's got gliding sites from Arizona to the Isle of Man. Visitors can find instructors (in case you actually want to learn about winging through the air before trying it) and tour home pages of hang-gliders like Bob Mackey, an electronic materials and processes Ph.D. student who has been hang-gliding since 1982. This looks like a great way to meet people who love to hang around in the air.

Smilin' Jack's Airport Page

http://www.inlink.com/~jack/index.html

This site, by Jack "Smilin' Jack" Irwin, boasts a wide array of links devoted to all things aviation. He flies for Trans-World Airlines (which, ironically, doesn't have a Web site yet), and the page starts with the pilot's checklist (cute touch). There's links to more than 60 airlines—well, if you count Starship Airlines, anyway—and a section devoted to aviation schools and other aviation-minded individuals. And no pilot would do well to ignore the weather, so there's a short list of sources to keep you flying.

Soaring Society of America
http://acro.harvard.edu/SSA/ssa_homepg.html

Almost 15,000 members strong, the Soaring Society of America promotes plane gliding and soaring, especially in the U.S., but also internationally. Their home page is filled with the sort of information that would interest, well, folks interested or involved in soaring. A clickable U.S. map will help you figure out where to go gliding in Alabama, say. The magazine article archive is also good for the likes of "How 'Frostbite' Ferguson Got His Name" by Tim Barr, which may provide discussion fodder for Bob Burchard's "Soaring: is it declining in popularity?" And if you want to hook up with gliding clubs or related Web sites, those opportunities are here too. A good take off point, maintained by ubiquitous aviation Webmaster Günther Eichhorn.

Football

Georgie's SCORE
http://www2.nando.net/SportServer/SCORE/users/
francisg.html

This branch of NandO's Sports Server offers the latest U.S. pro and college football updates in quick-hitting fashion. An exhaustive breakdown of NFL action—archived game stories, stats, quotes, and previews on each team—promises to put for pay fantasy football info services on waivers. Free registration is required for access to plentiful AP features such as: "Broncos' Backups Busy Boys." NCAA polls, game briefs, and conference breakdowns fill out the college portion of this gridiron info feast.

The National Football League Info Web
http://www.cs.cmu.edu/afs/cs/user/vernon/www/
nfl.html

Info Web is an easy way for fans to survey NFL sites on the Net. From "NFL Sidelines" (the league's official home page) to "Satish Nair's first round draft picks since the AFL-NFL merger" and Mark Gaither's "Pool Entry Form," it's an online gridiron extravaganza. The direct links to teams, newsgroups, etc., are so many woes to be heaped on football widows, who can now become Web football widows. Our sympathies to them, and a tip of the helmet to Webmaster Vernon Harmon.

Notre Dame Football
http://www.nd.edu/~ndsi/

From the Fighting Irish sports information department, here's history, news, and lots, lots more on the most successful college football program of the 20th century. You'll read about legends such as The Four Horsemen, Knute Rockne, and . . . Jamey Sotis of Prior Lake, Minn. (he's the leprechaun mascot). Full page spreads on each current player are included, with seven categories of Lou Holtz "philosophy," such as: "At most places, the football coach feels like a czar . . . Not at Notre Dame. I'm just here to keep an eye on things for a while."

Texas A & M Bonfire Page
http://entcweb.tamu.edu/camera.htm

Not to be outdone by The Trojan Room Coffee Machine, the Aggies of Texas A & M here provide live video coverage of the bonfire site symbolizing their "burning desire" to win the annual football game with arch rival U. of Texas. As of our last visit, the "build" was just about to begin (read: the main image was of an open field), but we're told thousands of fans per day (Aggie and otherwise) access the page from all over the world, leading up to a "frenzy" of visits during the actual burn of their six-tier, 5,000-7,000 log construction. Among other features, visitors can check out a (fast loading) past-photo archive, plus fascinating history, such as how the 1994 pyre collapsed and had to be re-built due to an 18-inch rainstorm. This page has college times written all over it.

Golf

The 19th Hole
http://www.sport.net/golf/

Here's some consolation if you're stuck at a computer terminal but long to be teeing it up. With pin placement by Texas golf enthusiast "Jimbo" Odom IV, the site offers complete tournament updates, player profiles, "Sandy Bunker's Golf Tips," etc. We like "The Golfers Wake Up Call," a comic strip created by a late-night person "inspired by my ability to get up at any hour to play golf and my inability to get up early to go to work." Sound familiar? Get golf updates during the big events and check out some of the golf jokes (gee, only a million or so) in the lounge. Southpaws may link to the National Association of Left-Handed Golfers, too. Unusual scorecard collection; good links to other "cool golf sites."

golf.com

http://www.gdol.com/

When your daily 18 holes just aren't enough and you still need to be the ball, check out golf.com. Produced in collaboration with Golf Digest magazine, GolfWorld, and NBC Sports, this is (ready for the inevitable pun) a comprehensive, colorful links index. With lowdowns on the PGA, LPGA, and Seniors tours, surfing duffers can access current golf publications, reports on classic courses like Riviera in Los Angeles (e.g. The second hole is a slight dog leg right, so the ideal t-shot is left of center and long), and, naturally, there's a virtual pro shop. Then, if you're one of those neophytes who still hasn't mastered the game, "Ask Jeff Maggert," and the pro will give you tips online, no charge! A well-groomed site that's well worth playing a around on.

GolfWeb

http://www.golfweb.com/

Having joined forces with Gold Digest, this site promises to be "the most comprehensive and entertaining World Wide Web golf resource." And we wouldn't argue. It's beautifully presented with photo-links to a Chicago golf guide, Eye Cue putter manufacturers, the winning scorecard from John Daly's final round at the 1995 British Open, and much more. And the coverage of major events like the Ryder Cup includes daily notebooks and photographs, making this site a must for fans frustrated by chintzy television coverage. A great feature is OnCourse, an index of more than 14,000 golf courses throughout the United States that includes comments from other players.

iGOLF—The Players' Exchange
http://www.igolf.com/

Interactive media and original editorials are here offered from the approach that: "In the days of King Arthur nobody thought the worse of a young knight if he suspended all his social and business engagements in favor of a search for the Holy Grail . . . Why, then, blame the man of today for a zealous attention to the modern equivalent, the Quest of Scratch?" iGOLF is part newsroom, part clubhouse, pro-shop, historical archive, and picture gallery. InterZine Productions' snappy layout serves up an interview with Ken Venturi readily as, say, the legend of Augusta National owing its existence to a fateful meeting between Alister Mackenzie and Bobby Jones, which would never have come about had Jones' not bombed out of the 1929 U.S. amateur at Pebble Beach. Whether you enjoy the game's sublime aspects, or just want a peek at the leader board, iGOLF is right on.

Great Outdoors

All Outdoors
http://www.alloutdoors.com/Default.html

Fishermen trolling the Web could do well to aim their virtual crankbaits toward this online hunting and fishing 'zine, whose depth is as impressive as any Michigan lake. A host of specialized mini-zines is at the Newsstand, and Adventure Travel features a nifty search engine for preparing traveling anglers and hunters. It isn't perfect, mind you—according to this there are no barracuda in Nevada. Still, this is a very current periodical, with plenty of discussion of hunting and angling news, gear, destinations and appropriate tips of the hat to tradition and good times.

Hiking and Walking Homepage
http://elaine.teleport.com/~walking/hiking.html

Here's a fine guide and info index for those who put one foot in front of the other for the pure joy of it. Via newsgroups and club links, it'll hook you up with walkers and hikers around the world, point to trails in Britain (or wherever), and allow you to order that reflective safety belt for those nighttime constitutionals. And there's soooo much more! For psychological insights, click on Connecting With Nature, and should the kids not share your volksmarch enthusiasm, read "Walking Without Whining," among other articles. The assemblers of this page evidently prefer to remain anonymous, yet they've provided pedestrians with an excellent resource.

Lou Bignami's Fine Fishing Magazine
http://www.finefishing.com/finefish2/

"Big" Lou commands the vessel, but he has lots of help from other writers to create this classy online fishing magazine. Lou's editorializing sets the tone for this 'zine, combining up-to-date knowledge of high-tech fishing wizardry with the "old school" philosophy of simplicity and sublimity. Fishing reports, articles, how-to guides on fishing techniques and a good bit of piscatorial humor offer a friendly helping hand to any fisherman, no matter how advanced. Beginners may be stymied with talk of nymphing ("just another form of fly-fishing") and Girdle Bitches, but keep reading and at least some things become clear. For those less interested in the act than in the meal, recipes and grilling hints are a regular catch here. This is an all-around fine fishing magazine, stocked with more than a day's worth of reading.

Rock 'N Road
http://www.rocknroad.com/

This site takes its name, and much of its elegantly searchable information, from rock climber Tim Tuola's book. Yet, more than text-based precipice primers, it features an interactive map of North America. Click California, or, for instance, Minnesota—a state not necessarily known for awesome crags ("roughly 50 lakes for every climbing area")—and you get guides to the likes of Shovel Point in Tettegouche State Park, complete with specs (e.g. Height: 100', Rock Type: Rhyolite), ratings, and directions. British Columbia, Alaska, and other regions, as one might imagine, are even more replete with helpful information. Scattered throughout to enhance the site are breathtaking photos and quips like: "It's not the high cost of living . . . it's the high cost of living high." With our only qualification being that it doesn't take the entire world into account, we'd agree that Rock 'N Road does indeed offer "Everything a climber could ever want . . ." from a Web site!

Hockey

The Goaltender Home Page
http://ucsu.colorado.edu/~norrisdt/goalie.html

These pages are devoted to "the most demanding position in the realm of sport"—the hockey goaltender. University of Colorado grad student Doug Norris (yes, he's a goaltender, but he's a roller hockey player who's just learning to ice skate) has created a superior resource that's a must-see for serious NHL fans. You can read about players like the often-stitched Terry Sawchuck, whose career almost ended on his 18th birthday in 1947 when he took a swinging stick in the eye. (Doctors said Sawchuck might not play again, but he was back on the ice in a month and was that year's top rookie in the United States League.) If you make your way to Norris's personal home page, you'll find the math student's own tables for rating the relative strengths of pro teams. Using the "Norris Power Indices," you can attempt to calculate the likely point spread of any NHL matchup.

Le Coq Sportif: Guide to Hockey
http://www.canadas.net/sports/Sportif/

This bi-weekly 'zine offers in-depth National Hockey League reportage on each and every team. After a little free registration, visitors gain access to current standings, boxscores, archived stats, and informative articles such as: "Obstruction Rule? What? Where?" Greats of the Game features profiles of rink luminaries like Terry ("The scars on his face said it all.") Sawchuck, and Hector "Toe" Blake—a great player for the Canadiens, before winning 8 Stanley Cups in 13 seasons as their head coach. Between regular issues, Web Extra serves up late breaking stickin' skater scoops. For breadth and quality of NHL coverage, Le Coq Sportif is well into a power play.

NHL Open Net
http://www.nhl.com/

The official Web site of the National Hockey League is the place for fans who prefer their statistics fresh and their HTML steaming. The NHL has unleashed a sizzling Web experience, with end-to-end Netscape-compatible frames technology and hard-hitting RealAudio sound bites of those players who always seem to give "110 percent." You'll find some interesting PR on the league's Nike-sponsored NHL Youth Street Hockey program and a celebrity All-Stars squad that gets actors such as Jason Priestley of TV's "90210" on the ice. But the real star here is what the NHL has more of than anything else: statistics. First there are all the ways you can examine the current-season standings, including a look at each team's performance at home and on the road. Then there are historical stats, such as the end-of-season standings for every year since 1917 and the names of all 304 inductees to the Hockey Hall of Fame. This is a big site from a team of webmasters who clearly like to give 110 percent.

WWW Hockey Guide
http://www.hockeyguide.com/

As a jumpstation for sources of hockey news and information on the Web, Joe Tremblay's WWW Hockey Guide has all the angles covered. Visitors will find one of the most comprehensive collections of links to amateur, NHL, and international hockey resources on the Net. For example, the entry for the NHL's Colorado Avalanche (the former Quebec Nordiques) includes links to the Nordiques Usenet newsgroup, the club's official WWW site and the pages of fans Darrin Jeffers and Peter Forsberg. And then there are Avalanche links to the big sports network sites as well. You'll be taking a breather on the bench before you're halfway through this big site.

Ice Skating

Amateur Speedskating Union of the United States
http://web.mit.edu/afs/athena.mit.edu/user/j/e/jeffrey/speedskating/asu.html

The ASU is "the grassroots, non-profit, national organization that regulates speedskating throughout the (U.S.)," and its Web site features access to a clubs and associations network spanning the country from California to Maine. With a directory of competitions that also includes Canada, they promote speedskating as "a sport for everyone!" Anyone who's never set blades upon one of those distilled ice Olympic-type courses will learn, too, that conventional indoor rinks are well suited to short track speedskating, where packs of four to six athletes attain speeds of up to 35 mph, and negotiate the turns leaning at a 65-degree angle. (Have you imagined such "furious and exhilarating" action since Roller Derby?) This hypertext introduction to the sport may prove worthwhile to veterans as well.

A Canadian Figure Skating Page
http://www.skate.org/can/

Thanks in large part to the Tonya and Nancy sideshow of a few years back, the popularity of figure skating's gone through the roof. And, as evidenced by this site, Americans certainly don't have a corner on the market. Here, you'll get the low-down on Canadian stars like Kurt Browning, Elvis Stojko, Brian Orser, and Elizabeth Manley. In addition, you'll find a calendar of upcoming figure skating competitions, tours, shows, and exhibitions. Most fun, though, is the exhaustive list of skater biographies. Also includes a list of agents, fan clubs, and training rinks for several skaters.

The Figure Skating Page
http://frog.simplenet.com/skateweb/

Yale U. research programmer Sandra Loosemore has, indeed, created the Figure Skating Page for fans and skaters alike. It's a comprehensive e-index, offering access to stars such as Oksana Baiul and Elvis Stojko (their Web sites and addresses, anyway), as well as technical skating resources, ticket information, the Ames (Iowa) Figure Skating Club, you name it. And after browsing a historical photo archive, clue in to Tonya Harding's Top 10 Excuses (thanks to Dave Letterman). This is also a good starting point for artistic roller skating and other skating forms.

A Kurt Browning Fan Page
http://www.skate.org/browning/

Forget all those goofy ice skating shows that are currently airing on network TV. This site contains so many images and movies of Canadian skater extraordinaire Kurt Browning that you'll feel like you're actually rinkside. Here, you'll find photos of Browning performing and chatting with other skaters, as well as Quicktime movies of him doing a double axel and triple toe loop/triple toe loop combination. Also includes information about his biography "Forcing the Edge," his television work, and his competitive history and record. Links to other ice skating-related sites.

Miscellaneous

Colorado Boomerangs
http://pd.net/colorado/

It's not surprising that Colorado Boomerangs is a company in Colorado that makes boomerangs. What is surprising is that their Web presence is a great use of the Internet to promote a product. Along with a well-presented catalog of their wares (every one guaranteed to return), the site provides a complete tutorial on throwing and links to other boomerang-related resources on the Net. Not in the market for a boomerang? Visit just to marvel at all the variations on the classic V-shaped boomerang, including the "Delicate Arch" and "Kilimanjaro."

Juggling Information Service
http://www.juggling.org/

Juggling (de Jonglage to you Francophiles) takes center stage at this mesmerizing site. Who knew there was so much juggling on the Internet? For that matter, who knew that juggling was so complicated? Browse through some back issues of "Juggler's World" or maybe step into the picture gallery, where you'll see a shot of Felix the Cat juggling four mice. You'll also find links to the homepages of jugglers around the world. One can even buy juggling software with features like per-hand dwell ratio control and pattern change control with history browser. Woo!

We're still just trying to keep from dropping the oranges. This breezy page delivers the goods without losing a sense of fun; don't be surprised if your mood is altered. And pass the oranges.

Martial Arts Resource Site
http://www.floor6.com/MARS/MARS.html

Webmaster Stacy Behrens of Lehigh University got tired of repeatedly hunting down martial arts texts and information; so he's assembled everything ever published on the subject, and made it available here. Okay, maybe not everything, but we're here to tell you this straight HTML site is loaded with enough stuff to transform martial arts enthusiasts (pick a style, any style) into virtual black-belts and Ph.D.s. That includes everything from "What is Wing Chun?" (hint: not a rock group) to classical e-texts such as Sun Tzu's "The Art of War," essays on ki breathing, "The Art of Making Mistakes," even "The Difference Between Karate and Sex." (Simpler costumes?) Admirably thorough, with pointers to newsgroups and related sites as well, this is definitely a collection to flip over.

Schneid's Volleyball Page
http://www.xnet.com/~schneid/vball.shtml

If there's a more complete volleyball Web page than what the otherwise anonymous Schneid has put up . . . well, that's not likely, or maybe even possible. With text links listed over blue background, it's not fancy, but talk about extensive! Here are enough diagrammed offensive & defensive schemes, drills (e.g. Four Person Pepper, Setter Triangle, Chaos . . .), and skill primers ("Basic Attack Footwork" by Tom Wilson . . .) to turn a novice Web surfer into a wise old coach. Check out reviews of the best balls, ankle supports, and other equipment, or, for fun, Mark Theissen's volleyball action photo portfolio. Then it's back to business with more nutrition, fitness, and sports medicine resources (e.g. Jump Training and Plyometrics, The Anterior Cruciate Ligament Page) than a body has a right to free of charge. An excellent site for coaches, volleyball players, and fitness enthusiasts in general!

Motor Sports

The Karting Web Site
```
http://www.callamer.com/~pete/karting/
index.html
```

Here's access to practically everything you could want to know (or at least all that's available on the Web) about karting—that miniature sort of Indy Car-like racing, in which pre-teens as well as 39 year old Webmaster Pete Muller are eligible to participate. Assorted FAQs serve as a good introduction to the sport, while tech articles (e.g. "Tecumpseh vs. Briggs Raptor"), race news & schedules, plus classified ads should interest veterans of the tracks. Hey, there's even a section on Karting Humor, which doesn't include Charlie Tackett's article on "The Danger of Long Hair"! Frequently updated with good reading and networking resources for wannabe karters as well as seasoned enthusiasts.

NASCAR Online
```
http://www.nascar.com/
```

Produced by Starwave (of ESPNET SportsZone fame), this official National Association for Stock Car Auto Racing (NASCAR) site is a news & features trove for the Winston Cup, Busch, and Craftsman Truck Series. Each team has its own dedicated page; Wally Dallenbach and other drivers are known to stop by for online Q & A; and the NASCAR Theater offers exciting sights (video) and sounds, for instance, of Terry Labonte holding off teammate Jeff Gordon to win the First Union 400. Step into the Garage for racing perspectives from "under the hood," or check out the Store to order Jeff Gordon caps and other sanctioned merchandise. A complete resource for fans, presented with flair to spare.

PPG Indy Car World Series
```
http://www.indycar.com/
```

Fans of the PPG (Pittsburgh Plate Glass Co.) Indy Car World Series circuit will be hard pressed to find a more informative Web site than this one. It's also quite interactive. Schedules include ticket info and pointers to various racetracks from Cleveland to Queensland, while there are enough individual driver and team profiles to wear out the tread on your mouse. That's not to mention all the salable Indy Car merchandise, accessible newsgroups, and so on. Done up in mostly black and blue, these pages are pretty to look at too.

RaceNet

http://www.primenet.com/~bobwest/index.html

Motorsport fans will appreciate this fan site's full field of auto racing features. It begins with a photo archive, including the "Damn Yankee 'Cuda Funnycar'" and "Start of the 1966 Le Mans 24 Hours." We went right to the "Racing Freebies" section, where we learned that some of the stuff required a toll call (geez!). If you're ears are a little too sensitive for the raceway, you can sample the "awesome" sound of Bobby Unser's Hotel Tropicana Special Novi during qualifying for a past Indy 500. There's trivia (John Surtees was the first Can-Am Champion) and retrospectives on classic drivers like Juan Manuel Fangio and A.J. Foyt. An exhaustive list of related links include "FerrariNet" and "Formula One On-Line." Fresh rubber all around.

Olympics

6th Games of the Small
European States

http://www.restena.lu/jpee/p1.html

How the heck are San Marino and Liechtenstein supposed to compete against Germany, Russia, and the United States in any sport? (One word: steroids.) In lieu of illegal drugs, however, these small guys get together in their own competition. This site—in Luxembourg, like the 6th edition of the games themselves—has all of the information about competitors, schedules, and records. But you gotta feel for San Marino and Liechtenstein—they're hard pressed to compete with Cyprus and Iceland, too.

Britannica Sporting Record:
The Olympic Games
http://sports.eb.com/

Thanks to the folks at Encyclopedia Britannica, here's a complete Olympics information resource. While limited to the summer games as of our last visit, a winter edition is in the works. In addition to an Olympic overview article written by 1924 gold medalist (and main Chariots of Fire character) Harold Abrahams, fans get background on each sport, biographies of competitors ranging from Mohammad Ali to Lyudmila Turishcheva, plus the complete results of every event contested since the modern era began in 1896. The database is elegantly searchable (e.g. by countries like Cote d'Ivoire, or individual athletes such as Carl Lewis), making this a virtually indispensable Olympic almanac.

The Olympic Movement
http://www.olympic.org/

This is the official Web site of the International Olympic Committee (IOC)—the umbrella organization which serves as "supreme authority" over the Summer and Winter Olympic Games. (They're also the ones who sold out the amateur ideal, allowing professionals to compete, but we'll grind our axes elsewhere.) In addition to a complete overview of the IOC and its subsidiary organizations—collectively known as the Olympic Movement—this is a place to check out pertinent news releases, grandiose mission statements and all manner of other official stuff. For fun, follow links to future Olympic sites in cities like Sydney and Salt Lake, or virtually tour the Olympic Museum in Lausanne, Switzerland. And be sure to catch that rousing Olympic theme music by clicking on the flaming torch.

Sydney 2000 Olympic Games
http://www.sydney.olympic.org/

It's not too early to make plans for the first Olympics of the third millennium. (Or the last one of the 20th century, if you're one of those stick-in-the-muds who insist the 21st century doesn't begin until 2001.) This is the official Web site for these summer games, which might rather be called "early spring" games, as that'll be the season from Friday 15 September to Sunday 1 October 2000 in Sydney, Australia. While it will no doubt develop as schedules and facilities take shape, this site already offers overviews of plans for, say, the Olympic Stadium (within walking distance of the Olympic Village), as well as detailed fact sheets on everything from the Sports (a first triathlon will be contested) to Travel and Freight Grants. Also, given Australia's proximity to the ozone hole and genuine conscientiousness, here's an inspiring Environmental Guidelines feature.

Personal Fitness

The Body Project
http://www.bodyzine.com/

Intended "to provide a symposium of information on the human body," with an eye toward foiling health industry hucksters, this 'zine offers articles and features on physical fitness and overall wellness. A recent issue included interesting food facts from consumer activist/nutritionist Keith Klein, such as that "bugs are in almost everything you eat!" (He allays our fears too, though.) That was in addition to discussion on the amazing health benefits of garlic (with recipes), an interactive Fat Loss Forum, Phil Kaplan's guide to cycle training, and a carrot-in-front-of-nose photo gallery featuring Arnold Schwarzenegger and other "fitness models." A generous read, with past issue archives, "FitLinks," and desktop shopping too.

Fitness Partner Connection Jumpsite
http://primusweb.com/fitnesspartner/

Two personal trainers and a computer nerd—er—a Web page expert created this index of over 450 links to exercise and wellness sites. Those are categorized under Training & Sports, Nutrition & Health, Publications, and on. A Plyometric FAQ (under Strength & Bodybuilding), for instance, included exercises for increasing vertical leaping ability, and there's even a link to the Skydive Archive—hence the "Jumpsite" pun. Beyond brief annotations for so many pointers, you won't find lots of original content here. Yet, for fitness buffs it should make a fine bookmark.

LifeMatters
http://lifematters.com/

A group of licensed marriage and family therapists in California pooled their backgrounds in counseling, biofeedback, physical education and T'ai Chi to create this forum for you who'd take responsibility for your own health and well-being. Articles and discussion areas are smartly presented on a variety of topics. Those include personal fitness, community relations, parenting and those other kind of relationships—namely, the ones that spawn sayings like: "You can't love someone else unless you love yourself first." Another series of articles, for instance, explores the "Mid-Life Transition." Empowering stuff here, for averting crises and taking charge of one's existence.

Weightlifting Page
http://www.cs.unc.edu/~kyle/weights.html

Who could ignore references from Benjamin Franklin and Thomas Jefferson? These American luminaries both, in their own way, promoted a "strong body." This particular page is a cross between a fanzine and a how-to guide. For the novice, we recommend "Zen and the Art of Weightlifting," which explains that lifting weights won't automatically make you a Greek god or goddess. That takes "years of training, gallons of chemical aids and dietary arrangements that would make most normal humans blanch," Kyle Wilson writes. The results can be impressive, as seen in the many photos here. And instead of strictly weightlifting links, the site includes fitness, nutrition, and general health. Those sculpted figures on the cover of Flex aren't that unfamiliar; with a little work, you could be there, too. (OK, a lot of work.)

Running

Dr. Pribut's Running Injuries Page
http://www.clark.net/pub/pribut/spsport.html

Runners suffering maladies from plantar fasciitis to simple over-training will appreciate the insights offered in this virtual diagnosis/treatment manual. Author Stephen M. Pribut is a podiatrist, so feet get lots of the attention, but a quick once over the HTML home page should point you toward pertinent information on common running ailments in the knees, ankles, and other areas. Biomechanic vernacular (e.g. during the mid-stance subphase, "the leg is externally rotating and the foot is supinating at the subtalar joint") can be daunting, but hey, so is running a marathon!

Internet Resources for Runners
http://www.nauticom.net/users/kenecon/

Here's a virtual community for amateur runners: that is, those who pick 'em up and put 'em down for the pure love of it. A snazzy interface (with room for advertisers) serves up for sale running gear (e.g. the Dor Sew Bug Free Shirt), along with pointers to clubs, newsgroups, and racing info. Labeled skeletal muscular system and foot structure graphics support the Injuries Resource Library, while access to the likes of Train Right (coaching software for Windows) and Runner's World magazine is also provided. An excellent index!

Portland Marathon
http://www.teleport.com/~pdxmar/

This complete and colorful electronic brochure provides a great overview of the Portland Marathon, which Runner's World called "the best people's marathon in the West(ern U.S.)" After previewing a graphic profile of the new "faster" course, visitors can download a registration form, check out a photo of the finishers' medals, for instance, and more. Beginners will appreciate info on the Portland Marathon Clinic, and, if 26 miles 385 yards isn't enough of a challenge for you, see the related events page for details on the "24 hour Ultra." Past results and other "Rose City" resources are also accessible.

Runner's World Online
http://www.runnersworld.com/

Runner's World monthly's excellent electronic edition is great for pertinent daily news updates, an articles archive, plus assorted other worthwhile features. Those include a shoe buyer's guide (where you can determine your foot type), training tips such as "Fat-Burning Workouts," and interesting nutrition advice on, conversely, say, the benefits of "Fat As Fuel?!" There's a special Women's Running section, and an interactive forum for sounding off on everything from Lasse Viren's Olympic Gold Races to how many miles your pair of Nike Air Triax lasted before the heel blew out. Competition info and a directory of related sites make this a complete resource (which they hope to keep free of charge!) for fitness enthusiasts.

Shooting

Sporting Adventures
http://www.spav.com/default.html

For fisherfolk, hunters, and other outdoor sportspeople, here are various resources to facilitate your next adventure. Those include an online store selling Fenwick and Penn products, and a searchable lodge/guide service database featuring over 1400 options—from East End Waterfowling (not to be confused with East River water fouling) in New York State to (we're not kidding!) deep sea fishing out of Deadwood, South Dakota. The Launchpad to related sites is also good, but a nominal membership fee is required for complete access here, such as to hundreds of JPEG photos, and "Tall Tales" of some guy landing a 10-pound rainbow trout.

Ultimate Weapons Systems
http://www.uws.com/

They bill these "tactical weapon" sales as suited to law enforcement, but the page seems aimed less at police than at those who'd like to take law into their own hands. Still, they have quite an amazing selection. The online catalog is rife with rifles and stocks and scopes, plus accessories such as flash suppressers (always essential to self-defense). Video tapes for order include

"Rock 'n' Roll #3 Sexy Girls and Sexy Guns," the "John Shaw Combat Shotgun Seminar." We feel safer already!

United States Practical Shooting Association
http://www.uspsa.org/

"Diligentia, Vis, Celeritas" (Accuracy, Power, Speed) is the motto of the USPSA, an official organization for governing and promotion the unabashedly macho sport of practical shooting. Its site has general information about this pursuit, which tests "the ability to use a pistol in its primary intended purpose of self-defense." The how-to pages here detail the sort of skills you'd expect James Bond to have: there are pointers on Gun Grip, Body Position, Eye Dominance, and the like. An extensive list of links to local organizations for practical shooters includes groups from Texas to Thailand (really!); you can also check here for the dates, locations, and results of major practical shooting matches.

Skiing

Cross-Country Ski World
http://www.weblab.com/xcski/

Cross-Country Ski World may be the ultimate source of Nordic skiing information on the Web. The site is hosted by Web Engine Laboratories of Mountain View, California, but it's really a collaborative work harnessing the efforts of cross-country buffs throughout North America — most of them fans of competitive skiing. Visitors will find the latest results from important U.S. and international races, and the site's X-C Ski Education Journal is billed as "the definitive resource for high-end skiers and ski educators." In a recent edition, former U.S. ski team coach John Estle recalls the history of the "skating" stride that has changed the face of competitive cross-country skiing. (Unlike some commentators, Estle doesn't give former U.S. Olympic medalist Bill Koch all the credit for developing the ice-skating-like stride that now dominates the sport.)

GoSki!
http://www.goski.com/

This "ultimate snow sports guide" is one of the more complete ski and snowboard resources we've seen. Its Global Resort Directory allows you to search out, say, helicopter skiing accommodations in New Zealand, while a Nordic link will point you toward a page devoted to cross-country skiing around Madison, Wisconsin. The latest snow conditions are reported here, with embellishments like "almost live" weather-cam shots from Crested Butte, Colorado. Electronic Editions' interface does a swell job of managing all this stuff, including shopping opportunities, user contributed reports and reviews, and advice from "experts" (e.g. a moto-skier, a proud papa, an aviator, and a snowman!). This is a great stop for those who'd otherwise be "shredding" the Web for such resources.

SkiNet
http://www.skinet.com/

When you're the publisher of magazines whose titles, like Ski and Skiing, are nearly as indistinguishable as their contents, it makes sense to combine the two to create one big snowbound destination on the Web. Times Mirror Magazines may be trying to increase circulation of the paper versions of these publications, but there's no skimping on the information available here for free. A survey of gourmet kitchens at ski resorts across North America puts Deer Valley, Utah, at the top of the list. Those who actually ski will find training tips and product reviews (the heated ski socks seemed like a good idea) culled from the magazines. What you can get here that you can't get in the printed versions, however, are the up-to-date reports on snow conditions at major ski centers.

SnoWeb
http://www.snoweb.com/

This page "for skiers by skiers" is a fine worldwide guide. You can peruse the e-version of Alpine World Magazine, get rental info on a Tyrolian Village cabin, plan runs on a map of

Kittlefjall in Sweden, or order a discount lift ticket card electronically . . . and that's just among the first four menu items! Can't figure out what to do during the summer months in Europe and the United States? A link reminds you that when it's summer north of the equator, it's winter in places like South Africa, where you'll find Tiffindell Ski and Mountain Resort. We also found links to the Mount Hood Academy for racers, Chile's Villarica-Pucon resort, and even Buck Hill, featuring a 309 foot vertical drop just a few miles south of Minneapolis! It's, well, cool.

Soccer

eurosoccer.com
http://www.eurosoccer.com/

England's Guardian newspaper and the commercial sponsors of the 1996 European soccer championships present this definitive site for the biggest show in the sport outside of the World Cup itself. Not only is the massive site made easy to navigate, but just in case you still can't figure it out there's a whole page explaining how to get around. The heart of the site is the Guardian's daily (yes, daily) magazine with all of the latest Euro soccer dope. The site even includes up-to-date betting odds (Italy remained the favorite at 5-1 when we put our money down). This one's a must-bookmark for soccer nuts.

Mark Wheeler's U.S. Soccer Page
http://www.cs.cmu.edu/~mdwheel/us-soccer/

This page "for soccer fans by soccer fans" is excellent! You'll find data on Americans playing abroad, the Women's World Cup, a "way cool" US Soccer Fanzine, and many other links. Covers various levels of play, too. Did you know that six professional soccer leagues operate in the United States? No? Then we'll list them . . . just kidding. Among the great links is a list of the top male and female high school players and what colleges they chose to attend. The unofficial fan club of the U.S. team, called "Sam's Army," can tell you what hotels the team stays at when it travels. Other fans will appreciate the list of "Pubs in US and Canada which show LIVE English soccer." Use of hands is permitted to applaud this fine site.

Soccer America Online
http://www.socceramerica.com/

The most established American soccer magazine goes digital here. 25-year-old Soccer America is the best and maybe the only periodical source of info on the U.S. soccer scene. Stateside soccer, contrary to what the rest of the soccer-watching world might think, is highly active, albeit a little ragged. The U.S. has not one but five count 'em five professional soccer leagues (including the nascent Major League Soccer, which is set to start play in 1996). Of course, three of them play the indoor version of the game, designed to quench the American craving for high scoring. In any case, Soccer America covers them all in its Web version, along with the various U.S. national teams (men's, women's, Olympic, etc.) and collegiate soccer.

Soccernet
http://soccernet.com/

With the resources of England's Daily Mail newspaper, Soccernet is perhaps the definitive site for Premier League coverage. The Mail updates the site every day with news and gossip emanating from each of the Premiership's 20 clubs, plus all of the necessary match reports and club histories. If you like British sarcasm, you'll enjoy weekly columns by insufferably dry correspondent James Foulerton. For devotees of English football, Soccernet is the equivalent of ESPN Sportszone—without the subscription fees.

Sports News and Information

ESPN SportsZone
http://espnet.sportszone.com/

Dah duh DOM! Dah duh DOM! Okay, there's still no catchy theme music, but cable sports colossus ESPN (in cahoots with Starwave Communications) has tossed up a state-of-the-art complement to your daily sports page. (Sure, it used to be free, but as they added extra stuff (like more columnists, AP photos and better NFL previews), the word "subscription" started popping up for complete access. Still, most of the stuff sports fans want is still free: photos of Steffi Graf jumping into her serve at Wimbledon, late-breaking hockey stories, boxscores, and more. The page also offers regular columns from anchor Keith Olbermann, sports nut Frank Deford, and others. As announcer Dan Patrick says of a swished jump shot, SportsZone is . . . Good!

The NandO Sports Server
http://www.nando.net/SportServer/

For a look at today's starting pitchers, "baseline to baseline coverage of the pro tennis circuit," Indonesian Open semi-final badminton results, and oh so much more, explore this mega-hyper-sportspage from the Raleigh News and Observer. Though you'll have to register for access to some links, if it happened on the field, court, or rink, you'll find at least a recap here. "Ghosts of Basketball Server Past" revealed to us, among other brilliant images, a photo of Randolph Childress stealing the rock from North Carolina A & T's Phillips Allen during the 1995 NCAA Tournament. Other cool stuff: great Associated Press stories and pictures, and "In the Press Box," a collection of columns and reader e-mail. This page is a bona fide contender for ESPN SportZone's heavyweight belt!

NASCAR Online
http://www.nascar.com/

Produced by Starwave (of ESPNET SportsZone fame), this official National Association for Stock Car Auto Racing (NASCAR) site is a news & features trove for the Winston Cup, Busch, and Craftsman Truck Series. Each team has its own dedicated page; Wally Dallenbach and other drivers are known to stop by for online Q & A; and the NASCAR Theater offers exciting sights (video) and sounds, for instance, of Terry Labonte holding off teammate Jeff Gordon to win the First Union 400. Step into the Garage for racing perspectives from "under the hood," or check out the Store to order Jeff Gordon caps and other sanctioned merchandise. A complete resource for fans, presented with flair to spare.

World Wide Web of Sports
http://www.tns.lcs.mit.edu/cgi-bin/sports

It ain't too pretty, but the Webmasters at M.I.T. have created an oh so extensive and efficient index of the Net's sports resources. We're talking straight HTML presentation of many categories, yielding plain vanilla links to a multitude of sport sites. Diversity of coverage is what makes this page stand out from its counterparts, however. Fans can customize it to suit their interests, which could range from NBA basketball (come on, let's get creative!) to fishing, sports software, kite flying, rodeo, even jump rope! If it even remotely qualifies as a sports page, chances are you can get there from this excellent and searchable index.

Tennis

Corel WTA Tour
http://www.corelwtatour.com/

Corel (a computer graphics and CD-ROM company) is the title sponsor of the Women's Tennis Association tour, and this page serves up a complete guide thereon. On the front page, a sensitive (stadium) graphic invites you, say, to click the Gabi Sabatini picture for an exhaustive list of player bios, while related tennis links, stats, ticket & scheduling information are also available. With the other pages popping up in frames, and so much promotional material mixed in here, the overall effect is a bit too busy. (For instance, the News section recently touted Web site awards alongside a report from the French Open.) Still, fans and even journalists should find this a serviceable resource on those elite female racqueteers.

Tennis FAQ
http://www.mindspring.com/~csmith/
TennisFAQ.html

Thanks to its maintainers at Georgia Tech University, the Tennis FAQ will satisfy those in search of specific information on a range of the sport's prominent issues. Those include everything from who won the 1973 Wimbledon Men's Singles title (some guy named Kodes), to considerations for buying a new racquet, tennis elbow alleviation tips (e.g. "Relearn your strokes to remove 'wristy-ness'"), and way beyond. Find out how to rate your ability level on the USTA scale, and, yes, (finally!) here's an explanation of that crazy love, fifteen, thirty, forty scoring system! A good players' and professional fans' resource.

The Tennis Server
http://www.tennisserver.com/

The Tennis Server helps players "go to the Net" for all manner of tennis information and equipment. As a hyper-index for the well-strung faithful, it enthusiastically covers the entire court, so to speak, with news from the professional tours, rules, instruction, and lots more. Visitors can read exclusive columns on, say, "Attentional Control In Tennis," while Pete Sampras and other such players occasionally stop by for some interaction. Then, should you be in the market for another racquet, or, say, an accessory to hang your camcorder on the fence for post-match self-video-analysis, the Tennis Warehouse boasts an exhaustive inventory at the "absolute lowest prices anywhere."

Tennis Web
http://www.tennisw.com/tweb

While the original content score is still at love, when it comes to comprehensive WWW tennis indexes, we're talking game, set, match to Tennis Web! Whether you want to learn the rules, build a court in the backyard, check out a favorite college team, or join the Monica Seles fan club ... ready access is offered to a gamut of resources. Okay, that's except for "Restringing & Repair," plus a couple other categories that had yet to be filled in on our last visit. Then again, they make up for a few unforced errors with links to, say, "Tennis in Salzburg," shopping opportunities, Tennis Worldwide magazine, and more.

Water Sports

Global Oceanic Surf Links
http://magna.com.au/~prfbrown/tubelink.html

Some folks in Australia have done it ... created the definitive (real, as opposed to Net) surfing index, that is. It's beautiful, with scores of links listed under Southern Planetary Regions, Central Pacific Ocean, US East Coast, etc. It's all here, from the story of Mark Foo's Last Ride, to Nancy Emerson's Maui surfing school, Swedish Surfnet, shops, and beyond. Environmentalists will find plenty of interest, as well as poetic types who would consider the very "Nature of Surf" itself. We'll leave out "dude" and "totally," just to say it's awesome.

Mark Rosenstein's Sailing Page
http://community.bellcore.com/mbr/
sailing-page.html

Mark Rosenstein produces this premier example of a maritime page, the ultimate nautical site for sailing information. It's mostly a list of hypertext links to sites having anything remotely to do with ships and sailing. When Rosenstein can't find resources elsewhere on the Net, he archives it himself, storing everything from maritime history documents to boat design and online sailing texts. You'll even find resources on "land yachting" for users prone to seasickness. News of current and upcoming sailing races keeps it all fresh. Even if you don't sail, you can have some fun: visit the signal flags guide and make up your messages, like "My vessel is a dangerous source of radiation; you may approach from the left."

ScubaDuba
http://www.scubaduba.com/

Click your browser type and dive on into this vast sea of scuba diving resources, which cover virtually all aspects of the underwater sport. Choose from among "Advanced & Technical Diving," clubs, equipment, "Marine Life," and other categories on the left. Then, in the middle frame against an aquamarine backdrop, browse annotated links to, for instance: The Australian Coral Reef Society, Shipwrecks ("annual event held by the Niagara Divers' association of Ontario, Canada"), Underwater Photographs of the Philippines, even The Crappy Divesite List—for "those who like to dive and don't need to go to the Bahamas to do it." Along the way, naturally, you'll come upon sunken treasure and (yikes!) perhaps even a great white shark or two. ScubaDuba might already have reached its goal of being "the ultimate scuba diving site on the World Wide Web."

World of Speedo
http://www.World-of-SPEEDO.com/

Welcome to the World of Speedo, where swimwear can double as fashion wear. This unique site is a bit high on bandwidth usage, but it's well-designed if you can take it—animations add to the look, rather than being simply obnoxious. Read about the history of Speedo, from their redesigning of the current swimmer's costume in 1927 to the introduction of Lycra to the present; view the results of testing their new AquaBlade material in the Aquatic Technology section.

Wrestling

Jerry Yang's Sumo Information Page
http://akebono.stanford.edu/users/jerry/sumo/

Ah, sumo wrestling. You may think of it as the dignified national sport of Japan, or you may think of it as humongous guys colliding while wearing strange bathing suits. Either way this is interesting stuff, especially the list of frequently asked questions, which reveals that suspicion of fixing matches in Japan exists (just like our pro "wrestling"). To guard against it, "there is a rule that wrestlers from the same heya (stable) do not wrestle each other." You'll definitely also want to view the photos of these amazingly large gentlemen, such as yokozuna (grand champion) Akebono; he looks plenty mean in some of these shots. And Jerry Yang has added movies, too! Also includes tournament results and amusing commentary: "Musoyama . . . fights like an old lady."

Oregon Wrestling Report
http://www.wrestling.org/%7Emitchell/oregon/

If you're a fan of amateur (also known as "real") wrestling and you live in Oregon, well, you've found your Web home. This comprehensive site provides full coverage of the sport in that Pacific Northwest state on high school and college levels. Even women's results make it on line. Special attention goes to the Oregon State Beavers, "one of the premier Division One wrestling programs in the country," who get their own page. Of special interest are the interviews with and guest articles by prominent amateur wrestlers and coaches. In one, Southern Maryland Wrestling Club coach Bruce Gabrielson, mentor of numerous national champions, offers his views on "making weight," one of the major health hazards faced by young wrestlers who desperately shed pounds as they try to fit into their narrow weight classes.

Professional Wrestling Server
http://orion.it.luc.edu/~mlong/wrestling.html

Bodyslam your browser to the Web home of the rec.sport.pro-wrestling newsgroup, the center of Internet professional wrestling fandom. Download soundbites from some of those eloquent wrestler interviews—even a clip from "Classy" Freddie Blassie's hit single (not!) "Pencil Neck Geeks." Yeah, he really made such a recording. The "real names lists" are particularly intriguing. Lex Luger's real name is Larry Pfohl. Not too glamorous, especially for a guy who once went by the nickname "The Narcissist." Also fascinating is a link to the "finishing moves list," enabling fans to identify each grappler by his trademark coup de grace. Colonel DeBeers, for example, employed the fearsome-sounding "Touch of Death" while Terry Gordy was known for the "Oriental Spike," also known as the "Thumb to the Throat." Enlightening.

Wrestling Weekly
http://www.pacifier.com/~jharris/ww.html

As with so many pro wrestlers themselves, this site isn't much too look at, but it sure is beefy. All of the latest, hottest pro wrestling news from all of the "federations," and there are plenty of them. No glitz and PR here. This is the juicy insider stuff. Unfortunately, it doesn't make much use of the Web. It's basically a big text-only e-mail posting. But no matter. For what's going on behind the scenes of the squared circle, this is one of the only sites available.

World

Cities, States and Regions

The Arizona Guide

http://www.arizonaguide.com/clients/
MARIZO/000001/001.html

The Arizona Guide resembles a glossy tourist bureau magazine—not surprising, since this is the Arizona Office of Tourism's official site. It's thick with things to see and do, mainly divided into the state's seven "territories" (e.g. Canyon Country, Indian Country, High Country). Click on a territory and you'll find brief but informative write-ups about the area and its attractions. The travel section features tips and a few scary warnings, including the admonition that, "When hiking in the desert, it is advisable to stay on marked trails. Desert flora and fauna can make your dream vacation a nightmare." Yow! You'll also find pages devoted to weather, golf and that huge tourist pit, the Grand Canyon. The Arizona Guide is a terrific travel planning tool, heavy on the information but easy on the eyes.

London Calling Internet

http://www.london-calling.co.uk/

The distant echoes of the BBC (or the Clash) give this site its name. This well-done page presents London as the living city it is, not just a place full of old statues and royal family doodads. With counter-culture flavor, LCI dishes the UK skinny on everything from media news to film reviews, in a tone ranging from rudely irreverent to discreetly English. On British television: "If the BSC get wound up by the amount of sex & violence on the BBC, then surely Sky [a new satellite network] must seem like a vision of hell to them." A virtual tour of the Portobello Road Market captures some of the hustle and color of this unusual shopping district, while gems like the "The Pixel and Paper Art Gallery" keep you up-to-date on local artistry. Some naughty language, but still a swell place to visit.

Maui Interactive
http://www.maui.net/~kelii/MIA/MI.html

Virtual surfers will shoot the curl over this great-looking page from Maui-ites Stuart Helmintoller and Rick Leong, who are out to promote the island's many charms. Info on everything the Maui-bound could want (and then some) include a sunrise bike ride into a volcano (watch for erupting rock!), and a kayaking expedition in search of Moby Dick (watchers only, please). The Webmasters serve up a colorful interactive map of hot spots like "La Haina" (where you can enjoy a little sky-diving) and "Molokini," where the best of Maui is evidently underwater. Links to Maui Digital Magazine and a wealth of photo and art exhibits make this as much fun for the armchair traveler as it is for the real-timer.

The Polar Regions
http://www.stud.unit.no/~sveinw/arctic/

Svein Yngvar Willassen, "a lover of the cold and remote," put together this information station on Earth's polar regions. A self-described "computer communication nerd," Willassen includes cool links to "Blocks of Ice," where you may frolic with a furry seal and learn how thinning of the ozone layer has affected the Arctic's natural ecology. "The Great Explorers" chronicles explorations dating back to the early 20th century (when Robert Falcon Scott trekked the Antarctic), and shows off the likes of Roald Amundsen and Fridtjof Nansen. Though "Bears, Seals, and Penguins" sounds a lot like a hockey league lineup, it's actually a study of polar wildlife, with super shots— and a few eerie soundbites—of arctic beasts.

Countries and Continents

The Brasil Page
http://charlotte.acns.nwu.edu/rio/brasil.html

Bright graphics and comprehensive links combine to make
this a pleasant and thorough Brazilian resource. (Much of the
site is in Portuguese.) Direct links to government offices
include the Ministry for External Relations (kind of like the
State Department) and the Ministry for the Army. A
"Portuguese for Travelers" guide teaches vital phrases like
"Where is the bathroom?" and "I don't understand"; photo
essays, including a "Greenpeace Visits Brazil Photobook," show
off the country's life and beauty; and audio files resound the
cries of exotic birds and samba music. (There's even a link to a
Swedish samba page.) Odd humor turns up in the curious
recipe for "Mother-in-Law's Eyes," built around a pound of pit-
ted prunes. Museums, universities, publications, businesses . . .
what a site!

Latin World
http://www.latinworld.com/

Latin World is a Miami-based site that gathers together
political, cultural, and social resources on nations in Latin
America and the Caribbean. Little-known resources (like
extensive news sources in many of the countries and economic
sites) are commonplace here; the authors have done a great
job of finding the most useful sites. Each country has its own
sub-page where visitors can choose from a number of options.
Some, like Cuba, don't have a lot of entries in all the categories.
But others do and the "culture" section typically has plenty
of items, from newsgroups to travel stories. Every section
notes which languages each item is published in, too. This
should be your first stop when looking for Latin American
Internet sites.

Siam.NET
http://www.siam.net/

The magical kingdom of Thailand has a worthy Web home in Siam.NET. The country makes an equally wonderful destination for backpackers and first-class travelers alike, though the Web site, not surprisingly, is oriented toward the luxury-hungry. Golfers will be especially pleased with an entire section on Thailand's top courses—a tip-off as to the site's target demographic. Recreational divers will also be hooked by a section of their own, overflowing with the translucent blue waters of the Indian Ocean. Siam.NET captures Thailand's history with thumbnail essays on most of the country's major regions and beautiful pictures from one of Earth's most exotic lands as well as all of the usual nuts 'n' bolts travel info. Unfortunately, a section on the true glory of Thailand—food!—is only under development.

The Thai Heritage Page
http://www.cs.ait.ac.th/~wutt/wutt.html

This page gives a spicy taste of Thailand's rich culture and history, and serves as a tour guide to the modern-day "Land of Smiles." You'll be serenaded with a snappy tune from the country's "most popular singer" and shown a snapshot of "His Royal Highness Prince Mahidol of Songkhla holding His Majesty the King." (Back when the king was a baby, that is.) Learn about the Temple of the Emerald Buddha, then discover the high rises and shopping centers of Bangkok. And did you know that Thais consider it extremely rude to point your foot at a person? The affection the page shows for Thailand, and especially for the royal family, is quite touching and lifts this beyond the normal travelogue routine.

Cultures

The A—Z of Jewish and Israel Related Resources
http://www.maven.co.il/

This marvelous global collection is maintained by Webmaster Matthew Album, project coordinator for the British organization ANJY (A Network for Jewish Youth). This jump-station features sites ranging from the Abayudaya Jews of Uganda to the Zamir Chorale of Boston (so named after the Hebrew word for "nightingale"). A real variety of issues are tackled, from the horrors of the Holocaust (at least seven sites, including "Holocaust Denial & the Internet"), to the fundamentals of the "Jewish Belief Home Page," which offers selections from the Babylonian Talmud and Maimonides. Our personal favorite: a page "devoted to studying and collecting trivia relating to the Jewish religious/cultural odysseys of Shabtai Zisel ben Avraham, a.k.a. Bob Dylan." A masterful compilation.

Discover Turkey; Discover the Difference

`http://www.missouri.edu/~c584540/`

No, not the lunchmeat. Discover Turkey, the country. Not only is this a fine resource for learning about Turkey, with its maps, political information, and cuisine, it's a good place for home-sick Turks to keep up on news, poetry, and other reading (in Turkish, of course). The home page alone is a wealth of information, attesting that the country was the home of 10 of the greatest world civilizations, and providing a variety of other snippets from around the site.

Drum

`http://drum.ncsc.org/index.html`

Drum is a virtual resource with direct links to political, cultural and education news affecting African Americans. Access Black history information by month (like the first game of the National Negro Baseball League, played on May 2, 1920), browse Drum Arts to see works by painter Linda Fardan (and hook up with terrific links to other African art pages), or dig into programs at Howard University and Clark Atlanta. An excellent reference tool with good links too numerous to mention.

Hungary Online Directory
http://www.hungary.com/hudir/

A veritable Yahoo-style goulash of resources "related to
Hungary or Hungarian people," this site will definitely score
higher with Hungarian-speaking surfers. Still, English-speakers
fear not: of the 600 or so links here, many are in English rather
than Magyar. Almost 100 of those sites are devoted to universities and colleges, including Jozsef Attila University (those
Attilas get around), many with campus photos and English text.
And you'll split your sides laughing when you check out
Szamitogepgyulolok Tarsasaga. If you speak the language.

DICTIONARY

500 Essential Internet Terms You Should Know

Symbols and Numbers

@ In an *e-mail address*, a symbol used to separate the user name from the name of the computer on which the user's mailbox is stored (for example, frodo@bagend.org). Pronounced "at."

100% Pure Java A certification from *JavaSoft*, the Sun Microsystems venture founded to promote the Java programming language, that a given *Java* product conforms to the current cross-platform Java specification, contained in the current *Java development kit (JDK)*, and will therefore execute on any platform for which a Java interpreter has been developed. The 100% Pure Java program is intended to protect Java's "write-once, run anywhere" philosophy against proprietary versions of the language, which could contain extensions that would restrict Java programs to execution on a single platform.

AAMOF Abbreviation for "as a matter of fact." Commonly-used abbreviation on *Internet Relay Chat (IRC)*, *e-mail*, and *Usenet*.

abbreviation Commonly used shorthand in *Internet Relay Chat (IRC)*, *chat rooms*, *e-mail*, and *Usenet*. Examples include BRB for "be right back" and IMHO for "in my humble opinion."

absolute link A *hyperlink* that fully and precisely specifies the file location of the referenced remote document. An absolute link specifies the protocol (such as http:// or ftp://), as well as the name of the computer and the location of the referenced file within the computer's directory structure. See *Relative URL (RELURL)*.

ACAP See *Application Configuration Access Protocol.*

Acceptable Use Policy (AUP) An *Internet service provider (ISP)* policy that indicates which types of uses are permissible. Some services sharply restrict commercial use. Most forbid abusive network behavior, such as *spamming.*

account A contractual agreement between the user and the *service provider.* In return for network access, the user agrees to abide by the service provider's regulations and, in some cases, pay a fee.

acoustic coupler A *modem* with cups that fit around the earpiece and mouthpiece of a standard (not cellular) telephone receiver. The cups contain a microphone and a speaker that convert the computer's digital signals into sound, and vice versa. With the almost-universal use of modular jacks, *direct-connect modems* have supplanted acoustic modems in general use.

ActiveX The newest version of Microsoft Corporation's Object Linking and Embedding (OLE) technology, which enables applications to communicate with each other by means of messages passed with the aid of the computer's operating system (see interprocess communication). The previous version was called Component Object Model (COM). ActiveX adds features designed to enable the distribution of executable programs, called controls, via the Internet. To use these controls, a computer must be running an operating system that supports OLE, such as Microsoft Windows 3.1, Microsoft Windows 95, Microsoft Windows NT, or MacOS. Unlike *Java applets,* which run in a *sandbox* that protects the computer's file system, ActiveX controls can directly affect files. For this reason, ActiveX controls are packaged with *digitally-signed* certificates, which prove that the program emanates from a respectable software publisher (and will therefore presumably not do nasty things to one's computer). See *Java.*

ActiveX control An executable program that is designed to be distributed in Microsoft's *ActiveX* packaging, which includes *digitally-signed* certificates. To execute ActiveX controls, the user must be running a *Web browser* that supports ActiveX, as well as an operating system that supports Microsoft's Object Linking and Embedding (OLE) technology for interprocess communication—and in practice, that means Microsoft Windows and the Mac OS.

address 1. An *e-mail address*. 2. The location of a *host* on the network. See *IP address*.

address book In an *e-mail* program, a utility that enables users to store and retrieve *e-mail addresses* and other contact information.

address mask See *subnet mask*.

address resolution The automated process by which the LAN address of each workstation is converted into an *IP address.* The translation is needed because the Internet and LANs handle workstation addresses in different ways.

Adobe Acrobat A *cross-platform* document distribution program created by Adobe Systems. With Adobe Acrobat, a document publisher can create a file in Adobe's PDF (Portable Document Format) format. This file can be read on any computer system that can run an Adobe Acrobat reader. Versions of the reader are available for most popular computing formats, including Windows, Macintosh, and Unix.

Adobe PageMill A Web publishing program created by Adobe Systems. PageMill is a WYSIWYG editor, which enables Web authors to create Web pages without knowing any *HTML*. The program is available in Windows and Macintosh versions.

ADSL Acronym for Asymmetric Digital Subscriber Line. A digital telephone standard, available only in a few selected markets, that enables download speeds of up to 6 Mbps. The standard is asymmetric because upload speeds are markedly slower, reflecting the notion—common among commercial content providers—that most residential Internet users wish to consume rather than to originate content.

Advanced Research Projects Agency (ARPA) An agency of the U.S. Department of Defense (DoD), now called Defense Advanced Research Projects Agency (DARPA), and a major source of funding for important computer innovations. In the late 1960s and early 1970s, ARPA funded the development of the *ARPANET*, the *Internet's* predecessor, and the *TCP/IP* protocols, which have since provided the foundation for the emergence of a wide-area network (WAN) of global proportions.

AFAIK Abbreviation for "as far as I know." Commonly-used abbreviation on *Internet Relay Chat (IRC)*, *chat rooms*, *e-mail*, and *Usenet*.

AFK Abbreviation for "away from keyboard." Commonly-used on *Internet Relay Chat (IRC)* and *chat rooms*.

agent An automatic program that is designed to operate on the user's behalf, performing a specific function in the background. When the agent has achieved its goal, it reports to the user. In the future, agents may roam the world's computer networks, looking for information and reporting only when the information has been retrieved.

alias A secondary or symbolic name for a computer user or group of users. Group aliases provide a handy way to send *e-mail* to two or more people simultaneously.

AltaVista A *search engine* for keyword searches on the *World Wide Web (WWW)* created by Digital Electronics Corp. (DEC) and considered by many to be the most powerful available. Combining a huge database of Web resources with a flexible and very fast search program, AltaVista enables users to perform a simple search using natural language, or an advanced search using Boolean operators. One drawback of AltaVista is that untrained searchers may retrieve too many irrelevant documents (false drops). Better results can be obtained by using AltaVista's search-restriction features, including case-sensitive searching, field-based searches, and phrase searches. See *HotBot, Lycos.*

alt hierarchy One of several top-level *Usenet* classifications (hierarchies) of *newsgroups*. Alt (short for alternative) newsgroups can be created by anyone who knows the appropriate newsgroup origination commands, thus by-passing the voting procedures required to originate newsgroups in the *standard newsgroup hierarchies* (such as *comp, soc,* and *talk*). However,

Usenet administrators are not compelled to carry alt news-groups, and they are not available at all Usenet sites.

America Online (AOL) The largest *online information service* (with 2.5 million subscribers), headquartered in Vienna, Virginia. The firm's 1996 revenues exceeded US$1 billion. Offering a mix of news, sports, *chat rooms, e-mail,* computer support, *Internet* access, and fee-based services, AOL targets new computer users. AOL's major competitors include *CompuServe* and the Microsoft Network.

analog modem The most common kind of *modem* available today. Analog modems, unlike *digital modems,* are designed to communicate over *Plain Old Telephone Service (POTS)* lines. An analog modem converts a computer's digital data to an analog sound and sends it over the phone lines to another modem, which in turn converts the data back to digital form.

anchor In *hypertext,* a word, phrase, or image—usually demarcated by color, underlining, or both—that provides the gateway (called a link or *hyperlink*) to another document.

anonymous Originating from a concealed or unknown source. In *Usenet* and *e-mail,* anonymity cannot be assured by simply omitting one's signature or typing a phony name; the article's or message's *header* information shows where the message originated. Anonymity can be guaranteed only by sending the message through an *anonymous remailer.*

anonymous FTP In systems linked to the *Internet,* the use of a file-transfer program to contact a distant computer system to which you have no access rights, log on to its public directories, and transfer files from that computer to your own. When logging on to an anonymous FTP server, you should type anonymous as your name and your *e-mail* address as your password. For help in finding files to access via anonymous FTP, you can use *Archie, Gopher,* a *Wide Area Information Server (WAIS),* or the *World Wide Web (WWW).*

anonymous post In *Usenet,* an article that has been posted through an *anonymous remailer* so that the identity of the person posting the article is impossible to determine.

anonymous remailer   An *Internet* mailing service that strips an *e-mail* message of its originating header information, so that its origin cannot be easily determined. True anonymous remailers retain absolutely no information regarding the messages they relay; they should be distinguished from *pseudoanonymous remailers*, which retain origin information in order to facilitate replies to the message's originator.

AOL   See *America Online*.

API   See *application program interface*.

applet   In *Java*, a mini-program embedded in a Web document that, when downloaded, is executed by the browser. Both of the leading browsers (Netscape Communicator and Microsoft Internet Explorer) can execute Java applets. See *Java applet, Java application*.

Application Configuration Access Protocol (ACAP)   A proposed *Internet* standard that transfers crucial user configuration settings (including *address books, Bookmarks,* and options choices) to an Internet-accessible file. Because these settings are stored on the network instead of the user's computer, they are accessible no matter which computer is being used. ACAP will greatly benefit anyone who accesses the Internet from more than one computer.

application program interface (API)   In *Web servers*, the standards or conventions that enable a *hyperlink* to originate a call to a program that is external to the server (see *Common Gateway Interface (CGI), ISAPI,* and *NSAPI*).

Archie   An *Internet* tool for finding specific files that are available in publicly accessible *File Transfer Protocol (FTP)* archives. A major drawback of Archie is that you must know the precise spelling of some or all of the file names in order to retrieve the file. See *anonymous FTP*.

Archie gateway   A Web page that provides an easy-to-use interface to the *Archie* search service.

archive site   An *Internet*-accessible computer that serves as a repository for a large or complete collection of data, such as all the messages exchanged on a mailing list or *newsgroup*. Synonymous with FTP site because archive sites are frequently accessed by *FTP* programs.

ARPA See *Advanced Research Projects Agency*.

ARPANET A wide area network (WAN), created in 1969 with funding from the *Advanced Research Projects Agency (ARPA)*. Undergoing constant research and development in the early to mid-1970s, ARPANET served as the testbed for the development of *TCP/IP* (the protocols that make the *Internet* possible). Initially, the ARPANET was available only to government research institutes and to universities holding Department of Defense (DoD) research contracts. In 1983, ARPANET was divided into a high-security military network (Milnet) and an ARPANET that was recast as a research and development network, supervised by the National Science Foundation (NSF). NSF constructed a new TCP/IP-based network *backbone* called NSFNET and decommissioned the remnants of ARPANET in 1990.

article A contribution that an individual has written and posted to one or more Usenet newsgroups. There are two kinds of articles: original articles on new subjects, and *follow-up posts*. By means of *cross-posting*, an article can appear in more than one newsgroup.

article selector A *newsreader* feature in which the newsreader groups and displays the *articles* that are currently available for reading. *Threaded newsreaders* automatically sort the articles in such a way that you can see the *thread* of discussion; an article is followed immediately by all its *follow-up posts*.

AS See *autonomous system*.

ASN See *autonomous system number*.

assigned number A value associated with a specific protocol that is controlled by the Internet Assigned Numbers Authority (IANA). An example of an assigned number is the *port address* assigned to a specific network service, such as *Usenet* or *Internet Relay Chat (IRC)*.

Asymmetric Digital Subscriber Line   See *ADSL*.

AT command set   See *Hayes command set*.

at sign   See *@*.

attachment   A *binary file*, such as a program or a compressed word processing document, that has been attached to an e-mail message. The content of the file does not appear within the e-mail message itself. Instead, on the *Internet* it is encoded following the specifications of the *MIME* standard or older encoding standards called *BinHex* or *uuencode*. To include an attached document with an e-mail message, both the sender and receiver must have e-mail programs that are capable of working with the same encoding format. MIME is the most widely used format.

attachment encoding   The encoding format used to attach a *binary file* to an *e-mail* message. See *BinHex*, *MIME*, *uuencode*.

AU   In the Internet's *domain name system (DNS)*, an abbreviation for Australia.

AUP   See *Acceptable Use Policy*.

authentication   In a network, the process by which the system attempts to ensure that the person logging on is the same person to whom the *account* was issued. The sole means of authentication in most networks is the demand for a *password*, even though password-based authentication is known to have several serious security flaws.

auto-logon   A feature of *communications programs* that lets you automate the process of logging on to a *BBS* or *online information service*.

automatic name recognition   In databases and Web *search engines*, a feature that automatically detects that a supplied keyword is a person's name and restricts the search to capitalized names.

automatic speed sensing   A *modem* feature that lets the modem automatically determine the maximum speed at which a connection can be made. Performed during the *handshaking* period at the beginning of a call, modems with automatic speed sensing will fall back to the fastest speed the two connected modems, and line conditions, can support.

autonomous system (AS) In *Internet* network topology, a collection of *routers* that is under the control of a single administrative authority. Within an autonomous system, an administrator can create and name new *subdomains* and assign *IP addresses* and *domain names* to workstations on the network.

autonomous system number (ASN) In an *autonomous system (AS)*, an *IP address* that has been assigned by an automatic protocol to one of the workstations on the network.

avatar A graphical representation of a person that appears on the computer screen in an interactive game or communication system. The avatar's appearance, actions, and words are controlled by the person whom the avatar represents.

backbone In a wide area network (WAN), such as the *Internet,* a high-speed, high-capacity medium that is designed to transfer data over hundreds or thousands of miles. A variety of physical media are used for backbone services, including microwave relay, satellites, and dedicated telephone lines.

backbone site In *Usenet's* telephone-based store-and-forward network (see *Unix-to-Unix Copy Program (UUCP)*), a site that is centrally located on the article distribution network, such that the site administrator's decisions about which newsgroups to carry can affect the newsgroup selection available at dozens or even hundreds of downstream sites. The ability of these administrators to control and censor the newsgroup list collapsed with the migration of Usenet to the Internet via the NNTP protocol.

background communication Data communication, such as downloading a file from an online information service, that takes place in the background while the user concentrates on another application in the foreground.

background noise See *line noise.*

bandwidth The amount of data that can be transmitted via a given communications channel (such as a computer network) in a given unit of time (generally one second). For digital devices, bandwidth is measured in *bits per second (bps).* The bandwidth of analog devices is measured in cycles per second (cps).

bang A common slang term for a forward slash (/), especially when telling someone a *URL* ("Go to www-dot-Microsoft-dot-com-bang-search-dot-html").

base64 A data encoding method that converts a *binary file* into plain ASCII text, which can be transmitted via the *Internet* and other computer networks. This encoding method is used in *MIME.*

Basic Rate Interface (BRI) In the ISDN specification, the basic digital telephone and data service that is designed for residences. BRI offers two 64,000 bps channels for voice, graphics, and data, plus one 16,000 bps channel for signaling purposes.

baud A variation or change in a signal in a communications channel. See *baud rate* and *bits per second (bps).*

baud rate The maximum number of changes that can occur per second in the electrical state of a communications circuit. Under RS-232C communications protocols, 300 *baud* is likely to equal 300 *bits per second (bps),* but at higher baud rates, the number of bits per second transmitted is usually twice the baud rate because two bits of data can be sent with each change. Therefore, the transfer rate of modems, for example, is usually stated in bits per second (bps). See *modem.*

BBS Acronym for Bulletin Board Service. A small-scale *online information service,* usually set up by a personal computer hobbyist for the enjoyment of other hobbyists, and based on a single personal computer that is accessed by means of direct-dial modem links. A typical BBS includes topically-oriented discussion groups, file downloading, and games. The Internet's explosive popularity has eroded the popularity of BBSs, many of which have responded by making their resources accessible by means of direct Internet connections.

BCC See *blind carbon copy*.

binary file A file containing data or program instructions in a computer-readable format, unreadable to humans. The opposite of a binary file is an ASCII file.

binary newsgroup A Usenet newsgroup in which the articles contain (or are supposed to contain) binary files, such as sounds, graphics, or movies. These files have been encoded with *uuencode,* a program that transforms a *binary file* into coded ASCII characters so it can be transferred via the *Internet.* In order to use these files, it is first necessary to decode them (using a program called *uudecode,* or a *newsreader* that has built-in uudecoding capability).

binary transfer 1. In data communications generally, a file transfer protocol *(ftp)* that allows users to transfer *binary files* to and from a remote computer using terminal emulation software. 2. In *FTP,* a file download or upload that preserves *binary files* intact (unlike an ASCII transfer).

BinHex A method of encoding *binary files* so that the coded file contains nothing but the standard ASCII characters and can, therefore, be transferred to other computers via the *Internet.* The receiving computer must decode the file using BinHex-capable decoding software. BinHex is popular among Macintosh users. Note that BinHex is not a compression technique, and that a BinHexed file may actually be longer than the source file. For this reason, BinHexed files are generally compressed after they are encoded using the Macintosh standard compression program, StuffIt.

B-ISDN See *Broadband ISDN*.

BITNET A wide area network (WAN) that links mainframe computer systems at approximately 2,500 universities and research institutions in North America, Europe, and Japan. BITNET (an acronym for Because It's Time Network) does not use the *TCP/IP* protocols but can exchange *e-mail* with the *Internet.* BITNET is operated by the Corporation for Research and Educational Networking (CREN), with headquarters in Washington, D.C. To become a member of the network, an organization must pay for a *leased line* that connects to the nearest existing BITNET site, and it must also agree to let another institution connect with this line in the future. Faced with competition from the Internet, BITNET is slowly dying.

bits per second (bps) In asynchronous communications, a measurement of data transmission speed. In personal computing, bps rates frequently are used to measure the performance of *modems* and serial ports. A common modem speed is 28,800 bps.

blind carbon copy (BCC) A copy of an *e-mail* message that is sent to one or more persons without the knowledge of the other recipients. Also called blind courtesy copy (BCC).

bogus newsgroup In *Usenet*, a *newsgroup* that does not correspond to the site's list of approved newsgroups. Most *newsreaders* are programmed to detect such newsgroups and delete them automatically. Bogus newsgroups may originate from programming errors or somebody's effort to create the group by skirting the normal newsgroup creation process.

bomb See *mail bombing*.

Bookmark 1. To record the location of a desired Web page or passage in a word processing document so that the user can easily return to it later. 2. In *Netscape Navigator* or other *Web browsers*, one of the user's favorite places on the *World Wide Web*, someplace you'd like to visit again. Synonymous with *favorite* (the term used by *Microsoft Internet Explorer*) and *hotlist item* (*Mosaic*).

BOOTP Acronym for Bootstrap Protocol, an *Internet* protocol that enables workstations on a local area network to find their *IP address* dynamically.

Border Gateway Protocol An *Internet* protocol that defines the routing of Internet data between an *autonomous system (AS)* and the wider Internet. This protocol replaces the older *Exterior Gateway Protocol (EGP)*.

bot 1. In multi-user dungeons *(MUDs)* and *Internet Relay Chat (IRC)*, a character whose on-screen actions stem from a program rather than a real person. The term is a shortened form of "robot." Bots are frequently used for pranks or anti-social actions and are not welcome on most IRC servers. See *MOO.* 2. In Internet searching, an automated search agent that explores the Internet autonomously, and reports back to the user when the search conditions have been successfully fulfilled.

bounce   In *e-mail*, to come back marked as undeliverable (see *bounce message*).

bounce message   An *e-mail* message informing the user that an e-mail message could not be delivered to its intended recipient. The failure may be due to an incorrectly typed e-mail address or to a network problem.

bps   See *bits per second*.

BRI   See *Basic Rate Interface*.

Broadband ISDN (B-ISDN)   A high-*bandwidth* digital telephone standard for transmitting up to 1.5 Mbps over fiber optic cables. See *Basic Rate Interface (BRI), ISDN*.

browse   To look for information on the *World Wide Web (WWW)* by jumping from hyperlink to hyperlink.

browser   A program that enables the user to navigate the *World Wide Web (WWW)*. The two leading browsers are *Netscape Navigator,* part of Netscape Communication's *Netscape Communicator* package, and *Microsoft Internet Explorer (MSIE)*. A browser serves as the client for Web and other types of Internet *servers*. Synonymous with *Web browser*. Increasingly, browsers are becoming the interface of choice for all the various types of data accessible by means of networks based on Internet technology.

browsing   Following hyperlinks from one Web site to another. In the *World Wide Web (WWW)*, browsing is rarely effective for finding information on a specific topic (it's much better to use subject trees and search engines), but it's lots of fun. Also referred to as *surfing*. See *search engine* and *subject tree*.

BTW   In *online* conferences, an acronym for By The Way.

bulletin board system (BBS) See *BBS*.

bytecode A compiled Java program, with the extension .class, that can be executed by a *Java Virtual Machine (JVM)*. Unlike ordinary compiled languages, which produce machine language suitable for execution on a particular brand of computer, Java compilers produce an intermediary format, called bytecode, which can be executed on any computer capable of running a bytecode interpreter (such as a Java-compatible *browser*). However, because bytecode is interpreted, Java applications execute more slowly than programs designed specifically for a given type of computer (though not so slowly as true inter-preted code).

bytecode compiler A compiler that outputs a program in *bytecode* rather than machine code.

ca In the Internet *domain name system (DNS)*, the country code for Canada.

CA See *certificate authority*.

cache (Pronounced "cash.") A section of the hard drive that is set aside for storing recently-accessed Web pages. When you revisit one of these pages, the browser retrieves the page from the cache rather than the network, bringing about a consider-able improvement in apparent retrieval speed.

Café See *Visual Café*.

Call for Votes (CFV) A voting procedure that controls the creation of new Usenet newsgroups. Following a period of discussion, the call for votes is posted to the newsgroup news.announce.newgroups. During the voting period, any Usenet participant may vote for or against the new newsgroup's creation by sending *e-mail* to an independent tabulator (a vol-unteer). To pass, a newsgroup must receive at least 100 more Yes votes than No votes, and the number of Yes votes must be at least two-thirds of the total. If the newsgroup passes the vote, the newsgroup creation commands are issued and Usenet administrators are expected to carry the newsgroup, but there is no mechanism to force them to do so. The voting procedure does not apply to newsgroups outside the *standard newsgroup hierarchy*, such as the *alt hierarchy*.

cancelbot   In Usenet, a program that can hunt down a given individual's posts and remove them from the network. Cancelbots, such as the one used by the storied *Cancelmoose*, are frequently wielded against spammers, those who post unwanted messages to dozens or even hundreds of newsgroups, but they have also been used to try to silence unwanted opinion.

Cancelmoose   In *Usenet*, an individual, whose identity remains unknown, who takes upon himself the task of canceling articles that are inappropriately posted to a large number of *newsgroups* (this is called spamming). Although Usenet software ordinarily permits only the author of an article to cancel it (remove it from Usenet), Cancelmoose has devised ingenious software (called a *cancelbot*) that gets around this restriction, allowing him or her to cancel any person's articles. Although the Cancelmoose's actions are controversial, many Usenet participants believe that his or her actions are fully justified.

canonical name   The official name of an Internet *host,* as opposed to its aliases.

carpet bomb   See *spam.*

carrier detect signal   A signal sent from the *modem* to the rest of the computer to indicate that a connection has been made and the carrier tone has been established. The carrier detect (CD) light on *external modems* will illuminate when the carrier detect signal is sent.

cascade   In *follow-up posts* posted to *Usenet,* the accretion of quotation markers in messages that have been repeatedly quoted. Each time a message is quoted in a follow-up message, a newsreader adds quotation markers, as in the following:

>>>>>>Let's stop this thread.
>>>>>I agree.

>>>>Me too.
>>>You shouldn't post just to say, "Me too."
>>I agree.
>Me too.
Aargh!

cascading style sheet (CSS) An HTML specification of
document formats in which specific formatting attributes (such
as alignment, text style, font, and font size) are assigned to specific HTML *tags,* so that all subsequent uses of the tag in the
same page take on the same formats. Like a style sheet in a
word processing document, CSS enables a Web designer to
make a single change that affects all the text marked with the
same tag. The Level 1 definition of cascading style sheets is
defined by the *World Wide Web Consortium (W3C)*, but competing definitions are being pushed by Netscape. See *JavaScript style
sheet (JSS)*.

Castanet A *push media* developed by Marimba that enables
computer users to "tune" to *Java* software delivery channels.
When updated versions of a program become available, the
software is automatically downloaded and installed without
the user's involvement. Castanet has been incorporated into
Netscape Communicator's Netcaster module, which also
delivers content to the desktop.

catch up In *Usenet*, a command commonly implemented in
newsreaders that marks all the current *articles* in a *newsgroup* as
read, even if you have not actually read them. When you access
the newsgroup again, you will see only the articles that have
come in since the last time you accessed the newsgroup.

CC See *courtesy copy*.

CCITT protocol A standard for the transmission of data
using a computer *modem*, serial port, or a network. The following protocols are in the V series: V.17, V.21, V.22, V.22bis, V.27ter,
V.29, V.32, *V.32bis*, *V.34*, *V.42*, and *V.42bis*.

Center for Innovative Computer Applications (CICA)
An Indiana University-based research center that fosters innovative research in computer visualization and artificial intelligence.

For *Internet* users, CICA is better known as the home of a massive Windows shareware archive, accessible by means of *File Transfer Protocol (FTP)*.

CERN Acronym for Conseil European pour la Recherche Nucleaire (European Laboratory for Particle Physics). A Geneva, Switzerland-based research center for advanced physics research. CERN is the birthplace of the *World Wide Web (WWW)*, which the center's computer staff began in 1989 as a collaborative network for high-energy physicists.

CERT Acronym for Computer Emergency Response Team. An *Internet* security task force that is designed to detect and respond rapidly to Internet security threats. Formed by the *Defense Advanced Research Project Agency (DARPA)* in 1988 in response to the infamous Internet Worm, CERT monitors Internet security and alerts system administrators concerning the activities of computer *crackers* and computer virus authors.

certificate An encrypted and *digitally signed* attachment to an *e-mail* message or downloaded file that attests that the received data really comes from its claimed source and has not been altered while it was en route. A certificate is virtually impossible to fake. To be considered valid, however, the certificate should be digitally signed by a *certificate authority (CA)*, an independent agency that uses some type of identity-checking procedure (such as viewing a driver's license) prior to signing the certificate. Synonymous with digital ID. See *personal certificate, public key cryptography.*

certificate authority (CA) A company that verifies the identity of individuals and issues *certificates* attesting to the veracity of this identity. To obtain a certificate, an individual may be asked to show identification, such as a driver's license.

CFV See *Call for Votes.*

CGI See *Common Gateway Interface.*

Challenge-Handshake Authentication Protocol (CHAP)
In *Internet* dial-up services that use the Point-to-Point Protocol *(PPP)*, a standard that prevents hackers from intercepting passwords. CHAP is used to verify the identity of the person

logging on by using a three-way handshake. After the link is established, the service provider's computer sends a "challenge" message to the user's computer, which must then consult a "secret" stored on the user's computer, as well as on the service provider's computer, but is never sent over the network. The user's computer then performs a calculation using the challenge as well as the secret. If the result does not match the service provider's calculation, the connection is terminated. This authentication method provides a very high degree of protection against previous password-based authentication measures, and is more secure than its predecessor, the *Password Authentication Protocol (PAP)*.

channel 1. On *Internet Relay Chat (IRC)*, a named, topically-focused forum where you can *chat* in real time with other computers. Synonymous with *chat room*. 2. In *push media*, a named link to a network-based transmitter to which a user can "tune." For example, you can tune to Corel's channel to receive automatic updates to the company's Java version of its Corel Suite software.

channel op (CHOP) On *Internet Relay Chat (IRC)*, a person who possesses *op* (operator) privileges, including the right to kick unruly users out of the channel.

CHAP See *Challenge-Handshake Authentication Protocol.*

chat In an *online information service, BBS,* or *Internet Relay Chat (IRC)*, to converse with other computer users by exchanging typed lines of text in a real-time conversation.

chat room In a *BBS* or *online information service,* a named, topically-focused forum or conference for online, real-time chatting. See *chat, channel.*

CHOP See *channel op.*

CICA See *Center for Innovative Computer Applications.*

ciphertext In *cryptography,* a message that has been encrypted so that it can be read only by the intended recipient, who possesses the *key* needed to decode the message. See *encryption, public key cryptography.*

clari In *Usenet,* an alternative hierarchy that includes dozens of read-only *newsgroups* containing wire service articles—the same ones that will appear in today's newspapers. These wire services include United Press International (UPI), Newsbytes, and TechWire. The Clari hierarchy is available only at those Usenet sites that have paid a fee to ClariNet, the organization that collates the wire service articles and posts them to the dozens of clari newsgroups. The articles posted to the clari newsgroups are copyrighted and cannot be redistributed without ClariNet's written approval.

Class A network On the *Internet,* a participating network that is allocated up to 16,777,215 distinct Internet addresses (called *IP addresses*). Current Internet addressing limitations define a maximum of 128 Class A networks.

Class B network On the *Internet,* a participating network that is allocated up to 65,535 distinct Internet addresses (called *IP addresses*). Current Internet addressing limitations define a maximum of 16,384 Class B networks.

Class C network On the *Internet,* a participating network that is allocated up to 256 distinct Internet addresses (called *IP addresses*). Current Internet addressing limitations define a maximum of 2,097,152 Class C networks.

CMC See *computer-mediated communication.*

CoffeeCup A non-WYSIWYG *HTML editor* that includes many resources for creating eye-catching Web pages quickly, including animated GIFs, *JavaScripts,* and *ActiveX controls.* The shareware program is available for Windows.

Collabra See *Netscape Collabra.*

com On the *Internet,* a top-level domain name that is assigned to a corporation or business. Top-level domain names come last in a given Internet computer's domain name (such as www.apple.com).

command mode A *modem* mode in which it takes instructions from other parts of the computer, such as the keyboard, instead of transmitting everything over the phone line. For

example, in command mode you could issue an instruction for
the modem to lower the volume of its speaker or dial a number. *Communications programs* usually handle the distinction
between command mode and *communications mode.*

Common Gateway Interface (CGI) A standard that
describes how *HTTPD*-compatible *World Wide Web (WWW)*
servers should access external programs, so that this data is
returned to the user in the form of an automatically generated
Web page. CGI programs, called scripts, come into play when a
Web user fills out an on-screen *form;* the form generates output
that is handled by the script, which brings other programs into
play as necessary. These may include a database search engine or
a mailer program. Common applications of CGI include providing a means for users to type and mail feedback, enabling
database searches, and creating *gateways* to other Internet services that are not directly accessible through the Web.

communications mode A *modem* mode in which everything sent to the modem, such as text from the keyboard, is put
onto the telephone line. Contrast with *command mode.*

communications program An application that turns your
computer into a terminal for transmitting data to and receiving
data from distant computers through the telephone system.

communications protocol The standards that govern the
transfer of information among computers on a network or
using telecommunications. The computers involved in the
communication must have the same settings and follow the
same standards to avoid errors.

comp hierarchy In *Usenet,* one of the seven standard newsgroup hierarchies; the comp.* newsgroups deal with every
conceivable aspect of computing, including artificial intelligence, computer-aided design (CAD), database systems, digital
telephony, graphics, the *Internet,* professional organizations, programming languages, networks, operating systems, specific
computer systems, and theory. The comp.binaries.* newsgroups
contain freeware and shareware programs.

compressed SLIP (CSLIP) An optimized version of the
Serial Line Interface Protocol *(SLIP),* commonly used to

connect PCs to the *Internet* by means of dial-up connections, that includes compression and produces improved throughput. Because of its *security* shortcomings, *Internet service providers (ISPs)* prefer to implement dial-up access using the Point-to-Point Protocol *(PPP)*.

CompuServe   The second-largest *online information service*, which offers many of the same services as *America Online*, including a file *downloading, e-mail*, news, up-to-the-minute stock quotes, an online encyclopedia, chat rooms, Internet access, and conferences on a wide variety of topics.

Computer Emergency Response Team (CERT)   See *CERT.*

computer-mediated communication (CMC)   Any communication between or among people that employs computers as a medium. Examples of CMC include *chat, e-mail, MUDs*, and *Usenet.*

connectionless protocol   In wide area networks (WANs), a standard that enables the transmission of data from one computer to another even though no effort is made to determine whether the receiving computer is online or able to receive the information. This is the underlying protocol in any *packet-switching network,* such as the *Internet,* in which a unit of data is broken down into small-sized *packets,* each with a header containing the address of the data's intended destination. In the Internet, the connectionless protocol is the *Internet Protocol (IP).* IP is concerned only with breaking data down into packets for transmission and reassembling the packets after they have been received. A *connection-oriented protocol* (on the Internet, TCP) works at another level to assure that all the packets are received. Research on computer networks has disclosed this design is highly efficient. See *TCP.*

connection–oriented protocol   In wide area networks (WANs), a standard that establishes a procedure by which two of the computers on the network can establish a physical connection that lasts until they have successfully exchanged data. This is accomplished by means of *handshaking,* in which the two computers exchange messages that say, in effect, "OK, I'm ready," "I didn't get that; please re-send," and "Got it, bye." In the *Internet*, the Transmission Control Protocol *(TCP)* is a connection-oriented protocol; it provides the means by which two Internet-connected computers can enter into communication with each other to ensure the successful transmission of data. In contrast, the Internet Protocol *(IP)* is a *connectionless protocol*, which enables the transmission of data without requiring handshaking.

connect speed   The data-transmission rate at which a *modem*, after performing a handshaking sequence with another modem and determining the amount of *line noise*, establishes a connection. The connect speed may be lower than the modem's top speed.

cookie   In the *World Wide Web (WWW)*, a small text file that the server writes to the user's hard disk without the user's knowledge or permission. The data in the cookie file enables one Web page to pass information to other pages, thus directly addressing a major shortcoming of the underlying Web protocol, *HTTP*. Many cookie applications benefit the user, for example, the shopping basket used by many online "shopping malls" would not function without cookies. However, direct marketing firms are using cookies to compile information about user's browsing habits in ways that have raised grave concerns among privacy advocates. *Netscape Communicator* enables users to switch cookies off.

cooperative network   A wide-area network (WAN), such as *BITNET*, in which the costs of participating are borne by the linked organizations.

Cougar   Code name for the next version of *HTML*, currently under review by the *World Wide Web Consortium (W3C)*. Building on the achievements of HTML 3.2, Cougar will incorporate a better mechanism for representing information about the document (such as authenticating the author's name by means of digital signatures), support locally executable scripting languages such as *JavaScript*, formally specify frames tags, extend forms (with particular attention to providing access for people with disabilities), specify the means for including objects (such as *Java applets*), and additional improvements to support the international usage of HTML.

courtesy copy (CC) In *e-mail*, a copy of an e-mail message that is sent to one or more addresses. These addresses are included in the header information that the message's recipient sees. In a *blind carbon copy (BCC)*, the recipient does not know who, if anyone, has received copies of the message.

cracker A computer hobbyist who gets kicks from gaining unauthorized access to computer systems. Cracking is a silly, egotistical game in which the object is to defeat even the most secure computer systems. Although many crackers do little more than leave a "calling card" to prove their victory, some attempt to steal credit card information or destroy data. Whether or not they commit a crime, all crackers injure legitimate computer users by consuming the time of system administrators and making computer resources more difficult to access. In the press, the term "cracker" is used synonymously with "*hacker*," but hacking has a completely different meaning and plays a valuable role in computing. See *hacker ethic*.

cross-platform Able to operate on a network in which the workstations are of dissimilar make (for example, Macintoshes, Windows systems, and Unix computers). *Netscape Communicator* is a cross-platform browser because there are versions of the program for all three major computing formats, and the program conforms to cross-platform standards, which do not lock users into proprietary standards.

cross-post To *post* a contribution to two or more *newsgroups* simultaneously. Cross-posting is rarely warranted and is a favorite tactic of spammers, who post unsolicited, unwanted, and off-topic advertisements to hundreds or even thousands of newsgroups at a time.

cryptanalysis The science of breaking encrypted messages, both to determine the strength of encryption techniques and to provide the nation with a military advantage.

cryptography The science of coding messages so that they cannot be read by any person other than the intended recipient. Cryptography dates back to ancient Rome, but it has always been plagued by the messenger problem: if you want to send an encrypted message to somebody, then you must also somehow send the key that is needed to decode the message. There is always the threat that the key could be intercepted en route without your knowing, thus defeating the purpose of encryption. Possibly the most significant event in the history of cryptography is the recent invention of *public key cryptography*, which completely eliminates the need to send a key via a separate, secure channel, and enables two people who have never before communicated to exchange virtually unbreakable messages. See *cryptanalysis*.

CSLIP See *compressed SLIP*.

CSO name server An *Internet*-accessible white pages directory that an organization makes available. Listing the names, telephones, and *e-mail* addresses of all the organization's employees, a CSO name server provides an alternative to the telephone directory. The acronym CSO stands for Computing Service Office (CSO), a unit of the University of Illinois, where the original name server software was developed.

CSS See *cascading style sheet*.

CU-SeeMe An *Internet* conferencing program, created by White Pine Software, that enable users of systems equipped with digital cameras (such as QuickCam or Apple AV) to engage in real-time video conferences with up to 8 people at a time.

cybersex A form of long-distance eroticism made possible by a real-time computer *chat room;* synonymous with compusex. To stimulate your virtual partner, you relay a favorite sexual fantasy or describe in vivid terms what you would be doing if the person were actually present.

cyberspace The virtual space created by computer systems. One definition of space is "a boundless three-dimensional extent in which objects and events occur and have relative position and direction." In the 20th century, computer systems are creating a new kind of space that fits the previous definition, called cyberspace. (The prefix "cyber" refers to computers.) Cyberspace can take the form of elaborate virtual reality worlds or relatively simple *e-mail*.

D

DARPA See *Defense Advanced Research Project Agency (DARPA)*.

data-compression protocol In *modems*, a standard for automatically compressing data when it's sent and decompressing data when it's received. With data compression, you can realize gains of up to 400 percent in effective transmission speed. The two most common data-compression protocols are *V.42bis* and MNP-5. See *CCITT protocol*.

data encrypting key In *SSL* and other *security* protocols that begin a secure connection with public key encryption, a symmetric encryption key that is used to encrypt the transmitted data after a secure *key* exchange has taken place.

datagram The preferred *Internet* term for a data *packet*.

data modem A *modem* that can send and receive data, but not faxes. Compare to *fax modem*.

data transfer rate The speed, expressed in *bits per second (bps)*, at which a *modem* can transfer, or is transferring, data over a telephone line.

DBA See *dynamic bandwidth allocation*.

declarative markup language (DML) In text processing, a markup language—a system of codes for marking the format of a unit of text—that indicates only that a particular unit of text is a certain part of the document, such as an abstract, a title, or an author's name and affiliation. The actual formatting of the document part is left up to another program, called a parser, which displays the marked document and gives each document part a distinctive format (fonts, spacing, etc.). An international standard DML is the Standard Generalized Markup Language *(SGML)*, which was little-known until a subset of SGML, the

HyperText Markup Language *(HTML)*, came into widespread use on the *World Wide Web (WWW)*. HTML is a declarative markup language, and the Web browsers in use by millions today are parsers for HTML.

decryption   In *cryptography*, the decoding of an encrypted message by means of a *key*. See *encryption*.

dedicated line   A telephone line, devoted to data communications, that has been specially conditioned and permanently connected. Dedicated lines are often *leased lines* from regional telephone companies or public data networks (PDN).

default home page   The *World Wide Web (WWW)* document that appears when you start your Web browser or click the Home button. Most Web browsers are set up to display the browser company's *home page*, but you can easily change this setting so that the browser displays a more useful default home page.

Defense Advanced Research Projects Agency (DARPA)
A unit of the U.S. Department of Defense (DoD), the successor to the *Advanced Research Projects Agency (ARPA)* that played a key role in the development of the *ARPANET*, the *Internet's* predecessor. DARPA is one of several U.S. agencies that participate in the High Performance Computing and Communications Program (HPCC).

delurk   In *Usenet*, to post a message in which you reveal your identity and confess that you have been reading the newsgroup for a long time without contributing anything. See *lurk*.

demodulation   In telecommunications, the process of receiving and transforming an analog signal into its digital equivalent so that a computer can use the information. See *modulation*.

dialer program   A program that dials an *Internet* service provider's number and establishes the connection. A dialer program is unlike a *communications program*, which transforms your computer into a terminal of a remote computer. Instead, the dialer program establishes the connection that fully integrates your computer into the Internet. Many service providers distribute preconfigured dialer programs that enable users to connect to their service without configuring or programming the dialer; if you cannot obtain a preconfigured dialer, you may have to write your own *login script,* which can be tedious for people who lack programming experience.

dialup access   A means of connecting to another computer, or a network like the *Internet,* with a *modem*-equipped computer.

dialup IP   A *dialup access* method that gives you full access to the Internet. By means of dialup IP (in conjunction with Point to Point Protocol [PPP] or Serial Line Internet Protocol [SLIP]), you can use graphical programs like *Netscape Navigator* to browse the *World Wide Web (WWW)* and collect *e-mail.* See *Internet service provider (ISP).*

dialup modem   In contrast to a *modem* designed for use with a *leased line,* a modem that can dial a telephone number, establish a connection, and close the connection when it is no longer needed. Most personal computer modems are dialup modems.

dictionary flame   In *Usenet,* a *follow-up post* that initiates or prolongs a controversy over the meaning of a word or phrase, such as "Second Amendment" or "right to life."

Diffie-Hellman public key encryption algorithm   A *public key encryption* algorithm that was created by the inventors of public key encryption, and subsequently named after them. Diffie-Hellman has not seen widespread use in comparison to *RSA public key encryption algorithm,* but is expected to come into much wider use because the inventor's patent is about to expire.

digest   An *article* that appears in a moderated *newsgroup* summarizing the posts received by the newsgroup's *moderator.*

digital cash   A proposed method of ensuring personal privacy in a world in which electronic commerce becomes common. In digital cash commerce, a person who maintains an electronic bank account could make online purchases, which would be debited automatically and transferred to the payee. The transactions would be secure for all three parties concerned—the bank, the payer, and the payee—yet none of these parties, nor any outside investigator, would be able to determine just what has been done with the money. Relying on *public key cryptography,* this technology alarms government and law enforcement officials, who see it as an open invitation to tax cheats and drug dealers. Lacking U.S. Department of Commerce certification, digital cash schemes are currently in an experimental stage; one *World Wide Web (WWW)* accessible service allows you to obtain $5 of pretend money that you can "spend" at participating Web pages. Synonymous with e-cash.

digitally signed   In *e-mail,* signed with a *certificate* that confirms that the person sending the message is actually who he or she claims to be. See *digital signature.*

digital modem   A communications adapter designed to connect one computer to another digitally. Digital modems are not really modems at all, since *modulation* and *demodulation* are necessary only for analog connections. Digital modems, such as IBM's WaveRunner, work with digital telephone systems such as the Integrated Services Digital Network *(ISDN),* and therefore have not achieved widespread use.

digital signature   An encrypted, tamper-proof attestation, usually attached to an encrypted *e-mail* message or a *certificate,* that the person or authority signing the certificate is confident that the message's originator is actually the person he or she claims to be. See *certificate authority (CA).*

digital transmission   A data communications technique that passes information encoded as discrete on-off pulses. Digital transmission doesn't require digital-to-analog converters at each end of the transmission.

direct-connect modem   A *modem* equipped with a jack like the standard jack found in a telephone wall outlet, both of which accept an RJ-11 plug. The modem can be connected directly to the telephone line using ordinary telephone wire, unlike an *acoustic coupler* modem designed to cradle a telephone headset.

dirty   Full of extraneous signals or noise. A dirty telephone line causes problems when you try to log on with a *modem* to a distant computer system or *BBS*. You'll know if the line's dirty; you'll see many garbage characters on the screen. Log off, hang up, and dial again.

distributed bulletin board   A collection of computer conferences, called *newsgroups,* automatically distributed throughout a wide area network (WAN) so that individual postings are available to every user. The conferences are organized by topic, embracing such areas as ecology, politics, current events, music, specific computers and computer programs, and human sexuality. See *follow-up post, Internet, moderated newsgroup, post, thread, unmoderated newsgroup,* and *Usenet.*

distribution   In *Usenet,* the geographic area throughout which you want your *post* to be distributed. With most systems, you can choose from world distribution (the default in most systems), your country, your state, your local area, or your organization.

DML   See *declarative markup language.*

DNS   See *Domain Name Service* or *domain name system.*

document type definition (DTD)   In *SGML,* a complete definition of a markup language that defines the elements of the document as well as the *tags* used to identify them. HTML is defined by a standard DTD maintained by the *World Wide Web Consortium (W3C).*

domain   On the *Internet,* the highest subdivision, usually a country. However, in the United States, the subdivision is by type of organization, such as commercial (.com), educational (.edu), or government (.gov and .mil).

domain name   In the system of *domain names* used to identify individual *Internet* computers, a single word or abbreviation that makes up part of a computer's unique name (such as watt.seas.virginia.edu). Reading from left to right, the parts of a domain name go from specific to general; for example, "watt" is a specific computer, one of several RS-6000 minicomputers in service at the School of Engineering and Applied Science (seas) at the University of Virginia (virginia). At the end of the series of domain names is the top level domain (here, edu), which includes hundreds of colleges and universities throughout the U.S. See *Domain Name Service (DNS)*.

Domain Name Service (DNS) A program that runs on an *Internet*—connected computer system (called a DNS server) and provides an automatic translation between domain names (such as watt.seas.virginia.edu) and *IP addresses* (128.143.7.186). The purpose of this translation process, called resolution, is to enable Internet users to continue using a familiar name (such as www.yahoo.com) even though the service's IP address may change.

domain name system (DNS) The conceptual system, standards, and names that make up the hierarchical organization of the *Internet* into named *domains*.

Dow Jones News/Retrieval Service An *online information service* from Dow Jones, the publishers of *The Wall Street Journal* and *Barron's,* that offers a computer-searchable index to financial and business publications and to up-to-date financial information, such as stock quotes.

download To transfer a file from another computer to your computer by means of a *modem* and a telephone line. See *upload*.

downloading Transferring a copy of a file from a distant computer to a disk in your computer using data communication links. See *file transfer protocol (ftp)* and *modem*.

DTD See *document type definition*.

dumb terminal See *terminal*.

dynamic bandwidth allocation (DBA) In *ISDN*, a method of allocating bandwidth on the fly so that the line can handle data and voice communications simultaneously. DBA works with the *Multilink Point-to-Point Protocol (MPPP)* and enables an ISDN user to accept a call on one of the lines even if both are being used to download or upload data. *See Basic Rate Interface (BRI)*.

ECPA See *Electronic Communications Privacy Act.*

edu A *domain name* denoting a U.S. college or university.

effective transmission rate The rate at which a *modem* that uses on-the-fly data compression communicates data to another modem. Data compression ensures that a given amount of data can be communicated at a given speed in a shorter amount of time than uncompressed data, so modems that use on-the-fly compression have higher throughput than modems that do not.

EGP See *Exterior Gateway Protocol.*

EINet Galaxy In the *World Wide Web (WWW),* a *subject tree* maintained by Enterprise Integration Network (EINet), a division of Microelectronics and Computer Technology Corporation. Like all subject trees, EINet Galaxy's coverage is limited by the ability of the staff responsible for maintaining it to find and classify useful new Web pages. The service also includes a *search engine* that helps users find the entries that the subject tree contains.

Electronic Communications Privacy Act (ECPA) A U.S. federal law, enacted in 1986, that prevents U.S. investigative agencies from intercepting *e-mail* messages, or reading such messages that are temporarily stored in interim storage devices (up to 180 days) without first obtaining a warrant.

electronic mail See *e-mail.*

element In *HTML,* a distinctive component of a document's structure, such as a title, heading, or list. HTML divides elements into two categories: head elements (such as the document's title) and body elements (headings, paragraphs, links, and text).

e-mail The use of a network to send and receive messages. Also called *electronic mail.*

e-mail address A series of characters that precisely identifies the location of a person's electronic *mailbox*. On the *Internet*, e-mail addresses consist of a *mailbox name* (such as rebecca) followed by an at sign (@) and the computer's *domain name* (as in rebecca@hummer.virginia.edu).

e-mail client A program or program module that provides *e-mail* services for computer users, including receiving mail into a locally-stored inbox, sending e-mail to other network users, replying to received messages, and storing received messages. The better programs include *address books, mail filters,* and the ability to compose and read messages coded in *HTML*. Synonymous with user agent.

emoticon In *e-mail* and *newsgroups,* a sideways face made of ASCII characters that puts a message into context and compensates for the lack of verbal inflections and body language that plagues electronic communication. Synonymous with smileys. For example:

:-)	Smile
:-D	Big (stupid) grin.
:-*	Kiss.
;-)	Wink
:-(	Frown
>:-(	Angry

encryption The process of converting a message into a ciphertext (an encrypted message) by using a *key*, so the message appears to be nothing but gibberish. However, the intended recipient can apply the key to decrypt and read the message. See *decryption, public key cryptography,* and *rot-13*.

entity In HTML, a code that represents a non-ASCII character, such as an accented character from a foreign language.

error-correction protocol In *modems,* a method for filtering out *line noise* and repeating transmissions automatically if an error occurs. Error correction requires the use of sending and receiving modems that conform to the same error-correction protocols. When error correction is in use, a reliable *link* is established. Two widely used error-correcting protocols are *MNP-4* and *V.42*. See *CCITT protocol*.

escape character In *Telnet*, a command (often Ctrl+[) that enables you to interrupt the link with the Telnet server so that you can communicate directly with your Telnet client. The escape character comes in handy when the Telnet server isn't responding.

escape code The series of characters that engages a *modem's command mode*. In the *Hayes command set*, the escape sequence consists of three plus signs (+++). Synonymous with escape sequence.

ETX/ACK handshaking See *handshaking*.

Eudora A pioneering *e-mail* program, now available for Windows and Macintosh computers, currently published by Qualcomm. The program includes *mail filtering* and other advanced utilities that simplify electronic mail management.

European Laboratory for Particle Physics (CERN) See *CERN*.

expect statement In a *communications program's login script*, a statement that tells the dialer to wait for the service provider's computer to send certain characters (such as "Please type your password").

expiration date In *Usenet*, the date at which a *post* is set to expire. The expiration date can be set in two ways: by the article's author, and by Usenet system administrators. On the expiration date, the article is deleted to conserve disk space for incoming articles. See *expired article*.

expired article In *Usenet*, an article that is still listed in the article selector, even though the Usenet system software has deleted the article because it has expired. You cannot read an expired article. See *expiration date*.

Exterior Gateway Protocol (EGP) An *Internet* protocol that defines the routing of Internet data between an *autonomous* *system (AS)* and the wider Internet. This protocol has been superceded by the *Border Gateway Protocol.*

external modem A *modem* with its own case, cables, and power supply, designed to plug into a serial port. See *internal modem.*

extraction The process of decompressing or decoding a compressed or encoded file. For example, extraction refers to the process of using *uudecode* to decode a file encoded for network transmission by *uuencode,* a Unix utility program.

extranet An *intranet* (internal TCP/IP network) that has been selectively opened to a firm's suppliers, customers, and strategic allies.

F2F In *e-mail,* a common abbreviation that means "face to face"—a real-life meeting.

fall back In *modems,* to decrease the *data transfer rate* to accommodate communication with an older modem or across a *dirty* line. Some modems also *fall forward* if *line noise* conditions improve.

fall forward In *modems,* to increase the *data transfer rate* if the quality of a connection improves. Some modems that *fall back* due to *line noise* can fall forward again if noise abates.

FAQ See *Frequently Asked Questions.*

favorite In *Microsoft Internet Explorer,* a saved *hyperlink* to which the user plans to return. Synonymous with *Bookmark* and *hotlist item.*

fax modem A modem that also functions as a fax machine, giving the computer user the capability of sending word processing documents and other files as faxes.

Fetch A popular *FTP client* for Macintosh Computers developed by Dartmouth College. The program is freeware.

Fidonet A set of data exchange standards and procedures that permit privately operated *BBSs* to exchange data, files, and *e-mail* internationally, using the world telephone system. At an agreed-on time when telephone rates are low, subscribing BBSs send e-mail messages and files to a regional host, which in turn distributes them to other bulletin boards. Responses, or echoes, eventually find their way back to the host bulletin board.

field-based search In a database or a Web *search engine,* a search that is restricted to a given field in the database. This is one of several methods that can be used to improve the recall and precision. The following table shows examples of the syntax used to perform field-based searches in *AltaVista:*

Field	Example
applet	applet:HoppingBunny
domain	domain:ca
from	from:"me@anywhere.com" (Usenet searches only)
host	host:"microsoft.com"
image	image:"Hale-Bopp"
keywords	keywords:GPS
link	link:http://www.pages.com/mypage.html
newsgroup	newsgroup:rec.boats.cruising (Usenet searches only)
site	site:www.microsoft.com
subject	subject:"keyboard shorcuts for Netscape" (Usenet searches only)
title	title:"Carpal Tunnel Syndrome"

file transfer protocol See *ftp.*

File Transfer Protocol (FTP) See *FTP.*

finger An *Intérnet* utility that enables you to obtain information about a user who has an *e-mail* address. Normally, this information is limited to the person's full name, job title, and address. However, the user can set up finger to retrieve one or more text files that contain information (such as a resume) that the user wants to make public.

firewall A *security* procedure that places a specially programmed computer system between an organization's local area network (LAN) and the *Internet.* The firewall computer prevents *crackers* from accessing the internal network. Unfortunately, it also prevents the organization's computer users from gaining direct access to the Internet. The access that the firewall provides is indirect and mediated by programs called *proxy servers.*

flame 1. In *Usenet* and *e-mail,* a message that contains abusive, threatening, obscene, or inflammatory language. In e-mail, a slang term meaning to lose your self-control by writing a message that uses derogatory, obscene, or inappropriate language. See *flame bait, flame war, moderated newsgroup,* and *rave.* 2. To write an abusive, threatening, obscene, or inflammatory e-mail message or Usenet post out of anger.

flame bait In a *newsgroup,* a posting that contains opinions that prompt *flames*—abusive remarks and personal attacks—and may ultimately launch a *flame war.* Flame-bait topics include abortion, homosexuality, and the desirability of using Microsoft Windows 95 versus using Macintosh. True flame bait unintentionally elicits such responses; when such postings are made intentionally, the post is more properly called a *troll.* See *moderated newsgroup.*

flame war In *newsgroups, LISTSERVs,* and mailing lists, an unproductive and long-running debate marked by high emotion and little information. See *flame* and *flame bait.*

follow-up post In an online *newsgroup,* a contribution posted in response to a previous posting. Unlike a reply, a follow-up post is public and can be read by everyone in the newsgroup.

Follow-up posts form a *thread* of discussion. See *distributed bulletin board, netiquette, Usenet.*

forgery In *Usenet,* mailing lists, or *e-mail,* a message written by someone other than the apparent author. *Internet* software enables any person with a modicum of technical knowledge to forge messages. An old Usenet custom is a host of April Fool's Day forgeries, which are harmless enough, but many forgeries are intended to embarrass and harass.

form In HyperText Markup Language *(HTML)* and *World Wide Web (WWW)* documents, a set of document features (including fill-in text areas, drop-down list boxes, check boxes, and option buttons) that enable you to interact with a Web page. Not all *Web browsers* can interact with forms. See *forms-capable browser.*

forms-capable browser A *Web browser* that can deal with HyperText Markup Language *(HTML) tags* that create on-screen, interactive *forms,* including fill-in text boxes, option buttons, and drop-down list boxes. Some early *Web browsers* could not interact with forms; the leading programs, such as *Microsoft Internet Explorer* and *Netscape Navigator,* have no trouble with these features.

forum See *newsgroup.*

Forum of Incident Response and Security Teams (FIRST) A unit of the *Internet Society (ISOC)* that coordinates the activities of several Computer Emergency Response Teams *(CERTs)* worldwide. FIRSTs purpose is to bring these teams together to foster cooperation and coordination when security-related incidents occur and to promote the sharing of information concerning the security perils facing the Internet.

frame 1. In data communications, a unit *(packet)* of data that is transmitted via the network. 2. In a *browser,* a section of the window that has been partitioned off to display a separate document. This is done with frame *tags.*

freenet A community-based bulletin board system *(BBS),* usually based in a public library, that attempts to make useful resources available to the local citizenry. Such resources include transcripts of city council meetings, access to the local library's card catalog, the names and addresses of community organizations, and, increasingly, access to the *Internet*. In keeping with the freenet's public-service orientation, access is free or very inexpensive.

Frequently Asked Questions (FAQ) In *Usenet*, a document automatically posted to a *newsgroup* at regular intervals and designed to assist new users. A FAQ contains a list of the questions that are commonly posted to the newsgroup, together with the answers that have emerged from the newsgroup participants collective experience.

FrontPage See *Microsoft FrontPage.*

ftp A standard that ensures the error-free transmission of program and data files through the telephone system. When written in lowercase, ftp refers to any *protocol,* such as *XMODEM, Kermit,* or *ZMODEM.* Compare to the Internet standard, *FTP.*

FTP Acronym for File Transfer Protocol. An *Internet* standard for the exchange of files. FTP (Uppercase letters) is a specific set of rules that comprise a file transfer protocol *(ftp)* (lowercase letters).

FTP client A program that is able to assist the user to upload or download files from an *FTP site.* There are many standalone FTP clients, and FTP downloading capabilities are built into *Web browsers* such as *Netscape Navigator.*

FTP server In the *Internet,* a *server* program that enables external users to *download* or *upload* files from a specified directory or group of directories.

FTP site An Internet *host,* running an FTP server, that makes a large number of files available for downloading. See *anonymous FTP.*

G

gateway A means by which users of one computer service or network can access certain kinds of information on a different service or network. For example, *Internet e-mail* users can exchange mail with *CompuServe* users by means of a gateway. Similarly, people using *Web browsers* can access the Archie service by means of a Web page that functions as an Archie gateway.

GEnie Developed by General Electric, an *online information service* that, like *CompuServe,* offers many of the attractions of a bulletin board system *(BBS)* and up-to-date stock quotes, conferences, *Internet e-mail,* home shopping, and news updates.

global kill file In a *Usenet* newsreader program, a file containing words, phrases, names, or network addresses that you have identified as signals of an unwanted message (such as "Make Money Fast!"). The program screens incoming articles for these signals and automatically deletes the articles before you even see them. A global kill file performs this function in all newsgroups, while a newsgroup *kill file* deletes unwanted messages only in specific newsgroups.

Gopher In Unix-based systems linked to the *Internet,* a menu-based program that helps you find files, programs, definitions, and other resources on topics you specify. Gopher was originally developed at the University of Minnesota and named after the school mascot. The *World Wide Web (WWW)* has made Gopher and other text-based Internet search tools obsolete, although some Gopher servers are still operating.

gopherspace In *Gopher,* the enormous computer-based "space" that is created by the global dissemination of Gopher-accessible resources. A search tool called *Veronica* enables you to search Gopherspace for directory titles and resources that match key words you supply.

gov A *domain name* denoting a government office or agency.

gzip A Unix compression program, created by the Open Software Foundation (OSF) and free from patent restrictions, that is widely used to compress files on the *Internet*. Files compressed with gzip have the extension .gz.

hacker 1. A computer enthusiast who enjoys learning everything about a computer system or network and through clever programming, pushing the system to its highest possible level of performance. 2. In the press, synonymous with *cracker*. 3. An adept programmer.

hacker ethic A set of moral principles that were common to the first-generation *hacker* community (roughly 1965—1982), described by Steven Levy in *Hackers* (1984). According to the hacker ethic, all technical information should, in principle, be freely available to all. Therefore, gaining entry to a system to explore data and increase knowledge is never unethical. However, destroying, altering, or moving data in such a way that could cause injury or expense to others is always unethical. In increasingly more states, unauthorized computer access is against the law. See *cracker* and *cyberspace*.

handle In a computer *chat room* or *Internet Relay Chat (IRC)*, an alias or pseudonym.

handshaking A method for controlling the flow of serial communication between two devices so that one device transmits data only when the other device is ready. In *hardware handshaking,* a separate wire sends a signal when the receiving device is ready to receive the signal; *software handshaking* uses special control characters. Devices such as serial printers use hardware handshaking because they are close to one another and can use a special cable. Because the telephone system doesn't have an extra wire available, the telephone connections that *modems* use require software handshaking. The two software handshaking techniques are ETX/ACK, which uses the ASCII character Ctrl+C to pause data transmission, and

XON/XOFF, which uses Ctrl+S to pause and Ctrl+Q to resume transmission.

hardware error control Physical modem circuits that implement an error-correction *protocol*, such as *MNP-4* or *V.42*. The alternative (found in less expensive modems) is software error control, which requires the computer's central processing unit (CPU) to monitor the data stream for errors.

hardware handshaking In a serial data communications device such as a *modem*, a method of synchronizing two devices in a communications channel by means of separate physical circuits, which are used to send signals indicating that a device is ready to receive data. Compare *software handshaking*, in which this task is performed by inserting information into the data stream.

Hayes command set A standardized set of instructions used to control *modems*, introduced by Hayes, a pioneering modem manufacturer. Common Hayes commands include the following:

AT	Attention (used to start all commands)
ATDT	Attention, dial in tone mode
+++	Enter the command mode during the communication session
ATH	Attention, hang up

Hayes-compatible modem A *modem* that recognizes the *Hayes command set*.

header In *e-mail* or a *Usenet* news *article*, the beginning of a message. The header contains important information about the sender's address, the subject of the message, and other information.

helper program A supplementary program that enables a Web browser to handle multimedia files, such as animations, videos, and sounds. When the browser encounters a file it cannot read, it examines the file's extension. The browser then consults a lookup table that tells it which helper program to start. When the helper program starts, it runs as a separate program, unlike *plug-ins*, which extend the capabilities of the browser and can often display the multimedia data within the browser window.

hierarchy   In *Usenet*, a category of *newsgroups*. Within the standard newsgroups, for example, seven hierarchies exist: *comp, misc, news, rec, sci, soc*, and *talk*. The term hierarchies suggests the way that newsgroups are internally categorized. For example, the rec.* hierarchy includes many newsgroups pertaining to hobbies and recreation; the rec.comics.* hierarchy contains several newsgroups for comic collectors; and the rec.comics.elfquest newsgroup focuses on Wendy and Richard Pini's Elfquest comics. See *alt hierarchy, local Usenet hierarchy*, and *standard newsgroup hierarchy*.

history list   In a Web browser, a window that shows all the Web sites that the browser has accessed during a given period, such as the last 30 days.

hit   An externally originated request for a specific file, such as a graphic or *HTML* page, by means of the HyperText Transfer Protocol *(HTTP)*. Servers record the number of hits a Web site receives, but this is not identical to the number of unique individuals who have accessed the site; because many pages contain graphics, *Java* applets, sounds, and other resources, retrieving one page may require as many as a dozen or more hits.

holy war   A protracted and often incendiary debate within the computing community regarding the merits of a particular computer, operating system, or programming style. Holy wars tend to strike outsiders as ridiculous.

home page   1. In any *hypertext* system, including the *World Wide Web (WWW)*, a document intended to serve as an initial point of entry to a *web* of related documents. Also called a welcome page, a home page contains general introductory information, as well as *hyperlinks* to related resources. A well-designed home page contains internal navigation buttons that help users find their way among the various documents that the home page makes available. 2. The start page that is automatically displayed when you start a *Web browser* or click the program's Home button. 3. A personal page listing an individual's contact information, contact information, and favorite links, and (generally) some information—ranging from cryptic to voluminous—about the individual's perspective on life.

home server In *Gopher,* the server that the Gopher client program is configured to display automatically when you start the program.

host In the *Internet,* any computer that can function as the beginning and end point of data transfers. An Internet host has a unique Internet address (called an *IP address*) and a unique *domain name.*

HotBot A *search engine* for keyword searches on the *World Wide Web (WWW),* created by *Wired* magazine, that produces markedly better results when used for free text searching than competing search engines. HotBot retrieval lists are generally shorter and contain more relevant items than the longer lists produced by *AltaVista* and *Lycos.* To restrict the search further, searches can use case-sensitive searching and phrase searches.

HotDog An *HTML editor* published by Sausage Software that offers a number of features attractive to authors of complex sites, including a project manager that automatically opens all the files of a site and uploads them via *FTP* in a manner that preserves their location within the server's directory structure.

hotlist In a *Web browser,* a list of favorite *World Wide Web (WWW)* sites that a user saves for future use while browsing. To retrieve hotlist items, you select the item that you want in a menu or dialog box and then choose the Go To command or its equivalent. In *Netscape Navigator,* the hotlist items are called bookmarks, and the hotlist is called the bookmark list. In *Microsoft Internet Explorer,* the preferred term is favorites list.

hotlist item In a *Web browser's hotlist,* a stored *URL* that enables the user to quickly return to the URL just by choosing the item from a menu. Synonymous with *favorite* and *Bookmark.*

HoTMetaL A stand-alone *HTML editor,* created by SoftQuad Systems, for Microsoft Windows 95 systems. Widely distributed as shareware, HoTMetaL is also available in a professional version called HoTMetaL Pro.

HTML Acronym for HyperText Markup Language. A *declarative markup language (DML)* for marking the portions of a document (called elements) so that, when accessed by a program called a *Web browser*, each portion appears with a distinctive format. HTML is the markup language behind the appearance of documents on the *World Wide Web (WWW)*. HTML is standardized by means of a *document type definition (DTD)* composed in the Standard Generalized Markup Language *(SGML)*. HTML includes capabilities that enable authors to insert *hyperlinks*, which when clicked display another HTML document. The agency responsible for standardizing HTML is the *World Wide Web Consortium (W3C)*.

HTML 1.0 The original *HTML* specification, drafted in 1990. Because it contains certain *tags* that are no longer used, this specification is considered obsolete. The *HTML 3.2* specification is now considered authoritative. Also known as HTML Level 1.

HTML 2.0 A now-obsolete *HTML* specification that described HTML practice, as of mid-1994, and formalizes these practices as an *Internet Draft*. The major updates from *HTML 1.0* are the inclusion of forms and the removal of certain little-used *tags*. The *HTML 2.0* specification does not include many practices, such as tables and the *Netscape extensions,* that have arisen since its release.

HTML 3.0 An older *HTML* specification that would have greatly extended HTML relative to the 2.0 standard. However, this specification did not line up well enough with prevailing Web practice and has been superseded by the current recommended standard, 3.2.

HTML 3.2 The HTML specification that is (at this writing) recommended by the *World Wide Web Consortium (W3C),* the organization responsible for standardizing Web practices. HTML incorporates many widely-used and called-for features, including tables, subscript and superscript characters, text flow around images, *Java applets,* and style sheets. See *Cougar.*

HTML editor   A program that provides assistance in preparing documents for the *World Wide Web (WWW)* using the *HTML*. The simplest HTML editor is a word processing program that enables you to type text and add HTML *tags* manually. Stand-alone HTML editors provide automated assistance with HTML coding and display some formats on-screen. See *HoTMetaL* and *HotDog*.

HTTP   The *Internet* standard that supports the exchange of information on the *World Wide Web (WWW)*. By defining *Uniform Resource Locators (URLs)* and how they can be used to retrieve resources (including not only Web documents but also *FTP*-accessible files, *Usenet newsgroups,* and *Gopher* menus) anywhere on the Internet, HTTP enables Web authors to embed *hyperlinks* in Web documents. HTTP defines the process by which a Web client, called a *browser,* originates a request for information and sends it to a *Web server,* a program designed to respond to HTTP requests and provide the desired information. HTTP 1.0, in widespread use, has many shortcomings, including an inefficient design and slow performance. A new specification, HTTP 1.1, directly addresses these issues and will result in improved network performance, but *servers* will have to be updated.

httpd   See *HyperText Transfer Protocol Daemon.*

HTTPS   1. A variation on the *HTTP protocol* that provides *SSL security* for online transactions using the *World Wide Web (WWW)*. 2. A *Web server* for Microsoft Windows NT created and maintained by the European Microsoft Windows NT Academic Centre (EMWAC) project, at the University of Edinburgh. The server is available through *anonymous FTP* and incorporates several unique features, such as the capability to search *Wide Area Information Server (WAIS)* databases in response to browser queries.

hyperlink   In a *hypertext* system, an underlined or otherwise emphasized word or phrase that, when clicked with the mouse, displays another document.

hypermedia   A *hypertext* system that employs multimedia resources (graphics, videos, animations, and sounds).

hypertext A method of preparing and publishing text, ideally suited to the computer, in which readers can choose their own paths through the material. To prepare hypertext, you first "chunk" the information into small, manageable units, such as single pages of text. These units are called nodes. You then embed *hyperlinks* (also called anchors) in the text. When the reader clicks on a hyperlink, the hypertext software displays a different node. The process of navigating among the nodes linked in this way is called *browsing*. A collection of nodes that are interconnected by hyperlinks is called a *web*. The *World Wide Web (WWW)* is a hypertext system on a global scale.

HyperText Markup Language See *HTML*.

HyperText Transfer Protocol See *HTTP*.

HyperText Transfer Protocol Daemon (httpd) A *Web server* originally developed at the Swiss Center for Particle Research *(CERN)* and originally called CERN httpd. Subsequently, httpd was developed independently at the *National Center for Supercomputing Applications (NCSA)* for UNIX systems. An important innovation in the history of Web servers, NASA httpd introduced *forms*, clickable *image maps*, *authentication*, and key word searches. Most of these features are now taken for granted in other Web servers. An adaptation of the program for *Microsoft Windows 95*, called Windows httpd, is available.

Hytelnet A *hypertext*-based guide to the *Telnet*-based resources accessible on the Internet, including libraries, *freenets*, bulletin board systems *(BBS)*, and other information sites. A *World Wide Web (WWW)* gateway version is available.

I

IAP See *Internet access provider*.

ICMP See *Internet Control Message Protocol*.

IDEA See *International Data Encryption Algorithm*.

IIOP   See *Internet Inter-ORB Protocol.*

image map   In *HTML,* a graphic that has been coded so that specific regions of the graphic are associated with specific *URLs.* When the user clicks one of these regions, the browser initiates a *hyperlink* jump to the associated document or resource.

IMAP   See *Internet Message Access Protocol.*

IMAP4   Acronym for Internet Message Access Protocol Version 4.

IMHO   In a *chat room* or *Usenet,* an acronym for In My Humble Opinion.

include   To quote someone's *e-mail* or *Usenet* message within one's own message.

index   A Web page that gathers together the leading or best hyperlinks in a particular topical area.

Infobahn   A term preferred by some for the so-called *Information Superhighway,* a high-speed information system that would link homes, schools, and offices with high-bandwidth local delivery systems and backbone systems capable of gigabit-per-second speeds.

information service   See *BBS* and *online information service.*

Information Superhighway   An envisioned information infrastructure that will bring high-speed computer networking within the reach of homes, schools, and offices. The term is misleading in that the freeways, high-speed backbone networks, already exist; what is lacking is a good system of local roads. The current telephone system does not have the bandwidth to deliver high-speed digital services to the home; a capital investment on the order of $325 billion would be necessary to replace the existing telephone lines with high-speed fiber optic cables. The replacement will occur, but we will be decades into the 21st century before it is complete.

Infoseek   A *search engine* for keyword searches on the *World Wide Web,* created by Infoseek Corporation. Searchers can choose from Ultraseek, an unusually capable Web search engine, or Ultrasmart, which displays links to subject categories that are possibly relevant to the supplied search keywords. The search engine is capable of case-sensitive searches, *automatic name recognition, field-based searches,* phrase searching, and automatic detection of word variants.

initialization string   Certain commands from the *Hayes command set,* issued to the modem by a *communications program* at the beginning of a communication session, that establishes an active configuration. Initialization strings enable communications programs to work smoothly with a variety of modems, and often you can choose an initialization string appropriate for your modem from a list provided in your communications program.

in-line image   A graphic that has been placed so that it appears on the same line with text. In *HTML*, in-line images are defined by the IMG tag, which specifies the source of the graphic, its alignment (top, middle, or bottom), and the text to display if the document is accessed by a text-only browser.

Integrated Services Digital Network   See *ISDN.*

Interior Gateway Protocol   An *Internet* standard *(protocol)* that governs the routing of data within an *autonomous system (AS)*—a network or group of networks that is under a single administrator's control.

internal modem   A *modem* designed to fit into the expansion bus of a personal computer. See *external modem.*

internal navigation aid   In a series of related *World Wide Web (WWW)* documents, the hyperlinks or clickable buttons that provide users with a way of navigating through the documents without getting lost. If you see a Home button on one of the pages in a web, for example, you can click it to return to the web's *welcome page.* This is different from clicking the browser's Home button, which displays the browser's default *home page.*

International Data Encryption Algorithm (IDEA)   An *encryption* technique that employs a 128-bit *key* and is considered by most *cryptanalysts* to be the most secure encryption algorithm available today.

internet A group of local area networks (LANs) that have been connected by means of a common *communications protocol* and *packet* redirection devices called *routers,* so that, from the user's perspective, this group of networks seems as if it is one large network. Note the small "i"—many internets exist besides the *Internet,* including many *TCP/IP-* based networks that are not linked to the Internet (the Defense Data Network is a case in point).

Internet An enormous and rapidly-growing system of linked computer networks, world-wide in scope, that facilitates data communication services such as remote login, file transfer, electronic mail, the World Wide Web, and newsgroups. Relying on *TCP/IP,* the Internet assigns every connected computer a unique *Internet address,* also called an *IP address,* so that any two connected computers can locate each other on the network and exchange data. Although there are Internet connections in virtually every country in the world, the network is still predominantly English-speaking and most users live in English-speaking countries. Within English-speaking countries, the Internet is best seen as a new public communications medium, potentially on a par with the telephone system or television in ubiquity and impact. The Internet is the largest example in existence of an *internet.*

Internet access provider (IAP) A company or consortium that provides high-speed access to the Internet to businesses, universities, nonprofit organizations, and Internet service providers (ISPs), who in turn provide Internet access to individuals. Some IAPs are also ISPs.

Internet address The unique, 32-bit address assigned to a computer that is connected to the Internet, represented in dotted decimal notation (for example, 128.117.38.5). Synonymous with *IP address.*

Internet Control Message Protocol (ICMP) An extension to the original *Internet Protocol (IP)* that provides much-needed error and congestion control. Using ICMP, for example, routers can "tell" other routers that a given branch of the network is congested or not responding. ICMP provides an echo function that enables *PING* applications to determine whether a given *host* is reachable.

Internet Draft   A working document of the Internet Engineering Task Force (IETF), a unit of the Internet Architecture Board (IAB). Internet Drafts are unofficial discussion documents, meant to be circulated on the *Internet,* that are not intended to delineate new standards.

Internet Explorer   See *Microsoft Internet Explorer.*

Internet Inter-ORB Protocol (IIOP)   An Internet standard (protocol) that enables interoperability between Internet clients and CORBA servers, on the one hand, and between CORBA clients and Internet servers on the other. CORBA, an acronym for Common Object Request Broken Architecture, is a middleware standard for large-scale, multi-platfrom local area networks. In a CORBA-based network, programmers create an object (a mini-program with a well defined function) just once and make this available throughout the network. Using CORBA standards, programs can request functionality from an object; for example, if a program needs to perform a statistical analysis, it can request a copy of the object that makes this possible, and this functionality becomes available seamlessly. IIOP extends this functionality throughout the Internet.

Internet Message Access Protocol (IMAP)   In Internet *e-mail,* one of two fundamental *protocols* (the other is *POP3*) that governs how and where users store their incoming mail messages. IMAP stores messages on the mail server rather than facilitating downloading to the user's computer, as does the POP3 standard. For many users, this standard may prove more convenient than POP3 because all of one's mail is kept in one central location, where it can be organized, archived, and made available from remote locations. IMAP4 is supported by *Netscape Messenger,* the mail package in *Netscape Communicator,* and by other leading e-mail programs.

Internet Protocol (IP) In *TCP/IP,* the standard that describes how an Internet-connected computer should break data down into *packets* for transmission across the network, and how those packets should be addressed so that they arrive at their destination. IP is the connectionless part of the TCP/IP protocols; the *Transmission Control Protocol (TCP)* specifies how two Internet computers can establish a reliable data link by means of *handshaking.* See *connectionless protocol* and *packet-switching network.*

Internet Relay Chat (IRC) A real-time, Internet-based chat service, in which one can find "live" participants from the world over. IRC requires the use of an IRC client program, which displays a list of the current IRC channels. After joining a channel, you can see what other participants are typing on-screen, and you can type your own repartee.

Internet Server Application Programming Interface See *ISAPI.*

Internet service provider (ISP) A company that provides Internet accounts and connections to individuals and businesses. Most ISPs offer a range of connection options, ranging from dial-up modem connections to high-speed *ISDN.* Also provided is *e-mail, Usenet,* assistance with publishing material on the *World Wide Web (WWW).* See *Internet access provider (IAP).*

Internet Society (ISOC) An international, not-for-profit organization that seeks to maintain and broaden the *Internet's* availability. Created in 1992, ISOC is governed by an elected board of trustees. The organization sponsors annual conferences and has numerous publication programs. The Internet Society coordinates the activities of the Internet Architecture Board (IAB), the Internet Engineering Task Force (IETF), the Internet Engineering Steering Group (IESG), the Internet Engineering and Planning Group (IEPG), the Internet Assigned Numbers Authority (IANA), and the Internet PCA Registration Authority (IPRA).

InterNIC A consortium of two organizations that provide networking information services to the *Internet* community, under contract to the National Science Foundation (NSF).

Currently, AT&T provides directory and database services, while Network Solutions, Inc., provides registration services for new *domain names* and *IP addresses*.

InterSLIP   A *freeware* program, created by InterCon Systems Corp., that provides Serial Line Internet Protocol *(SLIP)* connectivity, including a dialer program, for Macintosh computers. InterSLIP requires *MacTCP.*

intranet   A computer network designed to meet the internal needs of a single organization or company that is based on *Internet* technology *(TCP/IP)*. Not necessarily open to the external Internet and almost certainly not accessible from the outside, an intranet enables organizations to make internal resources available using familiar Internet. See *extranet.*

IP   See *Internet Protocol.*

IP address   A 32-bit binary number that uniquely and precisely identifies the location of a particular computer on the *Internet*. Every computer that is directly connected to the Internet must have an IP address. Because binary numbers are so hard to read, IP addresses are given in four-part decimal numbers, each part representing 8 bits of the 32-bit address (for example, 128.143.7.226). On networks and *SLIP/PPP* connections that dynamically assign IP numbers when you log on, this number may change from session to session.

IPv6   The Next Generation Internet Protocol, also known as IPng, an evolutionary extension of the current Internet protocol suite that is under development by the Internet Engineering Task Force (IETF). Ipv6 was originally intended to deal with the coming exhaustion of *IP addresses,* a serious problem caused by the Internet's rapid growth. However, the development effort has broadened to address a number of deficiencies in the current versions of the fundamental Internet protocols, including *security,* the lack of support for mobile computing, the need for automatic configuration of network devices, the lack of support for allocating bandwidth to high-priority data transfers, and other shortcomings of the current protocols. An unresolved question is whether the working committee will be able to persuade network equipment suppliers to upgrade to the new protocols.

IPng See *IPv6*.

IP number See *Internet address*.

IRC See *Internet Relay Chat*.

ISAPI Acronym for *Internet Server Application Programming Interface*. An *application program interface (API)* that enables programmers to include links to computer programs, such as database searches, in Web pages. ISAPI is designed to work with Microsoft Information Server. ISAPI provides the same functionality as *Common Gateway Interface (CGI)*, but with markedly improved functionality and reduced overhead; ISAPI requests make full use of the Windows programming environment, and the called programs remain resident in memory in case they will be needed again.

ISDN A world-wide standard for the delivery of digital telephone and data services to homes, schools, and offices. ISDN services fall into three categories: *Basic Rate Interface (BRI)*, *Primary Rate Interface (PRI)*, and *Broadband ISDN (B-ISDN)*. Designed as the basic option for consumers, Basic Rate Interface offers two 64,000 bit per second channels for voice, graphics, and data, plus one 16,000 bit per second channel for signaling purposes. Primary Rate ISDN provides 23 channels with 64,000 bits per second capacity. Broadband ISDN, still under development, would supply up to 150 million bits per second of data transmission capacity.

ISOC See *Internet Society*.

ISP See *Internet Service Provider*.

J++ A programming environment for *Java* programming created by Microsoft Corporation. The package includes all the tools needed to create *Java applets* and *Java applications* efficiently, including a compiler and debugger.

Java   A *cross-platform* programming language created by Sun Microsystems that enables programmers to write a program that will execute on any computer capable of running a Java interpreter (which is built into today's leading *Web browsers*). Java is an object-oriented programming (OOP) language that is very similar to C++, except that it eliminates some features of C++ that programmers found to be tedious and time-consuming. Java programs are compiled into *applets* (small programs designed to be executed by a browser) or applications (larger, stand-alone programs that require a Java interpreter to be present on the user's computer), but the compiled code contains no machine code. Instead, the output of the compiler is *byte-code,* an intermediary between source code and machine code that can be transmitted via computer networks, including the Internet.

Java applet   A small program (applet) that is designed for distribution on the *World Wide Web (WWW)* and for interpretation by a Java-capable *Web browser,* such as *Microsoft Internet Explorer* or *Netscape Navigator.* Java applets execute within the browser window and seamlessly add functionality to Web pages. However, their functionality is restricted due to *security* restrictions, which prevent applets from gaining access to the computer's file system. See *Java application.*

Java application   A Java program that, unlike a *Java applet,* executes in its own window and possesses full access to the computer's file system. To run a Java application, the user's computer must be equipped with a stand-alone Java interpreter, such as the one included with the *Java Development Kit (JDK).* If Java applications are written in conformity to Sun's 100% Pure Java specifications, they will run on any computer that is capable of running a Java interpreter.

JavaBean   A reusable object, created with *Java* and in conformity to Sun's 100% Pure Java specifications, that is packaged according to the JavaBeans specifications. A JavaBean differs from a Java applet in that it has persistence (it remains on the user's system after execution). Additionally, Beans are capable of communicating and exchanging data with other JavaBeans by means of interprocess communication.

Java Development Kit (JDK) A package of Java utilities and development tools, created by Sun Microsystems and distributed free of charge, that represents the de facto standard for the *Java* programming language. The package contains an interpreter that enables users to run *Java applications.*

JavaScript A scripting language for Web publishing, developed by *Netscape Communications,* that enables Web authors to embed simple *Java*-like programming instructions within the *HTML* text of their Web pages. Originally called LiveScript, JavaScript was made more Java-like after Netscape Communications realized that Java would succeed, but JavaScript lacks the powerful inheritance capabilities of Java and is, at best, a simple scripting language.

JavaScript style sheet (JSS) A proprietary extension to the *World Wide Web Consortium (W3C)* standards for *cascading style sheets (CSS).* JSS is designed to enable *JavaScript* programmers to create dynamic effects by including JavaScript instructions in the various style definitions.

JavaSoft A subsidiary of Sun Microsystems that is responsible for developing and promoting the *Java* programming language and related products.

Java Virtual Machine A Java interpreter and runtime environment for *Java applets* and *Java applications.* This environment is called a virtual machine because, no matter what kind of computer it is running on, it creates a simulated computer that provides the correct platform for executing Java programs. In addition, this approach insulates the computer's file system from rogue applications. Java VMs are available for most computers.

JDBC Acronym for Java Database Connectivity. A *JavaSoft*-developed *application program interface (API)* that enables Java programs to interact with any database program that complies with the SQL query language.

JDK See *Java Development Kit.*

JIT compiler Abbreviation for Just in Time compiler. A compiler that receives the *bytecode* from a *Java* application or *applet*, and compiles the bytecode into machine code on the fly. Code compiled with a JIT executes much faster than code executed by a Java interpreter, such as the ones built into popular *Web browsers*.

Jscript Microsoft's version of *JavaScript*; it is not completely compatible with JavaScript, however, and for this reason is not widely used.

JSS See *JavaScript style sheet*.

Jughead In *Gopher*, a search service that enables you to search all of *gopherspace* for key words appearing in directory titles (not menu items). To search both directory titles and menu items, use *Veronica*.

K

K56plus One of two competing modulation protocols for 56 Kbps *modems*. The K56plus standard is backed by Lucent and Rockwell; the competing x.2 standard is backed by U.S. Robotics. The two standards do not work together. A decision concerning the 56 Kbps modem standard will be made by the International Telecommunications Union-Telecommunications Standards Section (ITU-TSS).

Kbps See *bits per second*.

Kermit An asynchronous *communications protocol* that makes the error-free transmission of program files via the telephone system easier. Developed by Columbia University and placed in the public domain, Kermit is used by academic institutions because, unlike *XMODEM*, Kermit can be implemented on mainframe systems that transmit 7 bits per byte.

key In *cryptography*, the procedure that is used to encipher the message so that it appears to be just so much nonsense. The key also is required for *decryption*. In *public key cryptography*, there are two keys, a private key and a public key. A user makes the public key known to others, who use it to encrypt messages; these messages can be decrypted only by the intended recipient of a message, who uses the private key to do so.

kick An action undertaken by an IRC *channel op* to expel an unwanted user from the channel.

kill file In a *Usenet* newsreader, a file that contains a list of subjects or names that you don't want to appear on the list of messages available for you to read. If you no longer want to read messages from Edward P. Jerk, you can add Ed's name to your *newsreaders* kill file, and his contributions will be discarded automatically before they reach your screen.

kiosk mode In a *Web browser*, a mode that zooms the program to full screen, permitting its use as an information navigation tool in a kiosk.

knowbot See *agent*.

leased line A permanently-connected and conditioned telephone line that provides wide area network (WAN) connectivity to an organization or business.

line noise Interference in a telephone line, caused by current fluctuations, poor connections in telephone equipment, crosstalk from adjacent lines, or environmental conditions such as lightning. Line noise may reduce the *data transfer rate* a *modem* can sustain, or may introduce garbage characters into the data stream.

link rot A slang expression for the tendency of *hyperlinks* to go stale (cease to function) when the page targeted by a hyperlink is moved or disappears entirely.

LISTSERV A commercial mailing list manager, originally developed in 1986 for BITNET mailing lists, that has since been ported to Unix, Microsoft Windows, and Windows 95. LISTSERV is marketed by L-Soft International. See *Majordomo.*

local Usenet hierarchy A category of *Usenet newsgroups* that is set up for local distribution only, for example, within the confines of a company or university.

login In a computer network, the authentication process in which a user supplies a *login name* and *password.* Also spelled logon. Can also refer to the *login name* itself.

login name A unique name assigned to you by the system administrator that is used as a means of initial identification. You must type this name and also your *password* to gain access to the system.

login script In *dialup access,* a list of instructions that guides the *dialer program* through the process of dialing the service provider's number, supplying the user's login name and password, and establishing the connection.

log off The process of terminating a connection with a computer system or peripheral device in an orderly way.

log on The process of establishing a connection with, or gaining access to, a network or computer.

logon file A batch file or configuration file that starts the network software and establishes the connection with the network when you turn on the workstation.

lurk To read a newsgroup or mailing list without ever posting a message. See *delurk.*

Lycos A *search engine* for locating *World Wide Web* documents. Lycos, named after a particularly energetic night-hunting spider, relies on an automated search routine (called a *spider*) that prowls the Web, discovering new Web, *FTP,* and *Gopher* documents (about 5,000 per day). The additions become part of Lycos' huge database. For each document, Lycos indexes words in the title, headings, subheadings, all of the document's hyperlinks, the 100 most important words in the document, and the words in the first 20 lines of text. A searcher wishing to locate documents containing words buried more deeply in a page should use *AltaVista,* which indexes the entire document text. See *Infoseek.*

LYNX A full-screen, text-only *Web browser* for Unix computers, created by Lou Montoulli of the University of Kansas. LYNX is a full-featured Web browser but it cannot display *in-line images.*

MacHTTP A popular, easy-to-use *Web server* for Macintosh computers that can handle up to 10 simultaneous connections. A more powerful commercial version is called WebStar.

MacTCP A Macintosh utility program, developed by Apple Computer and included with System 7.5, that provides the *TCP/IP* support needed to connect Macintoshes to the Internet. A separate *communications program* is needed to connect via Serial Line Internet Protocol *(SLIP)* or Point-to-Point Protocol *(PPP).*

mail bombing A form of harassment that involves sending numerous large *e-mail* messages to a person's electronic *mailbox.*

mailbox The storage space that has been set aside to store an individual's *e-mail* messages.

mailbox name One of the two basic parts of a person's *e-mail address:* the part to the left of the at sign (@), which specifies the name of the person's *mailbox.* To the right of the @ sign is the *domain name* of the computer that houses the mailbox. A person's mailbox name often is the same as his or her *login name.*

mail client See *e-mail client.*

mail filter A filter program or utility within an *e-mail* program that screens incoming mail, and then sorts the mail into folders or directories based on content found in one or more of the message's fields.

mail gateway A computer that enables two mutually incompatible computer networks to exchange *e-mail*. America Online users, for example, can exchange e-mail with *Internet* users by means of a gateway. In some cases, gateways cannot handle *attachments*.

mail reflector See *LISTSERV.*

mail server A program that responds automatically to *e-mail* messages. Mail server programs exist that enter or remove subscriptions to mailing lists and send information in response to a request.

mailto In *HTML,* an attribute that enables Web authors to create a link to a person's *e-mail* address. When the user clicks the mailto link, the browser displays a window for composing an e-mail message to this address.

mail user agent See *e-mail client.*

Majordomo A popular freeware mailing list manager for Unix computer systems. See *LISTSERV.*

mall On the *World Wide Web (WWW),* a shopping service that provides Web publishing space for business *storefronts* (Web pages that describe retail or service offerings). Malls typically offer credit-card ordering by means of secure servers and shopping carts, which enable users to select purchases and pay for them all when they are finished shopping.

MAPI See *Messaging Application Program Interface (MAPI).*

Mbone An experimental method of distributing data packets on the Internet in which a server broadcasts data to two or more servers simultaneously. This technique, also called IP multicasting, moves data packets to their multiple destinations in streams rather than packets, and is therefore more suitable for real-time audio and video than the standard TCP/IP network. Special routers are required.

Mbps See *bits per second.*

message transfer agent (MTA)   A program that sends *e-mail* messages to another message transfer agent. On the *Internet,* the most widely used MTA is *sendmail.*

Messaging Application Program Interface (MAPI)   The Microsoft implementation of an *application program interface (API)* that provides access to messaging services for developers. MAPI Version 3.2 provides resources to programmers for cross-platform messaging that is independent of the operating system and underlying hardware and makes applications mail-aware. MAPI can send messages to and from *Vendor Independent Messaging (VIM)* programs.

Microcom Networking Protocol   See *MNP.*

Microsoft Exchange   A message-management program capable of managing faxes and several types of *e-mail* on a local area network. Microsoft Exchange Server provides enterprise-wide e-mail and groupware support for enterprises. Because many businesses are constructing *extranets* that require data exchange beyond the boundaries of the corporate LAN, Microsoft is migrating Exchange to an *Internet* protocol base; Exchange 5.0 supports *NNTP* news, *POP3* and *IMAP* mail, and other Internet protocols.

Microsoft FrontPage   A WYSIWYG editor for *HTML*, created by Microsoft, that combines advanced Web publishing with graphical site management. Some of the advanced features do not work unless your *Internet service provider (ISP)* is running the Microsoft FrontPage extensions for *Microsoft Internet Information Server.* The program is available for Windows and Macintosh systems.

Microsoft Internet Assistant   An *HTML editor* and *Web browser* add-on for Microsoft Word for Windows 6.0. Distributed free of charge, Microsoft Internet Assistant transforms Microsoft Word into a what-you-see-is-what-you-get (WYSIWYG) HTML editor, in which you see the results of the HTML *tags* rather than the tags themselves.

Microsoft Internet Explorer (MSIE)   A popular *Web browser* for Microsoft Windows and Macintosh computers. Competing effectively with the most popular browser package,

Netscape Communicator, the Internet Explorer suite includes e-mail and newsgroups via *Microsoft Outlook Express, push media* support with Webcaster, WYSIWYG HTML composing with a stripped-down version of *Microsoft FrontPage* called FrontPad, Internet telephony and videoconferencing with Microsoft NetMeeting, and streaming audio and video with Microsoft NetShow.

Microsoft Internet Information Server A *Web server*, created by Microsoft Corporation for Microsoft Windows NT systems, that offers excellent performance on a much less expensive hardware platform than competing Unix servers. Included is a built-in search engine for searching documents, management tools, *Microsoft FrontPage,* and ODBC support for searching external databases. Tightly integrated with Windows NT (and requiring Windows NT Server), this server is a good choice for companies that have adopted Windows widely and that have Windows technical expertise; *Netscape Enterprise Server* is better suited to *cross-platform* networks that include Unix systems.

Microsoft Mail A proprietary enterprise *e-mail* standard introduced by *Microsoft* with its enterprise messaging application, *Microsoft Exchange.* Microsoft is currently migrating mail formats to *Internet* protocols.

Microsoft Outlook Express An easy-to-use *e-mail* program, distributed with Internet Explorer, that includes advanced features such as filters and *S/MIME* encryption.

MIME Acronym for Multipurpose Internet Mail Extensions. An *Internet* standard that specifies how tools, such as *e-mail* programs and *Web browsers,* can transfer multimedia files (including sounds, graphics, and video) via the Internet. Prior to the development of MIME, all data transferred via the Internet had to be coded in ASCII text. See *uuencode* and *uudecode.*

MIME encoding In an *e-mail* message, a method of encoding *binary files* in conformance with the Multipurpose Internet Mail Extension *(MIME)* standard. In order to receive the Mail message, the user must be running an *e-mail client* that is capable of decoding this format. Another commonly used encoding format is *uuencode.*

MIME type   In Multipurpose Internet Mail Extensions *(MIME),* a code that specifies the content type of a multimedia file. The Internet Assigned Numbers Authority (IANA) controls the naming of MIME types. A Web browser detects MIME types by examining the file's extension; for example, a file with the extension *.mpg or *.mpeg contains an MPEG video.

misc hierarchy   In *Usenet,* one of the *standard newsgroup hierarchies,* containing newsgroups that do not fit in the other categories (comp, sci, news, rec, soc, and talk). Examples of misc newsgroups include misc.consumers, misc.kids.computers, and misc.writing.

MNP   Abbreviation for Microcom Networking Protocol. Any of 10 error-correction and *data-compression protocols* used by *modems.* MNP-1 is obsolete; MNP-2, MNP-3, and *MNP-4* are error-correction protocols used in the *V.42* international standard. *MNP-5* is an on-the-fly data-compression protocol used by most modern modems, and MNP-6 through MNP-10 are proprietary communications standards.

MNP-4   The most popular *error-correction protocol,* which filters out *line noise* and eliminates errors that can occur during the transmission and reception of data via *modem.* For error correcting to function, both modems—the one sending as well as the one receiving the transmission—must have error-checking capabilities conforming to the same error-correcting protocol.

MNP-5   The same *error-correction protocol* as *MNP-4,* as well as a data-compression protocol for computer *modems* that speeds transmissions by compressing (encoding, actually) data on the sending end and decompressing the data on the reception end. If the data isn't already compressed, gains in effective transmission speeds of up to 200 percent can be realized. See *data-compression protocol.*

modem   A device that converts the digital signals generated by the serial port to the modulated analog signals required for transmission over a telephone line and, likewise, transforms

incoming analog signals to their digital equivalents. The speed
at which a modem (short for modulator/demodulator) transmits data is measured in units called *bits per second (bps)*
(technically not the same as *baud*, although the terms are often
and erroneously used interchangeably). Modems come in various speeds and use various modulation protocols. The most
recent standard (at this writing), an addition to the V.34 standard, enables communication at 33.6 Kbps. Several proprietary
standards have been offered for 56 Kbps modems, including
U.S. Robotics' *x2* protocol. Two common standards for *error-
correction protocols* eliminate errors attributable to noise and other
glitches in the telephone system: *MNP-4* and *V.42*. For data-
compression, two standards predominate: *V.42bis* and *MNP-5*.

moderated newsgroup   In a distributed bulletin board system *(BBS)*, such as *Usenet*, a topical conference in which one
or more moderators screen contributions before the post
appears. The moderator's job, often mistaken for censorship, is
to ensure that postings adhere to the group's stated topic. A
moderator also may rule out discussion on certain subtopics if
postings on such subjects turn out to be *flame bait* (postings
likely to cause an unproductive and bitter debate with low
information content).

moderator   In *Usenet* and mailing lists, a volunteer who takes
on the task of screening messages submitted to a *moderated newsgroup* or moderated mailing list.

modulation   The conversion of a digital signal to its analog
equivalent, especially for the purposes of transmitting signals
using telephone lines and *modems*. See *demodulation*.

MOO   A type of Multi-User Dungeon *(MUD)* that incorporates a sophisticated, object-oriented programming language,
which participants can use to construct their own personalized
characters and worlds

Mosaic   A *Web browser* created by the *National Center for
Supercomputing Applications (NCSA)* and placed in the public
domain. Though Mosaic was one of the earliest Web browsers,
it has been superseded by *Netscape Navigator*. See *World Wide
Web (WWW)*.

MSIE   See *Microsoft Internet Explorer.*

MTA   See *message transfer agent.*

MUD   Acronym for Multi-User Dungeon. A MUD is a form of virtual reality designed for network use that offers participants an opportunity to interact with other computer users in real time. MUDs, originally developed to support online role-playing games (such as Dungeons & Dragons), have mostly been replaced by more flexible *MOOs.*

Multicast Backbone (Mbone)   An experimental system that can deliver real-time audio and video via the *Internet.* Capable of one-to-many and many-to-many transmission with low consumption of network resources, Mbone requires special software, which is installed on only a small number of the computers currently connected to the Internet. The Rolling Stones broadcast a concert on the Mbone during their 1994 Voodoo Lounge tour.

Multilink Point-to-Point Protocol   An *Internet* standard for *ISDN* connections between an *Internet service provider (ISP)* and an ISDN terminal adapter. MP fragments data packets before transmitting them via ISDN lines, greatly improving efficiency and overall throughput.

Multipurpose Internet Mail Extensions (MIME)   See *MIME.*

Multi-User Dungeon (MUD)   See *MUD.*

name server   In an *Internet*-connected local area network (LAN), a computer that provides the *Domain Name Service (DNS)*, that is, the translation between alphabetical domain names and numerical *IP addresses.* To establish a connection with an Internet service provider, you need to know the IP address of the name server.

National Center for Supercomputing Applications (NCSA)   A supercomputer research center, affiliated with the University of Illinois at Urbana-Champaign, that specializes in scientific visualization. NCSA most recently achieved fame as the birthplace of *NCSA Mosaic*, the popular *Web browser*.

NCSA Mosaic   A graphical *Web browser* created at the *National Center for Supercomputing Applications (NCSA)*. Available as freeware for noncommercial uses, NCSA Mosaic is available in versions for Microsoft Windows 95, Unix, and Macintosh computers.

net.abuse   Any action that interferes with peoples' right to use and enjoy Usenet, including flooding newsgroups with unwanted posts (also called *spamming),* conducting an organized forgery campaign, or carrying out an organized effort to prevent the discussion of an issue.

net.god(dess)   In *Usenet,* an individual whose lengthy Usenet experience and savvy online demeanor elevates him or her to heroic status. An example of a net.god is James "Kibo" Parry, who is said to have developed a Practical Extraction and Report Language (perl) script enabling him to detect when and where his name was mentioned in any article throughout Usenet's thousands of *newsgroups.* His witty responses to these articles and his ubiquity—at one time he claimed to post as many as two dozen articles per day—soon resulted in deification (and the creation of a newsgroup in his honor, called alt.religion.kibology).

netiquette   *Network* etiquette; a set of rules that reflect long-standing experience about getting along harmoniously in the electronic environment (*e-mail* and *newsgroups*). The basics of netiquette are as follows:

- Keep your messages short and to the point, abbreviate whenever possible, and don't include an extravagant *signature* at the bottom of your message that lists your name and electronic mailing address.

- Don't use ALL UPPERCASE LETTERS. This is considered to be "shouting." To emphasize a word, use asterisks as you would quotation marks.

- If you want to criticize, criticize the idea, not the person. Don't criticize a person's spelling or grammatical errors. Today's worldwide networks encompass users willing to learn English and trying to participate; they deserve encouragement, not criticism.

- Don't overreact to something you read online. If you get angry, don't reply right away. Go take a walk or, better yet, sleep on it. Electronic mail is easily forwarded. Don't say anything that you don't want to wind up on your boss's desk.

- Don't ask members of a newsgroup to censor a particular person's contributions, or disallow discussion of a topic that you find offensive; instead, create a *kill file* so that those messages don't appear on your screen.

- If you ask a question in a newsgroup, request that replies be sent to you personally, unless you feel that the replies would be of interest to everyone who reads the newsgroup.

- In electronic mail, be cautious in replying to messages that were sent to more than one subscriber. In some systems, your reply will be sent to each person who received the original, which may include every subscriber.

- Don't *cross-post* a message (send it to more than one newsgroup), or reply to a cross-posted message, unless you're genuinely following the discussion in each newsgroup and believe your message would prove of interest to readers of each of them.

- If you're *posting* something that gives away the plot of a movie, novel, or television show, put <SPOILER> at the top of your message. That way, people can skip reading it if they don't want to know whodunit.

- If you're posting something that some people may find offensive, such as an erotic story, use the command (available with most networks) that *encrypts* your text so that it looks like garbage characters. (In Usenet, for example, the command *rot-13* shifts each letter 13 characters, so that b becomes o.) To read such a message, use the command that *decrypts* the text. Any reader who is offended will have to take responsibility for having decrypted the message.

Also, use discretion when "getting personal" with other users. Stalking laws are now being interpreted to encompass e-mail messages. See *follow-up post, Internet,* and *net.police.*

netnews A collective way of referring to the *Usenet newsgroups.*

net.police In *Usenet,* a person or group of persons who take upon themselves the enforcement of Usenet traditions and *netiquette.* For example, the famed *Cancelmoose* applies an automated program (called a *cancelbot*) that seeks out and destroys advertisements that are posted to excessive numbers of *newsgroups.* See *net.abuse* and *spam.*

Netscape Application Programming Interface (NSAPI) See *NSAPI.*

Netscape Auto-admin A module included in *Netscape Communicator Pro* that enables *intranet* administrators to control up to 200 configuration settings in distributed copies of the Communicator package.

Netscape Catalog Server An *Internet* server for Microsoft Windows NT and Unix workstations that enables enterprises to publish complex, hierarchically organized document stores on the World Wide Web. Based on the respected freeware program called Harvest, Catalog Server automatically combs an *intranet* for readable documents of all types, classifies them according to predetermined rules, organizes them into predetermined categories, and makes them available by means of a Web browser. Users can navigate the hierarchical categories or search, much as they access information in *Yahoo.*

Netscape Certificate Server An *Internet* server for Microsoft Windows NT and Unix workstations that enables organizations to become, in effect, a *certificate authority (CA)* by disseminating *certificates* to valid users. The certificates can be used for *strong authentication* to the network, so that it is no longer necessary for the user to supply a different login name and password for every server that is accessed.

Netscape Collabra A module included in *Netscape Communicator* that enables users to access *Usenet* newsgroups. When linked to a *Netscape Collabra* server, the module takes on additional capabilities (see *Netscape Collabra Server*).

Netscape Commerce Server A *Web server* for Microsoft Windows NT and Unix workstations that is designed to enable enterprises to conduct electronic commerce over the Internet. *SSL* 3.0 security enables strong authentication by means of digital *certificates* as well as secure, encrypted communication. Compare with *Netscape Enterprise Server* and *Netscape FastTrack Server*.

Netscape Communications Corporation A publisher of *Web browsers*, *Web servers*, and related software, based in Menlo Park, CA. The company's *Netscape Navigator* browser, now part of the company's *Netscape Communicator* package, is currently the most popular browser on the Internet, but is facing a spirited challenge from *Microsoft Internet Explorer*. The firm reported 1996 sales of $20.9 million.

Netscape Communicator A package including the world's most popular *Web browser*, *Netscape Navigator*, that is available for Microsoft Windows, Macintosh computers, and a variety of Unix workstations. The Communicator package is intended for general Internet use and includes the following modules in addition to Navigator: *Netscape Collabra* (newsgroups), *Netscape Conference* (Internet telephony), Netscape Messenger *(e-mail)*, *Netscape NetCaster* (push media), and Netscape Page Composer (a *WYSIWYG editor* for Web publishing).

Netscape Communicator Pro A package containing all the applications included in *Netscape Communicator*, plus additional modules designed to make the package appealing for *intranet* use, including Netscape Calendar, Netscape Host On-Demand, and Netscape Auto-Admin.

Netscape Conference   An Internet telephony module, included with *Netscape Communicator,* that enables users to place voice calls via the Internet. Conference conforms to current *ITU-TSS* standards for teleconferencing and will interoperate with other standards-based telephony programs, such as Intel's Internet Phone.

Netscape Directory Server   A server for Microsoft Windows NT and Unix workstations that enables enterprises to publish white pages directories of employee *e-mail* addresses and telephone numbers. A variety of access control and authentication options enable administrators to hide sensitive internal information from anonymous external access. Directory Server conforms to the LDAP and X.500 protocols, and the white pages databases it creates can be accessed by any LDAP-compatible *e-mail* program.

Netscape Enterprise Server   A *Web server* for Microsoft Windows NT and Unix workstations that is expressly designed for enterprise computing, and especially for *intranets.* Support is included for IIOP object requests via Netscape Communicator, full text searching of all the documents accessible to the server, author-managed access control, and strong authentication by means of *certificates.* Compare with *Netscape Enterprise Server Pro, Netscape Commerce Server, Netscape FastTrack Server.*

Netscape Enterprise Server Pro   A version of *Netscape Enterprise Server* for Microsoft Windows NT and Unix workstations that includes a developmental copy of the Informix OnLine Workgroup Server or Oracle7 Workgroup Server database software, and also includes out-of-the-box solutions that enable organizations to create Web-to-database applications without programming.

Netscape extensions   A set of additions to the *HTML 2.0* standard that enables Web authors to create documents with tables, frames, and other features not supported by the 2.0 specification. Until competing browsers decided to support Netscape's unilaterally introduced *tags,* these features could be seen only by *Netscape Navigator* users. Most of the extensions have been incorporated into HTML version 3.2, but Netscape (like other browser publishers) has recently introduced new, non-standard tags that other browsers do not support.

Netscape FastTrack Server A *Web server*, created by Netscape Communications, that is designed to enable companies to establish an Internet presence quickly. Intended for installation and management by end users rather than programmers, the program features wizards that guide users through the most common configuration tasks. FastTrack Server is available for Microsoft Windows 95, Microsoft Windows NT, and Unix systems.

Netscape Messaging Server A *e-mail server* for Microsoft Windows NT and Unix workstations. The program supports LDAP services; *Simple Mail Transport Protocol (SMTP), POP3,* and *Internet Message Access Protocol (IMAP);* X.509v3 certificates; and richly formatted e-mail with HTML and MIME.

Netscape Navigator The leading *Web browser*, now available as part of Netscape's *Netscape Communicator* package. Navigator is much more than a Web browser in that it serves as an interpreter for *Java applets* and *JavaScript.* A *cross-platform* product, Navigator is available in versions for Windows, Macintosh, and Unix systems.

Netscape NetCaster A *push media* client, included with *Netscape Communicator*, that enables users to subscribe to Web sites so that the most recent version of these sites is automatically displayed, either in a *Netscape Navigator* window or a special, screen-filling window called the Webtop. In addition, users can "tune" to broadcasting "channels" to receive commercial content from providers such as ABC News. NetCaster incorporates Marimba's Castanet client, which enables users to tune to channels that disseminate *Java* programs; updates to these programs are transparent to the user.

Netscape SuiteSpot A package of *Web server* and related software that includes Netscape Enterprise Server, LiveWire Pro (a development tool for linking to external databases), Catalog Server (utilities for managing and maintaining catalogs of Internet and *intranet* resources), Media Server (delivers *streaming audio*), MailServer and Messaging Server (*e-mail* and groupware support), News Server and Collabra Server (internal and external *newsgroups*), Calendar Server (facilitates group scheduling), Directory Server (provides white pages support for an organization), Proxy Server (provides *intranet* users with external *Internet* access), and Certificate Server (enables organizations to create and manage digital *certificates* for authentication purposes). This product competes with Microsoft BackOffice, which is intended for Windows-based networks. Netscape SuiteSpot is intended for *cross-platform* networks that include Unix systems.

Network Information Center (NIC)   A system that contains a repository of *Internet*-related information, including *File Transfer Protocol (FTP)* archives of Requests for Comments (RFCs), Internet Drafts, For Your Information (FYI) papers, and other documents, including handbooks on the use of the Internet. There are numerous Network Information Centers, but the official repository of network information is the Defense Data Network NIC (DDN NIC). See *InterNIC.*

Network News Transfer Protocol   See *NNTP.*

newbie   In *Usenet,* a new user who nevertheless makes his or her presence known, generally by pleading for information that is readily and easily available in *Frequently Asked Questions (FAQ).*

news feed   In *Usenet,* a service that enables you to download the day's Usenet articles directly to your computer and to upload all the articles contributed by people using your computer. Not for personal computer users, a news feed dumps as much as 100 MB of Usenet articles per day into your system—far more than one person could fruitfully read. A news feed is for organizations that want to set up a Usenet site, a computer—usually a minicomputer—with enough storage space to handle the huge influx of articles. Such a computer also has the multi-user capabilities that enable as many as dozens or even hundreds of people to take advantage of Usenet.

newsgroup   In a bulletin board system *(BBS),* such as The WELL, or a distributed bulletin board system, such as *Usenet,* a discussion group that's devoted to a single topic, such as

Star Trek, model aviation, the books of Ayn Rand, or the music of the Grateful Dead. Users *post* messages to the group, and those reading the discussion send reply messages to the author individually or post replies that can be read by the group as a whole. The term newsgroup is a misnomer in that the discussions rarely involve "news"; discussion group would be more accurate, but the term newsgroup has taken root. Synonymous with forum. See *FAQ, follow-up post, local Usenet hierarchy, moderated newsgroup, net.god(dess), netiquette, thread,* and *unmoderated newsgroup.*

newsgroup reader   See *newsreader.*

newsgroup selector   In a *Usenet newsreader,* a program mode that presents a list of currently subscribed newsgroups, from which you can select one to read.

news hierarchy   In *Usenet,* one of the seven standard newsgroup hierarchies. The news hierarchy is concerned with Usenet itself; the various newsgroups deal with administrative issues, new newsgroups, announcements, and Usenet software. See *local Usenet hierarchy* and *standard newsgroups.*

newsreader   A client program that enables you to access a Usenet news server, subscribe to Usenet *newsgroups,* read the articles appearing in these newsgroups, and post your own articles or reply by *e-mail.* Many *Web browsers* (such as *Netscape Navigator*) include newsreader functions.

news server   A computer that provides access to *Usenet newsgroups.* To read Usenet newsgroups, you must tell your *newsreader* program or *Web browser* the domain name of an *NNTP* server. Your Internet service provider can provide you with the name of this server, if one is available.

NIC   See *Network Information Center.*

NNTP   Acronym for Network News Transfer Protocol. In *Usenet,* the standard that governs the distribution of Usenet newsgroups via the *Internet.*

NNTP server   See *news server.*

noise   See *line noise.*

NSAPI Acronym for Netscape Application Programming Interface. An *application program interface (API)* for Netscape *Web servers* that enables programmers to route Web information requests to external programs, such as databases.

offline Not connected to a network or available from a network.

OLTP See *online transaction processing.*

online Connected to a network or available from a network.

online information service A for-profit firm that makes current news, stock quotes, and other information available to its subscribers over standard telephone lines. See *America Online (AOL).*

online transaction processing (OLTP) In the *Internet,* the capturing and recording of electronic transaction information (including names, addresses, and credit-card numbers) in a database, so that all transactions occurring online can be audited and the resulting data summarized for management purposes.

op Common abbreviation for operator, as in "channel op" (a channel operator on *IRC*).

Open Shortest Path First See *OSPF.*

OSPF Acronym for Open Shortest Path First. An improved version of *Internet* protocol (standard) that governs the exchange of data using *TCP/IP* within an internal network (an *autonomous system*). A *router* running OSPF compiles a database of its own current connections, as well as those OSPF-compatible routers to which it is connected, and then uses a routing algorithm to determine the shortest possible path for the data.

P

packet   In a packet-switching unit, a unit of data of a fixed size—not exceeding the network's maximum transmission unit (MTU) size—that has been prepared for network transmission. Each packet contains a *header* that indicates its origin and its destination. See *packet-switching network*. Synonymous with *datagram*.

Packet Internet Groper (PING)   See *PING*.

packet-switching network   One of two fundamental architectures for the design of a wide-area network (WAN); the other is a circuit switching network. In a packet-switching network such as the *Internet,* no effort is made to establish a single electrical circuit between two computing devices; for this reason, packet-switching networks are often called connectionless. Instead, the sending computer divides a message into a number of efficiently sized units called *packets,* each of which contains the address of the destination computer. These packets are simply dumped onto the network. They are intercepted by devices called *routers,* which read each packet's destination address and, based on that information, send the packets in the appropriate direction. Eventually, the packets arrive at their intended destination, although some may have actually traveled by different physical paths. The receiving computer assembles the packets, puts them in order, and delivers the received message to the appropriate application. Packet-switching networks are highly reliable and efficient, but they are not suited to the delivery of real-time voice and video.

page   See *Web page*.

PAP   See *Password Authentication Protocol*.

password   An authentication tool used to identify authorized users of a program or network and to define their privileges, such as read-only, reading and writing, or file copying.

password aging   In a computer network, a feature of the network operating system (NOS) that keeps track of the last time you changed your *password*.

Password Authentication Protocol (PAP) An *Internet* standard providing a simple (and fundamentally insecure) method of authentication. The authenticating computer demands the user's *login name* and *password,* and keeps doing so until these are supplied correctly. Computer criminals who possess a known login name can gain unauthorized access by running password-guessing programs that supply a variety of known insecure passwords.

password protection A method of limiting access to a program, file, computer, or a network by requiring you to enter a *password*. Some programs enable you to password-protect your files so they can't be read or altered by others.

PCMCIA modem A credit-card-sized *modem* designed to connect to a PCMCIA slot, usually in a portable computer. The acronym stands for Personal Computer Memory Card Interface Adapter.

personal certificate A digital *certificate* attesting that a given individual who is trying to log on to an authenticated *server* really is the individual he or she claims to be. Personal certificates are issued by *certificate authorities (CA)*.

PGP See *Pretty Good Privacy.*

PING A diagnostic program that is commonly used to determine whether a computer is properly connected to the *Internet.*

pingable Able to respond to *PING;* an *Internet* site that is "alive" and should be able to respond to Internet tools such as *FTP* and *Gopher.*

Plain Old Telephone Service (POTS) An analog communications system, adequate for voice communication and slow data communication with *modems,* but without sufficient *bandwidth* to handle high-speed digital communications. Technologies like *ISDN* may replace POTS someday and provide higher bandwidth.

plug-in A program module that is designed to directly interface with, and give additional capability to, a proprietary application, such as Adobe PhotoShop or Netscape Navigator.

After installing the plug-in, the program takes on additional capabilities, which may be reflected in the appearance of new commands in the original application's menu system.

PMJI In online communications, shorthand for Pardon Me for Jumping In.

point of presence (POP) A locality in which it is possible to obtain dialup access to the network by means of a local telephone call. *Internet service providers (ISP)* provide POPs in towns and cities, but many rural areas are without local POPs.

Point-to-Point Protocol (PPP) See *PPP.*

Point-to-Point Tunneling Protocol (PPTP) See *PPTP.*

POP See *point of presence* or *Post Office Protocol.*

POP3 Also spelled POP-3. The current version of the *Post Office Protocol (POP)*, an *Internet* standard for storing *e-mail* on a mail server until you can access it and download it to your computer.

port On the *Internet*, a logical channel through which a certain type of application data is routed in order to decode incoming data and route it to the correct destination. Each type of Internet service, such as *FTP* or *IRC*, has a certain port number associated with it. Port number assignments are controlled by the Internet Assigned Numbers Authority (IANA).

port address A number that identifies the location of a particular *Internet* application, such as *FTP*, a *World Wide Web (WWW)* server, or *Gopher*, on a computer that is directly connected to the Internet. Regulated by the Internet Assigned Numbers Authority (IANA), port numbers are included in the headers of every Internet packet; the numbers tell the receiving software where to deliver the incoming data.

post In a *newsgroup*, to send a message so that it can be read by everyone who accesses the group.

postmaster In a network, the human administrator who configures the *e-mail* manager and handles problems that arise.

Post Office Protocol (POP) An *Internet e-mail* standard that specifies how an Internet-connected computer can function as a mail-handling agent; the current version is called POP3. Messages arrive at a user's electronic mailbox, which is housed on the service provider's computer. From this central storage point, you can access your mail from different computers—a networked workstation in the office as well as a PC at home. In either case, a POP—compatible e-mail program, which runs on your workstation or PC, establishes a connection with the POP server, and detects that new mail has arrived. You can then download the mail to the workstation or computer, and reply to it, print it, or store it, as you prefer. POP does not send mail; that job is handled by *SMTP.*

POTS See *Plain Old Telephone Service.*

PPP Acronym for Point-to-Point Protocol. One of the two standards for directly connecting computers to the Internet via dialup telephone connections (the other is SLIP). Unlike the older SLIP protocol, PPP incorporates superior data negotiation, compression, and error correction. However, these features add overhead to data transmission, and are unnecessary when both the sending and receiving modems offer hardware error correction and on-the-fly data compression. See *SLIP.*

PPTP Acronym for Point-to-Point Tunneling Protocol. An extension of *PPP* that enables remote users of a corporate local area network (LAN) to access the internal network by means of protocol tunneling, in which the LAN data is encapsulated within *TCP/IP* and encrypted for secure, confidential transmission via the Internet.

Pretty Good Privacy (PGP) A comprehensive cryptosystem for private *e-mail* created by Phil Zimmerman. PGP uses a *public-key encryption algorithm* for initial key exchange and employs the *International Data Encryption Algorithm (IDEA)* to encrypt data after keys have been exchanged. A unique feature of the PGP mail model is the use of circles of trust for authenticating the sender of a message; instead of validating digital signatures by means of a *certificate authority (CA)*, PGP instead enables users to digitally sign other peoples' certificates, attesting that they know them personally and can vouch that the signature in question really came from that person and no other.

PRI See *Primary Rate Interface*.

Primary Rate Interface (PRI) A high-capacity *ISDN* service that provides 23 64 Kbps channels and one channel for carrying control information. PRI is designed for business use.

Prodigy Internet A national Internet service provider (ISP) which offers access to the Internet through a digital, 56 Kbps network. Prodigy Internet allows members to personalize their home pages with news, sports, stocks, weather, and personal reminders. Prodigy Internet also provides 24 hour online support. http://www.prodigy.com

protocol In data communications and networking, a standard that specifies the format of data as well as the rules to be followed. Networks could not be easily or efficiently designed or maintained without protocols; a protocol specifies how a program should prepare data so that it can be sent on to the next stage in the communication process. For example, *e-mail* programs prepare messages so that they conform to prevailing *Internet* mail standards, which are recognized by every program that is involved in the transmission of mail over the network.

proxy A program that stands between an internal network and the external Internet, intercepting requests for information. A proxy is generally part of a broader solution to internal network security called a *firewall*. The purpose of a proxy is to prevent external users from directly accessing resources inside the internal network or, indeed, knowing precisely where those resources are located. The proxy intercepts an external request for information, determines whether the request can be fulfilled, and passes on the request to an internal *server*, the address of which is not disclosed to the external client. By disguising the real location of the server that actually houses the requested information, the proxy makes it much more difficult for computer criminals to exploit potential security holes in servers and related applications, which might enable them to gain unauthorized access to the internal network. This protection from outside attack comes at the price of imposing inconveniences (including configuration hassles and slower performance) on internal users who wish to access the external Internet. Sometimes (inaccurately) called *proxy server.*

proxy server In an *online service,* such as America Online, a server that has been configured to store Web pages that are frequently accessed by the service's members. When members request these pages, the server provides the copy it has stored rather than requesting the page from the external Internet. Members see Web pages more quickly and the network experiences lighter load, but these benefits come at a price: the displayed page may be out of date. This term is often used synonymously (but incorrectly) with *proxy.*

pseudoanonymous remailer In the *Internet,* an *e-mail* forwarding service that enables Internet users to send anonymous e-mail or to post anonymously to *Usenet.* These services maintain records that preserve the sender's true identity, so they are not truly anonymous. Compare *anonymous remailer.*

public key cryptography In cryptography, a revolutionary new method of *encryption* that does not require the message's receiver to have received the decoding *key* in a separate transmission. The need to send the key, required to decode the message, is the chief vulnerability of previous encryption techniques. In public key cryptography, there are two keys, a public one and a private one. The public key is used for encryption, and the private key is used for *decryption.* If John wants to receive a private message from Alice, John sends his public key to Alice; Alice then uses the key to encrypt the message. Alice sends the message to John. Anyone trying to intercept the message en route would find that it is mere gibberish. When John receives the message, he uses his private key to decode it. Because John never sends his private key anywhere or gives it to anyone, he can be certain that the message is secure. Public key cryptography places into the hands of individuals a level of security that was formerly available only to the top levels of government security agencies. Also called asymmetric key cryptography.

public key encryption   The use of *public key cryptography* to encrypt messages for secret transmission. Because public key encryption techniques consume enormous amounts of computer processing overhead, they are generally used only for the initial phase of a connection between the sender and receiver of a secret message. In this phase, the users establish their identities by means of *digital signatures,* and exchange the *keys* that will be used for symmetric key encryption using an encryption algorithm such as DES.

pull media   In the *Internet,* the traditional Internet services (such as FTP and the World Wide Web), in which users do not obtain information unless they expressly and deliberately originate a request for it. To attract users (and therefore justify advertising), content providers must "pull" users to the site. See *push media* and *Netscape NetCaster.*

push media   In the *Internet,* a series of new content delivery mechanisms, in which users subscribe to what amounts to a broadcasting service, which subsequently delivers content to the user's computer without the user having to make further requests for information. In contrast to *pull media,* which must attract the user to the site, push media can guarantee advertisers that subscribers will continue to receive updates and view advertising banners. Among the various push media models that have been developed are applications such as PointCast that deliver news, weather, and sports scores to the user's screen saver, and services such as *Castanet,* which employ a radio metaphor: The user "tunes" to a "channel," and content is delivered to the user whenever updates are available. The delivered content may appear in a special window that appears on the user's desktop. Castanet can also automatically deliver software and updates to software, and thus creates a new and potentially significant model for software distribution and maintenance. The ultimate push medium is e-mail *spamming,* in which e-mail advertisers send unsolicited e-mail advertisements to as many as millions of e-mail addresses.

R

rave   In *e-mail* and *newsgroups,* to carry on an argument in support of a position beyond all bounds of reason and sensitivity. Raving is annoying but isn't considered to be worthy of a *flame* unless the argument is couched in offensive terms.

RC4   A widely used symmetric key encryption algorithm developed by RSA Data Security, Inc. The algorithm's vulnerability to *cryptanalysis* (code-breaking) is highly dependent on the length of the key; a key of 40 characters or less can be easily broken, even by amateur cryptanalysts. This is the encryption method that is used by the Secure Sockets Layer *(SSL)* standard. U.S. Government export restrictions prevent the use of RC4 keys greater than 40 characters for exported products, which means—essentially—that supposedly "secure" programs based on 40-key RC4 encryption are, in fact, quite insecure and vulnerable to interception and decoding while they are being transmitted via the network.

rec hierarchy   One of the seven *standard newsgroup hierarchies* in *Usenet,* this category includes newsgroups relating to recreational interests, such as movies, comics, science fiction, or audio systems.

Relative URL (RELURL)   One of two basic kinds of Uniform Resource Identifiers *(URIs),* a string of characters that gives a resource's file name (such as merlot.html), but does not specify its type or exact location. Parsers (such as *Web browsers*) will assume that the resource is located in the same directory that contains the RELURL. See *URL.*

RELURL   See *Relative URL.*

Request for Comments (RFC)   An *Internet* publication that constitutes the chief means by which standards are promulgated (although not all RFCs contain new standards). More than 1,000 RFCs are accessible from *Network Information Centers (NIC).* The publication of RFCs is currently controlled by the Internet Architecture Board (IAB).

RFC   See *Request for Comments.*

rlogin A Unix utility that enables users of one machine to connect to other Unix systems via the Internet and gain full control over the other machine's operation. This utility is rarely implemented due to its obvious security perils.

rn In *Usenet*, a non-threaded *newsreader* for Unix systems. Written by Larry Wall in the mid-1980s, rn has been replaced by *threaded newsreaders* such as *trn, tin,* and nn.

rot-13 In *Usenet newsgroups,* a simple *encryption* technique that offsets each character by 13 places (so that an e becomes an r, for example). Rot-13 encryption is used for any message that may spoil someone's fun (such as the solution to a game) or offend some readers (such as erotic poetry). If the reader chooses to decrypt the message by issuing the appropriate command, then the reader—not the author of the message—bears the responsibility for any discomfort that may be caused by reading the message. Lately, rot-13 has fallen into disuse. See *netiquette.*

router In a *packet-switching network* such as the *Internet,* one of two basic devices (the other is a *host*). A router is an electronic device that examines each packet of data it receives, and then decides which way to send it onward toward its destination.

Router Information Protocol (RIP) An *Internet* protocol that routes data within an internal TCP/IP-based network based on a table of distances. A more recent and sophisticated version of this protocol is the OSPF Interior Gateway Protocol.

RSA public key encryption algorithm The most popular algorithm for *public key encryption* and a de facto world standard. RSA Data Security, Inc., holds a patent on this algorithm, which is confidential; nevertheless, the algorithm has been incorporated in a number of major *protocols,* including *S/MIME* and Secure Sockets Layer *(SSL).*

S

sandbox In *Java,* a safe area for the execution of *applets,* created by the *Java virtual machine,* in which applets cannot get access to the computer's file system.

SATAN   A network security diagnostic tool that exhaustively examines a network and reveals security holes. SATAN is a two-edged sword: in the hands of network administrators, it is a valuable tool for detecting and closing security loopholes. In the hands of intruders, it is an equally valuable tool for exposing remaining loopholes and gaining unauthorized access to a network.

sci hierarchy   In *Usenet's standard newsgroup hierarchy*, a category of *newsgroups* devoted to topics in the sciences. The category includes newsgroups that cover astronomy, biology, engineering, geology, mathematics, psychology, and statistics.

search engine   Any program that locates needed information in a database, but especially an *Internet*-accessible search service that enables you to search for information on the Internet. To use a search engine, you type one or more key words; the result is a list of documents or files that contain one or more of these words in their titles, descriptions, or text. The databases of most Internet search engines contain *World Wide Web (WWW)* documents; some also contain items found in *Gopher* menus and *File Transfer Protocol (FTP)* file archives. Compiling the database requires an automated search routine called a *spider* (forms filled out by Web authors) or a search of other databases of Internet documents. See *AltaVista, HotBot, InfoSeek, Lycos,* and *WebCrawler.*

security   The protection of valuable assets stored on computer systems or transmitted via computer networks. Computer security involves the following conceptually differentiated areas:

- **Authentication** (ensuring that users are indeed the persons they claim to be)

- **Access control** (ensuring that users access only those resources and services that they are entitled to access)

- **Confidentiality** (ensuring that transmitted or stored data is not examined by unauthorized persons)

- **Integrity** (ensuring that transmitted or stored data is not altered by unauthorized persons in a way that is not detectable by authorized users)

- **Nonrepudiation** (ensuring that qualified users are not denied access to services that they legitimately expect to receive, and that originators of messages cannot deny that they in fact sent a given message).

sendmail A Unix utility that sends *e-mail* over the *Internet* in accordance with the *SMTP* protocol. To create the message, you use an *e-mail client* such as *Eudora* or *Netscape Messenger*. Mail is received and stored by the programs conforming to the *Post Office Protocol (POP)*.

send statement In a *SLIP* or *PPP* dialer program's script language, a statement that tells the program to send certain characters. Send statements follow expect statements, which tell the program to wait until the service provider's computer sends certain characters to your computer.

server On the *Internet*, a program that supplies information when it receives external requests via Internet connections. See *Web server*.

service provider See *Internet service provider* and *Internet access provider*.

SGML Acronym for Standard Generalized Markup Language. A means of describing markup languages, such as the HyperText Markup Language *(HTML)*, which is widely used on the *World Wide Web (WWW)*. SGML can be used to define a *document type definition (DTD)*, which defines the elements of a specific type of document and the *tags* that can be used to display these elements with distinctive formats. A program called a parser is needed to read the tags and display the text appropriately. SGML is an open, international standard defined by the International Standards Organization (ISO).

shell account An inexpensive but limited type of Internet *dialup access*. A shell account does not directly connect your computer to the Internet. Instead, you use a *communications program* to access a computer, usually a Unix computer, on which you have established an account. After logging on to this computer, you get text-only access to this Unix computer's operating system (its shell). From the shell, you can run the

Internet tools that are available on the *service provider's* computer, such as a text-only *Usenet* newsreaders or the text-only *Web browser* called *Lynx*.

S-HTTP Acronym for Secure HyperText Transport Protocol. An extension of the HyperText Transport Protocol *(HTTP)* that supports secure commercial transactions on the Web. Secure HTTP provides this support in two ways: by assuring vendors that the customers attempting to buy the vendors' wares are who they say they are (authentication) and by encrypting sensitive information (such as credit-card numbers) so that it cannot be intercepted while en route. Secure HTTP was developed by Enterprise Integration Technology (EIT) and the *National Center for Supercomputer Applications (NCSA)*, with subsequent commercial development by Terisa Systems. *Netscape Communications* developed a competing security technology, the Secure Sockets Layer *(SSL)* protocol. Although S-HTTP is still used by some *Web servers*, SSL has emerged as the clear de facto stand—and for good reason. S-HTTP is an application-layer protocol, which means that it cannot support secure, encrypted exchange of other types of data, including *FTP* or *NNTP* resources.

sig Common abbreviation for *signature*.

SIG See *special interest group*.

signal-to-noise ratio In *Usenet*, the ratio between meaningful content and noise (ranting, raving, and *flaming*). A good *newsgroup* has a high signal-to-noise ratio; a poor newsgroup has a low one. A major advantage of *moderated newsgroups* is to ensure a high signal-to-noise ratio. The term was originally used in electrical engineering to describe the ratio of information to background noise in an electronic circuit.

signature In *e-mail* and *Usenet newsgroups*, a brief file (of approximately three or four lines) that contains the message sender's name, organization, address, e-mail address, and (optionally) telephone numbers. You can configure most systems to add this file automatically at the end of each message you send. *Netiquette* advises against long, complicated signatures, especially when posting to Usenet. See ASCII art.

Simple Mail Transport Protocol (SMTP) An *Internet* protocol that governs the transmission of *e-mail* over computer networks. SMTP is simple indeed; it does not provide any support for the transmission of data other than plain text. For this reason, the Multipurpose Internet Mail Extensions *(MIME)* provide support for *binary files* of many types, and *S/MIME* provides support for *encrypted* e-mail.

Skipjack A *public key encryption algorithm,* reportedly closely related to the Diffie-Hellman public key encryption algorithm, that the U.S. National Security Agency wants American citizens and others to use when they encrypt their Internet transactions. The algorithm contains a key recover scheme that would enable government investigators to obtain the decoding key from a (supposedly) independent authority, and only when "public safety" or "national security" was at stake. The algorithm has been ignored by the cryptographic industry because the government has refused to enable cryptographers to examine the algorithm, which some suspect to contain deliberate built-in weaknesses that would aid government surveillance of encrypted communications.

SLIP Acronym for Serial Line Internet Protocol. The earliest of two *Internet* standards specifying how a workstation or personal computer can link to the *Internet* by means of a dialup connection (the other standard is *PPP*). SLIP defines the transport of data *packets* through an asynchronous telephone line. Therefore, SLIP enables computers not directly connected to local area networks (LANs) to be fully connected to the Internet. This mode of connectivity is far superior to a *shell account* (a dialup, text-only account on a Unix computer) because it enables you to use the Internet tools of your choice (such as a graphical *Web browser*) to run more than one Internet application at a time and to download data directly to your computer, with no intermediate storage required.

SLIP/PPP A commonly used abbreviation for the two types of dialup Internet access that directly integrate your computer with the Internet: *SLIP* and *PPP.* See *shell account.*

smiley See *emoticon.*

S/MIME Abbreviation for Secure Multipurpose Internet Mail Extensions. An addition to the *MIME* protocol that supports the exchange of encrypted *e-mail* via the *Internet*. S/MIME uses RSA's *public-key encryption algorithm* for the initial authentication (which makes use of *certificates*); after the secure connection is established, an exchange of symmetric encryption algorithm keys occurs.

SMTP See *Simple Mail Transport Protocol*.

snail mail A derogatory term for the postal service. In an *e-mail* message, you might say "I'm sending the article to you by snail mail."

soc hierarchy In *Usenet,* one of the *standard newsgroup hierarchies*. The soc newsgroups deal with social issues, social groups, and world cultures.

socket In the *Internet* and Unix, a virtual *port* that enables *client* applications to connect to the appropriate *server*. To achieve a connection, a client needs to specify both the *IP address* and the *port address* of the server application.

software handshaking A method of flow control that ensures that the data that a *modem* sends does not overwhelm the modem with which it is communicating. In a software handshaking scheme, such as XON/XOFF handshaking, modems exchange special codes when they are ready to send and receive data.

spam Unsolicited advertising in a *Usenet* newsgroup or *e-mail*. The term is derived from a Monty Python skit.

special interest group (SIG) A subgroup of an organization or network, consisting of members who share a common interest. Common SIG topics include software, hobbies, sports, and literary genres such as mystery or science fiction.

spider A program that prowls the *Internet,* attempting to locate new, publicly accessible resources such as *World Wide Web (WWW)* documents, files available in public *File Transfer Protocol (FTP)* archives, and *Gopher* documents. Also called wanderers or robots, spiders contribute their discoveries to a database, which

Internet users can search by using an Internet-accessible *search engine* (such as *Lycos* or *WebCrawler*). Spiders are necessary because the rate at which people are creating new Internet documents greatly exceeds manual indexing capacity.

spoiler In a *Usenet newsgroup,* a message that contains the ending of a novel, movie, or television program, or the solution to a computer or video game. Network etiquette (or *netiquette*) requires that you encrypt such messages so that users can't read them unless they choose to do so. In *Usenet* newsgroups, the *encryption* technique is called *rot-13.*

SSL Acronym for Secure Sockets Layer. An *Internet* security standard proposed by *Netscape Communications* and incorporated into its *Netscape Navigator* browser and *Netscape Commerce Server* software. Unlike its chief competition, *S-HTTP,* SSL is application-independent—it works with all Internet tools, not just the *World Wide Web (WWW).* This is because SSL functions at the network layer rather than the application layer, and is thus available to any SSL-ready Internet application, including *newsreaders.* (Netscape has developed a secure SSL newsreader for private organizational newsgroups, called *Collabra.*) Applications that use SSL use *RSA public key encryption* and RSA *certificates* and *digital signatures* to establish the identities of parties to the transaction; after the link is established, a key exchange takes place, and RSA's *RC4* encryption technology (a symmetric key encryption algorithm) is used to secure the transaction. With the 128-bit *keys* used for SSL communication within the U.S., the encrypted transaction would be computationally infeasible to decode, so it is safe from snoopers and criminals. (The 40-bit version used in export versions of *Netscape Navigator,* however, is not secure, and should not be avoided for commercial transactions.)

Standard Generalized Markup Language See *SGML.*

standard newsgroup hierarchy In *Usenet,* a collection of categories that every Usenet site is expected to carry, if sufficient storage room exists. The standard *newsgroup hierarchy* includes the following newsgroup categories: *comp.*, misc.*, news.*, rec.*, sci.*, soc.*,* and *talk*.* A voting process creates new newsgroups within the standard newsgroup hierarchies. See *alt hierarchy* and *Call for Votes (CFV).*

start page   See *home page.*

storefront   In the *World Wide Web (WWW),* a Web document that establishes a commercial enterprise's presence on the Web. Typically, a storefront does not attempt to provide a complete catalog, but instead illustrates a few items or services that typify what the firm has to offer. Web marketing experience demonstrates that the most successful storefronts are those that offer some interesting "freebies," such as information or downloadable software. As security protocols become more widely used, customers will be able to use their credit cards safely to place orders. See *S-HTTP* and *SSL.*

stream   A continuous flow of data through a channel, in contrast to data delivery by means of *packets* (fixed, numbered, and addressed units of data that may arrive out of order).

streaming audio   An *Internet* sound delivery technology that sends audio data as a continuous, compressed stream that is played back on the fly. In contrast to downloaded sounds, which may not begin playing for several minutes, streaming audio begins almost immediately. To get acceptable sound quality, the user needs a fast modem connection (preferably 28 MHz or better). At best, though, the sound is that of a good AM radio—acceptable for voice, but only marginal for music. There is no universally supported streaming audio standard; the de facto standard is Real Audio.

streaming video   An *Internet* video delivery technology that sends video data as a continuous, compressed stream that is played back on the fly. Like *streaming audio,* streaming videos begin playing almost immediately. A high-speed modem is required. Quality is marginal; the video appears in a small, on-screen window, and motion is jerky.

strong authentication   In computer security, the use of authentication measures that go beyond supplying a reusable password. Strong authentication techniques include the use of *digital signatures* and *certificates,* tokens, and smart cards.

subdomain   In the *Internet's domain name system (DNS),* a domain that is subordinate to a domain name; for example, in the Web address http://www.virginia.edu/tcc, www. virginia.edu is the domain and tcc is the subdomain.

subject drift In *Usenet newsgroups*, the tendency of the subject lines of follow-up posts to become increasingly irrelevant to the articles' contents. Subject drift is an unintended consequence of *newsreader* software, which automatically echoes the original article's subject (a brief one-line description) when you write a follow-up post. As the discussion progresses into new territory, newsreaders keep echoing the same subject line, even though it soon becomes irrelevant to the subject actually being discussed.

subject selector In a *Usenet newsreader*, a program mode in which you have a list of articles, sorted by subject. Note that sorting by subject is not the same thing as sorting by threads; a *threaded newsreader* shows the precise relationship among articles and *follow-up posts*, while a subject-sorted newsreader merely alphabetizes the subjects (thus obscuring some of the relationships among articles in a thread). See *thread selector*.

subject tree In the *World Wide Web (WWW)*, a guide to the Web that organizes Web sites by subject. The term originates from many of the subject classifications (such as Environment or Music) having "branches," or subcategories. At the lowest level of the tree, you find *hyperlinks*, which you can click to display the cited Web document. See *Yahoo*.

subnet In the *Internet*, a segment of an Internet-connected local area network (LAN) that is differentiated from other segments by using an operation (called a *subnet mask*) that is performed on the networks *IP address*. Subnets share a common IP address with the rest of the network of which they are a part, but they can function autonomously. A subnet is a virtual unit, identified conceptually by using the addressing methodology, and is generally created to reflect valid organizational distinctions—even if the members of an organizational unit are in fact using two or more physically dissimilar portions of the network. For example, in a university, a single academic department can be assigned a subnet, even though some of the faculty connect to the Internet by using a high-speed Ethernet, and others by using an AppleTalk network.

subnet mask A transformation performed on an organization's *IP address* that enables the network administrators to create *subnets,* which are virtual subunits of the organization's physical network.

subscribe In *Usenet,* to add a *newsgroup* to the list of groups that you're reading regularly. Subscribed newsgroups appear in the *newsgroup selector,* enabling you to choose them easily. If you stop reading a newsgroup, you can *unsubscribe* to remove the newsgroup name from your subscription list.

surf To explore the World Wide Web serendipitously by following *hyperlinks* that seem interesting.

surfing Exploring the Web by following interesting links—to some, a monumental waste of time; to others, a joy.

sysop Abbreviation for system operator. A person who runs a *bulletin board system (BBS).*

T1 A high-bandwidth telephone trunk line that is capable of transferring 1.544 megabits per second (Mbps) of data. Compare to *T3.*

T3 A very-high-bandwidth telephone trunk line that is capable of transferring 44.7 megabits per second (Mbps) of computer data. Compare to *T1.*

table In *HTML,* a matrix of rows and columns that appears on a Web page, if the user is browsing with a table-capable browser (such *as Netscape Navigator).*

tag In *HTML,* a code that identifies an element (a certain part of a document, such as a heading or list) so that a *Web browser* can tell how to display it. Tags are enclosed by beginning and ending delimiters (angle brackets). Most tags begin with a start tag (delimited with <>), followed by the content and an end tag (delimited with </>), as in the following example:

```
<H1>Welcome to my home page</H1>
```

talk A Unix utility that enables users to engage in a typed, real-time conversation while they are online.

talk hierarchy In *Usenet,* one of the seven *standard newsgroup hierarchies.* The talk newsgroups are expressly devoted to controversial topics, and are often characterized by acrimonious debate. Topics covered include abortion, drugs, and gun control.

TCP Abbreviation for Transmission Control Protocol. On the *Internet,* the protocol (standard) that permits two Internet-connected computers to establish a reliable connection. TCP ensures reliable data delivery with a method known as Positive Acknowledgment with Re-Transmission (PAR). The computer that sends the data continues to do so until it receives a confirmation from the receiving computer that the data has been received intact. See *Internet Protocol (IP)* and *TCP/IP.*

TCP/IP Abbreviation for Transmission Control Protocol/Internet Protocol (TCP/IP), and a commonly-used phrase to refer to the entire Internet protocol suite.

TCP/IP network A network that uses the *TCP/IP* protocols, whether or not it is connected to the external *Internet.* See *extranet* and *intranet.*

Telnet An *Internet* protocol that enables Internet users to log on to another computer linked to the Internet, including those that cannot directly communicate with the Internet's *TCP/IP* protocols. Telnet establishes a "plain vanilla" computer terminal called a network virtual terminal.

terminal An input/output device, consisting of a keyboard and monitor, commonly used with multi-user systems.

thread A chain of *Usenet* postings on a single subject. Most *newsreaders* include a command that lets you follow the thread (that is, jump to the next message on the topic rather than display each message in sequence).

threaded newsreader A *Usenet newsreader* program that can group articles by topic of discussion, and then show where a given article stands in the chain of discussion. Often, this is done using indentation. See *thread selector.*

thread selector In a *Usenet newsreader*, a program mode in which you see articles sorted by *threads*. Many newsreaders use indentation to indicate that the indented article is a response to the one positioned above it. See *subject selector* and *threaded newsreader*.

tin A *Usenet newsreader* for Unix computers. Developed by Iain Lee, this *threaded newsreader* offers powerful features like its other Unix newsreader counterparts, but is much easier to use. See *trn*.

Transmission Control Protocol See *TCP.*

Transmission Control Protocol/Internet Protocol See *TCP/IP.*

transmitter In *push media*, a program that sends updated information to subscribers. An example is Castanet's Transmitter, which automatically downloads updates to *Java* programs installed on subscribers' computers.

trn A *Usenet newsreader* for Unix computer systems. A *threaded newsreader* that can show the chain of discussion in a news-group, trn is a successor to the widely used *rn*. Somewhat difficult to learn and use, trn is a powerful program that offers many advanced features (such as the ability to decode binary postings).

trolling In *Usenet*, posting a facetious message containing an obvious exaggeration or factual error. The troller hopes to trick a gullible person into posting a follow-up post pointing out the error.

Undernet One of several international Internet Relay Chat (IRC) networks, independent of other IRC networks.

Uniform Resource Identifier See *URI.*

Uniform Resource Locator See *URL.*

Unix-to-Unix Copy Program (UUCP) A network, based on long-distance telephone *uploads* and *downloads*. UUCP allows Unix users to exchange files, *e-mail,* and *Usenet* articles. In the 1980s, when *Internet* connectivity was hard to come by, UUCP played an important role in providing support for the Unix operating system.

unmoderated newsgroup In a distributed *bulletin board system (BBS)* such as EchoMail (*FidoNet*) or *Usenet* (Internet), a topical discussion group in which postings aren't subject to review before distribution. Unmoderated newsgroups are characterized by spontaneity, but some postings may be inflammatory or inconsiderate, and *flame wars* may erupt. See *moderated newsgroup* and *newsgroup.*

unordered list In *HTML,* a bulleted list created with <UL>_</UL> tags. Text tagged as an unordered list often appears bulleted.

unsubscribe In *Usenet,* to remove a *newsgroup* from your subscription list, so that it does not appear on the list of newsgroups you are actively following. You can also unsubscribe from a mailing list. See *subscribe.*

upload To send a file by telecommunications to another computer user or a *bulletin board system (BBS).*

URI Abbreviation for Uniform Resource Identifier. In the *HyperText Transfer Protocol (HTTP),* a string of characters that identifies an Internet resource, including the type of resource and its location. There are two types of URIs: *Uniform Resource Locators (URLs)* and *Relative URLs.*

URL Acronym for Uniform Resource Locator. In the World Wide Web, one of two basic kinds of Universal Resource Identifiers *(URI),* a string of characters that precisely identifies an *Internet* resource's type and location. For example, the following fictitious URL identifies a *World Wide Web* document (http://), indicates the domain name of the computer on which it is stored (www.wolverine.virginia.edu), fully describes the document's location within the directory structure (~toros/winerefs/), and includes the document's name and extension (merlot.html).

```
http://www.wolverine.virginia.edu/~toros/
winerefs/merlot.html
```

See *Relative URL*.

Usenet A worldwide computer-based discussion system that uses the Internet and other networks for transmission media. Discussion is channeled into more than 30,000 topically-named *newsgroups*, which contain original contributions called *articles*, as well as commentaries on these articles called *follow-up posts*. As follow-up posts continue to appear on a given subject, a *thread* of discussion emerges; a *threaded newsreader* collates these articles together so readers can see the flow of the discussion. Unix Usenet is accessed daily by more than 15 million people in more than 100 countries. See *NNTP*.

Usenet site A computer system—one with lots of disk storage—that receives a news feed and enables dozens or hundreds of people to participate in Usenet. Currently, approximately 120,000 Usenet sites exist, providing an estimated four million people with access to Usenet newsgroups.

User Datagram Protocol (UDP) One of the fundamental *Internet* protocols. UDP operates at the same level as the Transmission Control Protocol (*TCP*), but has much lower overhead, and is less reliable. Unlike TCP, it does not attempt to establish a connection with the remote computer, but simply hands the data down to the connectionless *IP* protocol. UDP comes into play when network *bandwidth* could be preserved by not making a connection (for example, when responding to a *PING* request).

UUCP See *Unix-to-Unix Copy Program*.

uudecode A Unix utility program that decodes a *uuencoded* ASCII file, restoring the original *binary file* (such as a program or graphic). A uudecode utility is needed to decode the binary files posted to *Usenet*. Programs with uudecoding capabilities are available for Macintosh and Microsoft Windows 95 systems, and are often built into Usenet *newsreaders*.

uuencode A Unix utility program that transforms a *binary file*, such as a program or graphic, into coded ASCII text. This text can be transferred by using the *Internet* or it can be posted to a *Usenet newsgroup.* At the receiving end, the *uudecode* utility decodes the message and restores the binary file. Programs with uuencoding capabilities are available for Macintosh and Microsoft Windows 95 systems, and are often built into Usenet *newsreaders.*

V

V.32bis An ITU-TSS *modulation protocol* for *modems* transmitting and receiving data at 14,400 *bits per second (bps).* Modems that use the V.32bis standard are very common, and can transfer data at 12,000 bps, 9600 bps, 7200 bps, and 4800 bps if needed.

V.34 An ITU-TSS *modulation protocol* for *modems* transmitting and receiving data at 28,800 *bits per second (bps).* V.34 modems adjust to changing line conditions to achieve the highest possible *data transfer rate.* A recent addition to the protocol enables transmission rates of up to 33.6 Kbps.

V.42 An ITU-TSS *error-correction protocol* designed to counter the effects of *line noise.* A pair of V.42-compliant *modems* will check each transmitted piece of data to make sure they arrive error-free, and retransmit any faulty data. The V.42 standard uses the Link Access Protocol for Modems (LAPM) as its default error-correction method, but will switch to MNP-4 if needed.

V.42bis An ITU-TSS compression *protocol* that increases the throughput of *modems.* V.42bis is an on-the-fly compression technique that reduces the amount of data a modem needs to transmit.

Vendor Independent Messaging (VIM) In *e-mail* programs, an *application program interface (API)* that lets e-mail programs from different manufacturers exchange mail with one another. The consortium of developers that designed VIM did not include Microsoft Corporation, which uses the *Messaging Application Program Interface (MAPI).* A VIM-to-MAPI dynamic link library (DLL) file makes it possible for the two interfaces to exchange messages.

Veronica In *Gopher,* a search service that scans a database of Gopher directory titles and resources (such as documents, graphics, movies, and sounds), and generates a new Gopher menu containing the results of the search. See *Jughead.*

VIM See *Vendor Independent Messaging.*

virtual community A group of people who, although they may have never met, share interests and concerns and communicate with each other via *e-mail* and *newsgroups.*

virtual corporation A means of organizing a business in which the various units are geographically dispersed, but actively and fruitfully linked by the *Internet* or some other wide area network (WAN).

Virtual Library In the *World Wide Web (WWW),* a subject tree in which volunteers take on the responsibility of maintaining the portion of the tree that is devoted to a specific subject, such as astronomy or zoology. The Virtual Library is a good place to look for academically oriented information on the Web. See *subject tree.*

Visual Café A programming environment for developing applications in Java, created by Symantec. Advanced features of the package include a class editor for editing general versions of objects (classes), visual drag-and-drop application development that enables programmers to quickly build user interfaces, a real-time interpreter and debugger, and a compiler that builds standalone Java applications that execute up to 25 times faster than previous Java code.

W3 See *World Wide Web.*

W3C See *World Wide Web Consortium.*

WAIS See *Wide Area Information Server.*

web In the *World Wide Web (WWW)* or any *hypertext* system, a set of related documents that together make up a hypertext presentation. The documents do not have to be stored on the same computer system, but they are explicitly interlinked, generally by providing internal navigation buttons. A web generally includes a *welcome page* that serves as the top-level document (*home page*) of the web. Synonymous (in practical usage) with site.

Web browser A program that runs on an *Internet*-connected computer and provides access to the riches of the *World Wide Web (WWW)*. Web browsers are of two kinds: text-only browsers and graphical Web browsers. The two most popular graphical browsers are *Microsoft Internet Explorer* and *Netscape Navigator*, the browser component of *Netscape Communicator*. Graphical browsers are preferable because you can see *in-line images*, fonts, and document layouts.

WebCrawler A *search engine* for locating *World Wide Web (WWW)* documents that is based at the University of Washington and supported by DealerNet, Starware Corporation, and Satchel Sports. Relying on an automated search routine (called a *spider*) that indexes all the words in the documents it finds, WebCrawler is slow to compile its database (which contains only 300,000 documents at this writing). However, the fact that it retrieves and indexes all the words in the document makes it unusually accurate when you're searching for words that may not appear in document titles or headings.

Web server In the *World Wide Web (WWW)*, a program that accepts requests for information framed according to the HyperText Transport Protocol *(HTTP)*. The server processes these requests and sends the requested document. Web servers have been developed for most computer systems, including Unix workstations, Microsoft Windows 95 and Microsoft Windows NT systems, and Macintoshes. See *HyperText Transfer Protocol Daemon (httpd)*, *MacHTTP*, *Netscape Commerce Server*, and *Netscape Messaging Server*.

Web site In the *World Wide Web (WWW)*, a computer system that runs a *Web server*, and has been set up for publishing documents on the Web.

welcome page In the *World Wide Web (WWW)*, a Web-accessible document that is meant to be the point of entry to a series of related documents, called a *web*. For example, a company's welcome page typically includes the company's logo, a brief description of the web's purpose, and links to the additional documents available at that site. Welcome pages are also called *home pages,* because they are the home page (the top-level document) of the series of related documents that makes up the web.

whois A Unix utility, run by a whois server, that enables users to locate the *e-mail* address, and often the telephone number and other information, of people who have an account on the same computer system. In Novell networks, a command that displays a list of all users logged on the network.

Wide Area Information Server (WAIS) A Unix-based system linked to the *Internet;* also, a program that permits the user to search worldwide archives for resources based on a series of key words. Users familiar with personal computer database programs are likely to find WAIS a less-than-satisfactory search tool, because WAIS generates a list of documents that's sure to contain many "false drops" (irrelevant documents that don't really pertain to the search subject). See *anonymous FTP.*

Winsock An open standard that specifies how a dynamic link library (DLL) should be written to provide *TCP/IP* support for Microsoft Windows 95 systems. An outgrowth of a "birds of a feather" session at a Unix conference, the Winsock standard—currently in Version 2.0—is actively supported by Microsoft Corporation.

World Wide Web (WWW) A global *hypertext* system that uses the *Internet* as its transport mechanism. In a hypertext system, you navigate by clicking hyperlinks, which display another document (which also contains hyperlinks). Most Web documents are created using the *HTML*, a markup language that is easy to learn and will soon be supplanted by automated tools. Incorporating *hypermedia* (graphics, sounds, animations, and video), the Web has become the ideal medium for publishing information on the Internet. See *Web browser.*

World Wide Web Consortium (W3C) An independent standards body, composed of university researchers and industry practitioners, that is devoted to setting effective standards to promote the orderly growth of the World Wide Web. Housed at the Massachusetts Institute of Technology (MIT), W3C sets standards for *HTML* and many other aspects of Web usage.

WWW See *World Wide Web*.

x2 An unratified *modulation protocol* for *modems* transferring data at 56.6 Kbps. At this writing there is a competing but incompatible protocol called *K56Plus*.

X.509 An international standard for digital *certificates*, maintained by ITU-TSS, that can be used for *strong authentication*. The latest version, X.509V3, helps to assure interoperability among software employing certificates.

XMODEM An asynchronous *file transfer protocol (ftp)* for personal computers that makes the error-free transmission of files through the telephone system easier. Developed by Ward Christiansen for 8-bit computers running Control Program for Microprocessors (CP/M) and placed in the public domain, the XMODEM protocol is included in most personal computer *communications programs* and commonly is used to download files from *bulletin board systems (BBSs)*.

XMODEM-1K A data transmission *protocol* that retains *XMODEM/CRC's* error-checking capabilities but has higher throughput. By performing a cyclic redundancy check (CRC) only on 1,024-byte blocks of data, transmission overhead is reduced. See *YMODEM* and *ZMODEM*.

XMODEM/CRC A version of the *XMODEM* data transmission *protocol* that reduces throughput but also reduces errors. XMODEM/CRC performs a cyclic redundancy check (CRC) on every two bytes transmitted—a more reliable scheme than the checksum technique employed by *XMODEM*. See *XMODEM-1K*, *YMODEM*, and *ZMODEM*.

Yahoo In the *World Wide Web (WWW)*, a popular subject tree created by David Filo and Jerry Yang of the Department of Computer Science at Stanford University. With a keen eye for the popular as well as the useful, Filo and Yang have created a directory of Web resources that currently includes nearly 35,000 Web documents. In 1995, Yahoo moved out of Stanford to www.yahoo.com, where it is supported by advertising. Yahoo reportedly performs 10 million searches each week.

YMODEM A *file transfer protocol (ftp)* that is an improved version of *XMODEM-1K*. YMODEM transfers data in 1,024-byte blocks and performs a cyclic redundancy check (CRC) on each frame. Also, YMODEM supports sending more than one file in sequence. See *YMODEM-g* and *ZMODEM*.

YMODEM-g A *file transfer protocol (ftp)* that leaves error-checking to protocols encoded on modem hardware, such as *V.42* and *MNP-4*, and is best used with high-speed modems in low *line noise* conditions. *ZMODEM* is usually a better choice than YMODEM-g.

Z

ZMODEM An asynchronous *file transfer protocol (ftp)* for personal computers that makes the error-free transmission of computer files with a *modem* easier. ZMODEM is a very fast protocol that lets you use wild-card file names for transfers. It's also well-liked because you can resume the transfer of a file if the first attempt is interrupted before completion. Next to *XMODEM*, ZMODEM is the most popular file transfer protocol and is included in most communications applications.

Build Your
Own Web
Address Book

Site Name _____

http:// _____

Notes _____

_____

Site Name _____

http:// _____

Notes _____

_____

Site Name _____

http:// _____

Notes _____

_____

Site Name _____

http:// _____

Notes _____

_____

Site Name _____

http:// _____

Notes _____

_____

Site Name _____

http:// _____

Notes _____

_____

Site Name _____

http:// _____

Notes _____

_____

Site Name _____

http:// _____

Notes _____

_____

Site Name _____

http:// _____

Notes _____

_____

Site Name _____

http:// _____

Notes _____

_____

Site Name _____

http:// _____

Notes _____

_____

Site Name _____

http:// _____

Notes _____

_____

Site Name _____

http:// _____

Notes _____

_____

Site Name _____

http:// _____

Notes _____

_____

Site Name _____

http:// _____

Notes _____

_____

Site Name _____

http:// _____

Notes _____

_____

Site Name _____

http:// _____

Notes _____

_____

Site Name _____

http:// _____

Notes _____

_____

Site Name _____

http:// _____

Notes _____

_____

Site Name _____

http:// _____

Notes _____

_____

Site Name _____

http:// _____

Notes _____

_____

Site Name _____

http:// _____

Notes _____

_____

Site Name _____

http:// _____

Notes _____

Site Name _____

http:// _____

Notes _____

Site Name _____

http:// _____

Notes _____

Site Name _____

http:// _____

Notes _____

Site Name _____

http:// _____

Notes _____

Site Name _____

http:// _____

Notes _____

Site Name _____

http:// _____

Notes _____

Site Name _____

http:// _____

Notes _____

_____

Site Name _____

http:// _____

Notes _____

_____

Site Name _____

http:// _____

Notes _____

_____

Site Name _____

http:// _____

Notes _____

_____

Site Name _____

http:// _____

Notes _____

_____

Site Name _____

http:// _____

Notes _____

_____

Site Name _____

http:// _____

Notes _____

_____

Site Name _____

http:// _____

Notes _____

Site Name _____

http:// _____

Notes _____

Site Name _____

http:// _____

Notes _____

Site Name _____

http:// _____

Notes _____

Site Name _____

http:// _____

Notes _____

Site Name _____

http:// _____

Notes _____

Site Name _____

http:// _____

Notes _____

Site Name _____

http:// _____

Notes _____

_____

Site Name _____

http:// _____

Notes _____

_____

Site Name _____

http:// _____

Notes _____

_____

Site Name _____

http:// _____

Notes _____

_____

Site Name _____

http:// _____

Notes _____

_____

Site Name _____

http:// _____

Notes _____

_____

Site Name _____

http:// _____

Notes _____

_____

Site Name _____

http:// _____

Notes _____

_____

Site Name _____

http:// _____

Notes _____

_____

Site Name _____

http:// _____

Notes _____

_____

Site Name _____

http:// _____

Notes _____

_____

Site Name _____

http:// _____

Notes _____

_____

Site Name _____

http:// _____

Notes _____

_____

Site Name _____

http:// _____

Notes _____

_____

Site Name _____

http:// _____

Notes _____

_____

Site Name _____

http:// _____

Notes _____

_____

Site Name _____

http:// _____

Notes _____

_____

Site Name _____

http:// _____

Notes _____

_____

Site Name _____

http:// _____

Notes _____

_____

Site Name _____

http:// _____

Notes _____

_____

Site Name _____

http:// _____

Notes _____

_____